Lecture Notes in Computer Science   3912

Commenced Publication in 1973
Founding and Former Series Editors:
Gerhard Goos, Juris Hartmanis, and Jan van Leeuwen

T0223275

Gary J. Minden   Kenneth L. Calvert
Marcin Solarski   Miki Yamamoto (Eds.)

Active Networks

IFIP TC6 6th International Working Conference, IWAN 2004
Lawrence, KS, USA, October 27-29, 2004
Revised Papers

 Springer

Volume Editors

Gary J. Minden
University of Kansas
Information and Telecommunications Technology Center
2335 Irving Hill Road, Lawrence, KS 66045, USA
E-mail: gminden@ittc.ku.edu

Kenneth L. Calvert
University of Kentucky
Department of Computer Science, Laboratory for Advanced Networking
Hardymon Building, 301 Rose Street, Lexington, KY 40506-0495, USA
E-mail: calvert@netlab.uky.edu

Marcin Solarski
Deutsche Telekom A.G.Laboratories
Ernst-Reuter-Platz 7, 10587 Berlin, Germany

Miki Yamamoto
Kansai University
Department of Electrical Engineering and Computer Science
3-3-35 Yamate-cho, Suita, Osaka 564-8680, Japan
E-mail: yama-m@ipcku.kansai-u.ac.jp

Library of Congress Control Number: 2007923238

CR Subject Classification (1998): C.2, D.2, H.3.4-5, K.6, D.4.4, H.4.3

LNCS Sublibrary: SL 5 – Computer Communication Networks and
Telecommunications

ISSN   0302-9743
ISBN-10   3-540-71499-5 Springer Berlin Heidelberg New York
ISBN-13   978-3-540-71499-6 Springer Berlin Heidelberg New York

Springer is a part of Springer Science+Business Media

springer.com

©2007 IFIP International Federation for Information Processing,Hofstraße 3,2361 Laxenburg, Austria
Printed in Germany

Typesetting: Camera-ready by author, data conversion by Scientific Publishing Services, Chennai, India
Printed on acid-free paper   SPIN: 12038831   06/3142   5 4 3 2 1 0

Preface

We are pleased to present to you the proceedings of the sixth Annual International Working Conference on Active Networks, which took place in October 2004 at The Information and Telecommunications Technology Center, The University of Kansas, USA. The proceedings of IWAN 2004 mark a transition between the funded active networking programs in Europe, Japan, and the United States and a strong, continued interest in the architectures of programmable networks.

The technical committee accepted 14 papers for presentation from 32 submitted papers. The papers are organized into sections on active network systems and architectures, security in active networking, active network applications, mobile active networks and active network management. Whereas the contributions on active network architectures and management build upon mature concepts devised in the previous years and are incremental follow-ups of the related research, the security considerations are of primary importance to the active networks practitioners. The papers on mobile applications of active networks, like TCP gateways between wireless and wireline networks, provide additional inspirations to the active network researchers.

Featured in the program were a keynote address by Jonathan M. Smith of DARPA and two invited papers, one by Takashi Egawa, Yoshiaki Kiriha, and Akira Arutaki on "Tackling the Complexity of Future Networks", and one by Bernhard Plattner and James Sterbenz, titled "Programmable Networks: Alternative Mechanisms and Design Choices". Based on the reviewer feedback, the authors of the paper "Dynamic Link Measurements Using Active Components", Dimitrios Pezaros, Manolis Sifalakis, Stefan Schmid and David Hutchison, all of Lancaster University, were awarded this year's Best Paper Award. During the two days of the conference there were several lively discussions, including one at the end of the first day on the scope and future of IWAN itself. The social event, barbecue at the Circle-S ranch, provided a most enjoyable venue for discussion and collegiality.

We would like to thank the members of the Program Committee for their excellent work in reviewing, selecting, and in some cases shepherding papers for the program. V. Rory Petty and F. "Ted" Weidling supported the Web site and conference organization.

We appreciate the work of all the authors, they are the core of this workshop and proceedings. The participation of all the attendees made an outstanding conference. Enjoy the fruits of all their labors. We trust you will find these proceedings interesting.

October 2004

Gary J. Minden
Ken Calvert
Marcin Solarski
Miki Yamamoto

Organization

IWAN 2004 was organized by The Information and Telecommunications Technology Center (ITTC) at The University of Kansas. We would like to acknowledge the support of our sponsors, The Information and Telecommunications Technology Center, The University of Kansas, and Hitachi Ltd., and we thank them for their contributions. Their support and the research presented in these proceedings continue to demonstrate international interest in active networking.

Executive Committee

General Chair   Gary J. Minden, The University of Kansas, USA

General Co-chairs   Tadanobu Okada, NTT, Japan
Bernhard Plattner, ETH Zürich, Switzerland

Program Co-chairs   Marcin Solarski, Fraunhofer FOKUS, Germany
Ken Calvert, The University of Kentucky, USA
Miki Yamamoto, Osaka University, Japan

Technical Program Committee

Stephane Amarger
Bobby Bhattacharjee
Matthias Bossardt
Bob Braden
Torsten Braun
Marcus Brunner
Ken Calvert
Hermann DeMeer
Takashi Egawa
Ted Faber
Mike Fisher
Alex Galis
Anastasius Gavras
Jim Griffioen
Robert Haas

Toru Hasegawa
Michael Hicks
David Hutchison
Javed Kahn
Andreas Kind
Yoshiaki Kiriha
Akira Kurokawa
Laurent Lefevre
John Lockwood
Douglas Maughan
Gary Minden
Toshiaki Miyazaki
Sandy Murphy
Scott Nettles
Bernhard Plattner

Guy Pujolle
Lukas Ruf
Nadia Shalaby
Yuval Shavitt
Marcin Solarski
James Sterbenz
Christian Tschudin
Naoki Wakamiya
Marcel Waldvogel
Tilman Wolf
Miki Yamamoto
Krzysztof Zielinski
Martina Zitterbart

Sponsoring Institutions

The University of Kansas
The Information and Telecommunications Technology Center
Hitichai

Table of Contents

Mobile Active Networks

Active Networking Management

GateScript: A Scripting Language for Generic Active Gateways

Hoa-Binh Nguyen and Andrzej Duda

LSR-IMAG Laboratory
Institut National Polytechnique de Grenoble
BP. 72, 38402 Saint Martin d'Hères, France
{Hoa-Binh.Nguyen,Andrzej.Duda}@imag.fr
http://drakkar.imag.fr

Abstract. In this paper, we present *GateScript*, a scripting language for active applications to be executed on generic active gateways. Unlike other active networking platforms, it offers a simple scripting language for expressing custom processing of packets at different protocol layers without the need for interpretation of complex protocol data structures. In this way, the user writes statements in a script-like language while using protocol-specific variables and predefined function calls acting on the packet's content. From a textual description, we automatically create a packet parser and reassembler for a given protocol. The parser decomposes PDUs arriving in an active application into protocol variables that can be used in the script language. After processing, outcoming packets are reconstructed from the protocol variables. *GateScript* also enables active applications to react to the state of the environment: they can receive events from monitors and test variables reflecting the state of the environment.

We have designed an architecture for a *generic active gateway* (GAG) that supports *GateScript*. An active application can dynamically install/remove a packet filter that intercepts relevant packets and passes them to the application. We have implemented *GAG* on Linux: its packet forwarding part is implemented in the kernel and all other components as user space processes.

1 Introduction

In our work, we address the problem of customizing user flows in active gateways at the border of the network infrastructure. Unlike traditional proxy nodes, active gateways provide transparent processing of data streams without the need of configuring client hosts. An active gateway may be placed in the access network, for example in the last router connected to a LAN. Many applications may benefit from custom processing physically located close to the client host, especially if it has limited resources. Consider for example small mobile devices that require some adaptation or reaction to changing conditions, and pervasive environments with various devices such as sensors or actuators—an active gateway can provide additional processing in the fixed network infrastructure. In

G.J. Minden et al. (Eds.): IWAN 2004, LNCS 3912, pp. 1–20, 2007.

some cases, we may even want to place the gateway functionality on the end system, so that the user can easily control, filter, or adapt flows arriving to the device.

We have designed and developed *GateScript*, a scripting language for easy programming of active applications that process packets in active gateways. Although there are several platforms for adding programmability to a network node, usually they are programmed in a full-fledged programming language such as Java [8,18], C [5,21], or TCL [1]. Moreover, many platforms require kernel modules or plugins to be developed [13,14], which can be done by experts, but it is too tedious for most of users. With *GateScript* we want to offer a simple scripting language for expressing custom processing of packets at different protocol layers without the need for interpretation of complex protocol data structures. In this way, the user just writes a script that uses variables relative to a given protocol and calls predefined functions working on the packet's content.

More specifically, *GateScript* provides a higher level view than traditional languages and automates the tasks of interpreting/constructing data packets. Coupling protocol variables to values in a received packet is automatically done by a packet parser generated from a formal description of a protocol. The variables available to script programs represent either protocol header fields (e.g. `$http.content_type` for a HTTP Reply or `$tcp.window` for a TCP segment) or elements of the packet data content (e.g. `$html.title` for the title HTML markup). When some values of variables are detected in a packet by the protocol parser, they are made available to a script program so it can take some action or modify them. Simple statements allow to test the values contained in a packet and invoke functions able to modify its content or perform other actions such as packet duplication or drop.

With *GateScript*, we also explore the possibility of coupling the behavior of an active gateway with the state of the environment. Some active applications that we call *proactive* are able to dynamically react and adapt to varying conditions [17]. They cooperate with *monitors*, special entities that observe the state of the network, routers, or hosts. *GateScript* proposes a statement for waiting for an event to execute some operations when a monitor signals an event.

To support *GateScript*, we have designed and implemented an architecture for a generic active gateway called *GAG*. An active application can install a packet filter that recognizes some packets according to the information in the packet header and passes them to the application. Then, it is parsed and the *GateScript* engine interprets the code of a script that processes the packet. Intercepting packets can be activated and disabled dynamically, so that there is no overhead for forwarding packets that do not require active processing.

We have implemented *GateScript* in Java and GAG on Linux. *GateScript* currently integrates two generators of packet parsers: one based on Flavor [6] oriented towards bitstream protocols and a second one based on JavaCC [12] for text oriented protocols. The packet forwarding part of *GAG* is implemented in the kernel and all other components, such as scripts written in *GateScript*, are user space processes. We have experimented with *GateScript* by implementing several example active applications enhancing the behavior of transport and application level protocols. Even if the performance was not our primary goal, we have evaluated the overhead of intercepting packets in *GAG* and compared the processing performance of *GateScript* with a standard HTTP Java-based gateway such as Muffin [15].

In this paper, we present the main features of *GateScript* and illustrate their use by some examples. We do not cover many other aspects such as secure deployment of scripts on active nodes, control of active applications, node administration, event generation by monitors, and experimentation with active applications specialized for different protocols.

The paper is organized as follows. Section 2 introduces the architecture of *GAG*. We describe *GateScript* in Section 3 and present its implementation in Section 4. Section 5 reports on our experience and presents a first evaluation of the prototype. We discuss the related work in Section 6. Finally, we draw conclusions in Section 7.

2 Generic Active Gateways

A generic active gateway needs to provide general support for processing the content of different data flows and customizing the behavior of protocols. We consider transparent gateways that are network nodes acting in a similar way to routers: data packets are not directly addressed to them, rather they are forwarded to a destination after processing some of them. The gateway forwards packets in a usual way based on standard routing tables or according to the effect of active packet processing.

Usually a gateway implementing active applications performs some packet parsing, processing, and reconstruction while all these functionalities are combined in the same piece of code. Our approach consists of separating packet parsing and reconstruction from data processing to make them generic so that they can be used for any bit oriented or textual protocol. The generic part of an active gateway can be specialized for a given protocol or data flow based on the structure of a PDU (*Protocol Data Unit*) defined by the protocol[1]. Examples of such a use are intelligent HTTP, RTSP, or SIP proxies, media transcoding gateways (e.g. from HTML to WML), or adaptation gateways (e.g. from MPEG to H.263).

An active gateway needs to support the following functionalities (we illustrate them with examples in the context of HTTP when relevant):

- Active applications need to execute some code upon the arrival of a packet or when the state of the system changes (e.g. when receiving a HTTP Reply, check for the MIME type of the message body and filter out all images). The

---

[1] We use the term of a packet to designate the PDU entering an active gateway. A packet may contain encapsulated PDUs defined by higher level protocols, e.g. a TCP segment containing a HTTP Reply. When describing the protocol parsing part within *GateScript*, we will use the term of a PDU.

code of an active application should involve variables variables proper to a given protocol (e.g. an active application should be able to test the MIME type of the HTTP message body).

- The value of a variable used in an active application should be set to the value of a PDU field assigned when a packet is received by the gateway (e.g. variable $http.content_type should be set to the value image/jpeg for a HTTP Reply containing a JPEG image).
- A rich library of functions able to process specific data types should be available to active applications (e.g. ReduceImageSize or TranscodeVideo for processing objects in a HTTP Reply).
- We need means for dynamically enable or disable processing of packets passing through a gateway to obtain good performance when custom processing is not required.
- Active applications require support for reacting to changes in their environment such as network congestion, host disconnection, lack of resources (e.g. when a client host changes the access network, it may request to change processing of packets, because of the increased available bandwidth).

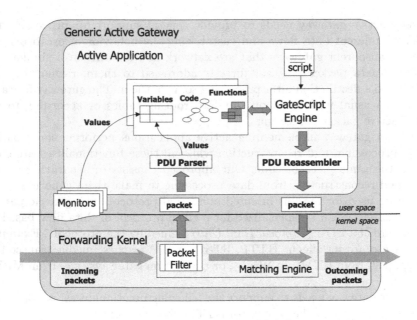

Fig. 1. Architecture of GAG

The architecture of *GAG*, a generic active gateway supporting *GateScript* is presented in Figure 1. *GAG* is composed of the following entities:

- *Active applications* that process some packet data. They are programmed using the *GateScript* scripting language. The script program involves variables proper to a given protocol or representing the state of the environment.

- A *GateScript engine* for executing a script program once the variables used in the program have their values assigned. It couples a script program with the variables recognized in data packets and with the functions able to process them.
- *Protocol variables* that represent fields defined in the PDU structure of a given protocol or some parts of the packet content. Protocol variables are predefined for any given protocol.
- A *PDU parser* for recognizing the structure of a given PDU contained in a packet, parsing the data contents, and setting up variables used by the script program of active applications.
- A *PDU reassembler* to reconstruct a data packet from the variables used by the script program (the inverse function to the PDU parser). The PDU parser and reassembler are automatically created from the description of a given protocol.
- *Processing functions*, an extensible library of useful functions that allow to process data packets. The functions are proper to a given protocol or to a data format. They are supposed to be developed by an expert Java programmer, because they may require an extensive knowledge of a protocol, system calls, and programming conventions (parameter passing, operations allowed on the *PDU context*, cf. Section 4).
- *Monitors* able to detect varying conditions in the environment (network, gateways, devices, services, hosts, users). In some cases it is important that an active application reacts to the change of the system state. A monitor can signal an active application by sending an event that can be tested in the script program.
- A *matching engine* that allows to dynamically install and uninstall *packet filters* responsible for intercepting packets and passing them to active applications. An active application can decide when to install or uninstall a packet filter so that when intercepting packets is not needed, there is no overhead of passing packets to the user space. Packets that do not match any filter are forwarded in the standard way.

Active applications can be loaded or unloaded dynamically into the active gateway. Some active applications that we call *proactive* cooperate with monitors and are able to dynamically react and adapt to varying conditions.

3   GateScript Language

GateScript is a scripting language for programming active applications that process packets in *GAG* gateways. Below we review the main constructs of the *GateScript* language (see Appendix for more formal description).

3.1   Statements

A *GateScript* program is composed of statements. Each statement can test the values of variables representing specific PDU fields and invoke appropriate functions. User defined variables can be declared and initialized using the set statement and substitute to their values when preceded by $. There are several types of statements:

- *assignment statement* to assign a value to a variable, e.g.

  ```
  set State $AckState;
  ```

- *conditional statement* to execute one of two groups of statements based on the test of a condition, e.g.

  ```
  if ($ip.destination_address = $Client) then
      WriteToCache;
  endif
  ```

- *function call* to invoke a function with some arguments, e.g.

  ```
  CheckIfExistPacket $tcp.Ack_Number
  ```

- *event statement* to wait for a condition related to an event and to execute a statement when the event is received, e.g.

  ```
  onEvent $EventName = "ClientDisconnects" then
      PacketFilter "add $ClientIPAddress";
  endEvent
  ```

When a monitor signals event ClientDisconnects, the application executes function PacketFilter to install a packet filter for intercepting packets containing the IP address of the client. In this way, the active application starts receiving packets on behalf of the client, which can be for instance stored in a cache for later delivery.

3.2 Variables

There are three kinds of variables:

- *user defined variables* that are not related to any protocol, e.g. variable $State given in the example above.
- *protocol-related variables* that represent PDU fields or data content values, e.g. variable $tcp.SYN representing the SYN TCP flag. The PDU parser assigns values recognized in a packet to such variables each time a new packet arrives in the gateway and is passed to the active application.
- *monitor variables* that represent the state of some environment conditions, e.g. variable $Disconnected becomes true if a client host probed by a monitor cannot be reached (we assume that we use a monitor able to detect such a condition).

In *GateScript* PDUs arriving in an active application are decomposed into protocol variables that can be processed in script statements. After processing packets are completely reconstructed from the variables on the way out.

Variables can be combined by using operators to form expressions. Function calls in expressions are separated from operators with square brackets.

3.3 Events

When a monitor detects a modification in the state of the environment, it signals an application with an *event*. An event has a name and a list of variables. Consider the following example: an application subscribes to a congestion monitor that detects congestion conditions in the network and passes some information about the available resources:

```
onEvent $EventName = "Congestion" then
   AdaptEncoding $AvailableBandwidth;
endEvent
```

The monitor signals the `Congestion` event and makes the current value of the available bandwidth accessible. Upon this event, the monitor invokes a function to adapt encoding.

3.4 Static Attribute

Statements may be static or not. A static statement is executed only once per execution of a script, whereas a non static statement is executed each time a packet is received and parsed. Such an execution semantics is needed when we want to initialize some variables or start monitors. It allows keeping a limited state during the execution of a script. Any statement can be static. As packet processing is the main goal of active applications, statements are not static by default. Consider the following example:

```
if ($tcp.SYN = 1) then
   static set Client $ip.destination_address;
   set State $SynState;
endif
```

If the active application receives a SYN TCP segment, it stores the IP destination address in the variable `$Client` and the current state of the connection in the variable `$State`. The first assignment will be executed only once, while the second one, every received SYN segment.

We can characterize *GateScript* as an active platform supporting limited statefull packet processing—limited by the script language itself, because the static attribute only allows initializing some variables of a script. However, if required, it is extendable by functions such as `WriteToCache`.

3.5 Examples

The following three examples concern pervasive environments in which computer devices connected via different types of networks provide the user with some augmented functionalities. Due to energy or capacity limitations pervasive environments and mobile components usually require some additional processing to be done in the fixed network infrastructure by a proxy node or a gateway.

The *GateScript* program presented below corresponds to TCP snooping [2]. It operates in a gateway located between the wired and the wireless parts of the network. It caches TCP packets in order to respond more quickly to ACK packets from a mobile client.

```
static set State 0;
static set SynState 1;
static set AckState 2;
static set EtablishedState 3;
if ($tcp.SYN = 1) then
    static set Client $ip.destination_address;
    set State $SynState;
endif
if ($tcp.SYN = 1) and ($tcp.ACK = 1) and
    ($State = $SynState) then
    set State $AckState;
    ForwardPacket;
    return;
endif
if ($State = $AckState) and ($tcp.ACK = 1) then
    set State $EtablishedState;
    ForwardPacket;
    return;
endif
if ($State = $EtablishedState) then
    if ($ip.destination_address = $Client) then
        WriteToCache;
    endif
    if ($ip.source_address = $Client) then
        if ([CheckIfExistPacket $tcp.ack_number]) then
            ForwardFromCacheToClient $tcp.ack_number;
            return;
        endif
    endif
endif
ForwardPacket;
```

The script performs TCP snooping for one TCP connection with a given client host. At the beginning, it defines four variables to represent the state of a TCP connection: $State, $SynState, $AckState, and $EtablishedState. For each segment during the three-way handshake, the state is modified. When the connection is established, the active application caches all the packets going to the given client host and forwards them to the destination. When it detects by means of the TCP ACK that the next not yet acknowledged segment resides in the cache, it forwards it directly to the client (the TCP ACK number corresponds to the next not yet received segment), and the ACK segment is dropped. In this way, the client quickly obtains a retransmitted segment from the gateway instead from the source.

The next example presents a caching service for a mobile host. It subscribes to a $PresenceMonitor that checks for the presence of a client host by periodically sending ICMP Echo Request. The state of the client host is represented in the variable $Disconnected updated by the monitor. When the state changes, an event is sent to the active application: ClientDisconnects or ClientConnects. Based on these events, the application enables or disables packet intercepting in the kernel. At the beginning, when the client host is connected, the application is running and packets go through the gateway without processing. When the monitor detects the disconnection of the client host, it signals the application that installs a packet filter for the IP address of the client. In this way, the application starts receiving packets. Each packet is stored in a cache. When the client host connects again, packets are forwarded to the host and the packet filter is deleted so that packets are no longer processed by the active application.

```
static set Client "client.host.edu";
static PresenceMonitor $Client;
onEvent $EventName = "ClientDisconnects" then
   PacketFilter "add $Client";
endEvent
onEvent $EventName = "ClientConnects" then
   PacketFilter "delete $Client";
endEvent
if $Disconnected then
   WriteToCache;
else
   ForwardCacheToClient;
endif
```

The following example shows an active application that detects high temperature and generates a fire alarm. First, it calibrates a raw measurement from a temperature sensor, then it tests to detect whether it is higher than a predefined threshold, and generates an event handled by applications that subscribed to it. If the temperature is low, the packet is dropped. We assume a simple packet structure with two fields: the sensor id and the raw measurement of the temperature.

```
static set FireAlarmThreshold 50;
set Temperature   [Calibrate $RawMesurement];
if $Temperature > $FireAlarmThreshold then
  GenerateEvent "FireAlarm" [GetLocalization $SensorID];
else
  DropPacket;
endif
```

The last examples illustrate a HTTP gateway developed using *GateScript*—it scans the HTTP traffic on behalf of a user and performs customization (filtering out ad banners, reducing image size, etc.). Table 1 lists the functions developed to process HTTP typed objects.

Table 1. Processing functions for HTTP

Name	Functionality
RemoveTag	Remove a tag
RemoveColor	Remove color information
ContentDiscard	Discard the data
ReduceImageSize	Reduce image size
ColorToGreyScale	Transcode to grey scale
ColorToBW	Transcode to black and white
JPEGToGIF	Transcode JPEG to GIF
GIFToJPEG	Transcode GIF to JPEG
BreakPage	Break page
FilterHtmlFrame	Filter out a frame
FilterHtmlTable	Filter out a table

The examples below deal with the content of Web pages. The first one filters images by removing all image tags from an HTML page and by discarding all image objects (RemoveTag function makes use of a HTML parser on a HTTP object of type text/html).

```
if $http.content_type contains "text/html" then
    RemoveTag "img";
endif
if $http.content_type contains "image" then
    ContentDiscard;
endif
```

The next example reduces the size of JPEG images by half if the original image is greater than 1 Kbyte.

```
if (($http.content_type = "image/gif") or
    ($http.content_type = "image/jpeg")) and
    ($http.content_length > 1000) then
        ReduceImage 0.5;
endif
```

4 Implementation of *GAG* and *GateScript*

4.1 *GAG* Prototype on Linux

We have implemented *GAG* on Linux (its first version was called ProAN [17]). Linux is a good candidate for such an active node because of its properties: packet forwarding support, loadable kernel modules, and the ease of modifying the kernel behavior. The forwarding part of our architecture with the matching engine is implemented in the Linux kernel. Each active application is implemented as a user space process and may receive packets belonging to a flow defined by some packet properties such as source or destination address. An active application may dynamically install and uninstall packet filters in the matching engine. When installed, a packet filter passes matching packets to the application.

The matching engine uses Netfilter [16], the support for custom processing of packets in the kernel. It allows users to hook extended modules in the packet forwarding path and to pass packets of a flow to a process in the user space for further processing. After processing packets are re-injected into the kernel, however the process cannot inject newly created packets into kernel so that some processing such as packet duplication is impossible with standard Netfilter.

Another limitation of Netfilter is that only one process in the user space may receive packets from the kernel. IP Queue Multiplex Daemon (`ipqmpd`) [11] adds the possibility of passing packets from different flows to different user processes. It communicates with user processes using sockets or other IPC mechanisms. This is inefficient, because packets must re-enter the kernel before arriving in the destination user process.

To obtain better performance of *GAG*, we have modified Netfilter to pass different packet flows directly to the right user process without going through the multiplexer daemon. We use `iptable` to mark packets with the corresponding process ID (PID) of the active application. When the `ip_queue` module receives the packets, it detects and forwards them directly to the right process. We have also modified the `ip_queue` module to support more than three modes of operation (drop a packet, pass the kernel metadata of a packet to the user process, pass the metadata and the packet payload to the user process)—the standard `ip_queue` module always keeps a copy of a packet passed to a user space process. A module can only modify the payload of packets and it is not possible for a module to inject newly created packets into the kernel. With our modification, when a packet is passed to a user space process in this mode, it uses a new verdict value (`NF_INJECT`) to inject a new packet into the kernel. Our version of the modified `ip_queue` currently supports 40 queues in the `ip_queue` module.

4.2 *GateScript* Implementation

We have implemented *GateScript* in Java. A user space process implementing each active application contains the *GateScript* engine as well as PDU parsers and reassembler. A script program is compiled into an intermediate form interpreted by the *GateScript* engine. The compilation is done only once per each application activation. Protocol variables exist in the intermediate form, however their values become assigned when a packet arrives in the application.

Internally, *GateScript* makes use of a structure containing the set of variables corresponding to a PDU: the *PDU context*. It is a hashed table with all protocol-related variables obtained from the parsing of a PDU. When a protocol parser receives a PDU, it parses it and creates a PDU context. The *GateScript* engine uses it when executing a program script and passes it to any invoked function, which can change the variable values or may add more variables if necessary (when developing functions, the programmer needs to carefully handle the PDU context).

Table 2. TCP/IP PDU described in Flavor

```
class TCP_IP {
unsigned int(4) ip.version;
unsigned int(4) ip.hdr_length;
unsigned int(8) ip.service_type;
unsigned int(16) ip.total_length;
unsigned int(16) ip.identification;
unsigned int(3)  ip.flags;
unsigned int(13) ip.fragment_offset;
unsigned int(8)  ip.ttl;
unsigned int(8)  ip.protocol;
unsigned int(16) ip.header_checksum;
unsigned int(32) ip.source_address;
unsigned int(32) ip.destination_address;
if (ip.hdr_length>5)
   { unsigned int(8) ip.options[(ip.hdr_length*4-20)]; }

unsigned int(16) tcp.source_port;
unsigned int(16) tcp.destination_port;
unsigned int(32) tcp.sequence_number;
unsigned int(32) tcp.ack_number;
unsigned int(4)  tcp.data_offset;
unsigned int(6)  tcp.reserved;
unsigned int(1)  tcp.URG;
unsigned int(1)  tcp.ACK;
unsigned int(1)  tcp.PSH;
unsigned int(1)  tcp.RST;
unsigned int(1)  tcp.SYN;
unsigned int(1)  tcp.FIN;
unsigned int(16) tcp.window;
unsigned int(16) tcp.TCP_Checksum;
unsigned int(16) tcp.urgent_pointer;
if (tcp.data_offset>5)
   { unsigned int(8) tcp.options[(tcp.data_offset-5)*4]; }

unsigned int(8) tcp.data[ip.total_length-(ip.hdr_length*4)
                         -(tcp.data_offset*4)]; };
```

We use Flavor [6] to describe the structure of bitstream oriented protocols such as IP, TCP, UDP, RTP, or X Window. The PDU description in Flavor is compiled to generate a C++ or a Java class, integrated with the *GateScript* engine to parse a bitstream, recognize the defined fields, and obtain their values. Table 2 presents the description of an IP packet containing a TCP segment in Flavor.

For text oriented protocols such as HTTP, FTP, SMTP, SNMP, RTSP, or SIP we generate parsers using JavaCC [12]. We describe a given protocol in a

Table 3. HTTP PDU described in JavaCC

```
options
{ USER_CHAR_STREAM = true; }

PARSER_BEGIN (HTTPResponseParser)
public class HTTPResponseParser
{ public Map PDUcontext; }
PARSER_END (HTTPResponseParser)

void HTTPParse(): {}
{{ PDUcontext = new HashMap(); }
Status_Line() <CRLF>
( Header() <CRLF> )*
<CRLF>
Message_Body()
}

void Status_Line() :
{ String version,reason_phrase;
int status_code; }
{ version = string()  <SPACE>
{ PDUcontext.put("version",version); }
status_code = number() <SPACE>
{ PDUcontext.put("status code",
                  new Integer(status_code)); }
reason_phrase = String();
{ PDUcontext.put("reason_phrase", reason_phrase); }}


void Header():
{ String header,value; }
{ header = string() ";" value = string()
{ header = header.replace('-','_');
PDUcontext.put(header,value); }}

void Message_Body():
{ byte[] data; }
{ data = byte_array()
{ PDUcontext.put("content",data); }}
```

syntax description file proper to JavaCC. Table 3 presents the description of the HTTP protocol. It defines the structure of the HTTP PDUs and couples the parser and reassembler with the *GateScript* engine by means of the *PDU context*. The header attributes become available for scripts in variables whose names are HTTP attributes (because of compatibility problems with Java, we replace dash with underscore, for example, the Content-Type header attribute is represented by the $http.content_type variable).

5   Evaluation

We have experimented with *GateScript* by implementing active applications enhancing the behavior of several protocols: an active gateway for HTTP that scans the HTTP traffic on behalf of a user and performs customization (filtering out ad banners, reducing image size), a multiplexer of the X Window protocol able to replicate a window of a remote application on different X displays, a SIP gateway that performs user defined actions on SIP INVITE messages, an MPEG adaptation gateway that monitors the RTCP reports to detect degrading reception conditions and transcode MPEG to H.263, and a snooping wireless adaptation gateway that acts at the IP and TCP layers in a 802.11 WLAN cell to provide statistical QoS by limiting the rate of TCP flows through modification of the announced window size.

Although the best performance was not our primary goal, we wanted to obtain a first evaluation to see if the overhead of *GateScript* is not too prohibitive compared to standard gateways. Therefore we separated *GateScript* from *GAG* and evaluated them independently. We have measured the performance of a HTTP gateway programmed using *GateScript* on a 1.06 GHz Pentium III PC with 248 MB RAM running Windows XP and compared with the performance of Muffin [15], a public Java HTTP proxy. In this experiment, our gateway operated as a proxy without the packet matching kernel: all packets go through a user process running *GateScript* engine. Both tested tools are entirely developed in Java and executed with Java 2 SDK 1.4.1.

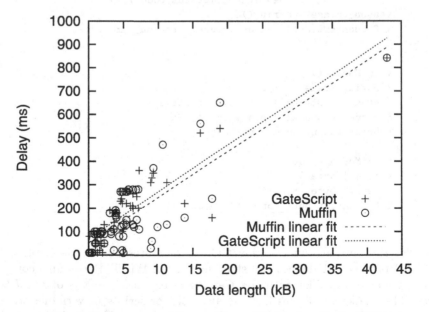

Fig. 2. Performance of Gatescript vs. Muffin, image elimination

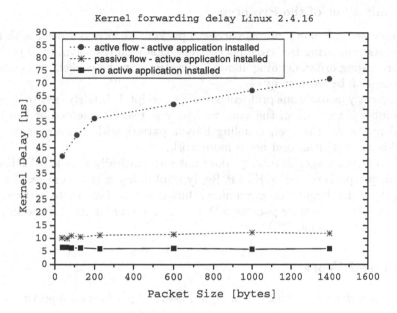

Fig. 3. Performance of passing packets to the user space

In the test, we have downloaded pages from a popular Web server through the gateways that processed HTTP Replies: each page has been analyzed and all images have been filtered out. Figure 2 compares the download delay for the *GateScript* gateway and Muffin in function of different page sizes. We can see that the overall performance in terms of delay remains comparable.

To evaluate the *GAG* implementation on Linux, we have measured the performance of packet forwarding and passing them to the user space on a 800 MHz Pentium III PC with 128 MB RAM running Red Hat 7.2. Figure 3 presents the delay of packet forwarding in function of the packet size for two cases: in the first one, packets enters the kernel and they are just forwarded to the destination (no active application installed); in the second case, a packet filter is installed to intercept packets and pass them to an active application (active flow - active application installed). It does not perform any processing and just re-injects packets into the kernel for further forwarding. The difference between the two curves represents the overhead of passing a packet to the user space. These results show that when an active application does not install a packet filter, data flows do not incur any performance penalty. We can also see from the figure that in the second case the overhead has only impact on data flows on which active applications need to perform useful processing: the delay for a passive flow (the flow for which packets are not intercepted by its packet filter) stays small even if the packets of an active flow are processed by the associated active application.

5.1   Limitations of the Prototype

At the moment only one script can access a packet. We have not dealt with multiple scripts processing the same packet yet—this requires solving the problem of the processing order, defining allowed operations on the packet, and eventual communication between scripts.

We currently use only one protocol parser per script. It is fairly easy to increase their number if they are of the same nature, e.g. two bit-oriented or two text-oriented protocols. However, coupling Flavor parsers with those generated by JavaCC is more difficult and needs more work.

At the current stage, GateScript does not automatically handle a PDU split over multiple packets, e.g. a HTTP Reply containing a large image. If really needed, it can be done by programming a function that keep state between two packet arrivals: it can store packets with fragments, reorder them if needed, and finally process the whole PDU.

6   Related Work

Research in active networking has brought in several platforms supporting active applications and services. Many of them use full-fledged programming languages such as Java ([8,18]), C ([5,21]), or TCL [1]. However, as said previously, we think that a specialized scripting language with automatic parsing of PDU fields like *GateScript* provides a more flexible tool for programming active gateways. As to Java, we consider it as an excellent language for developing *GateScript* internal functions, but we do not need all its complexity to program active applications, in which for example, the programmer would have to deal with exceptions and all Java keywords.

There are several other specialized languages for active networking platforms. PLAN [10] and *GateScript* have different objectives: PLAN is a language for programming active packets while *GateScript* is used for programming active applications that process regular (passive) packets in a transparent way.

Netscript [23] is a connector-oriented language for composing active applications from smaller components called Netscript boxes. The main difference between Netscript and *GateScript* is that Netscript is suitable for composing extensible routers with dynamic protocol stacks, while *GateScript* is mainly used to customize a flow at a given protocol layer without cumbersome interpretation of the incoming data and encoding the outgoing data.

Unlike several existing platforms that require developing kernel modules or plugins [13,14], we place custom processing in the user space. Other platforms such as ALAN [8] or AS1 [1] have adopted a similar goal, but they provide support for active services working mostly at the application layer. The *GateScript* support for packet processing in the user space does not limit the scope of programmability to application layer protocols—it can deal with packets of any layer ranging from network to application.

Adaptation proxies have been extensively studied in the context of HTTP and content distribution. *CacheL* is a language that enables creating customizable caching policies based on different cache events and a set of prede-fined actions [3]. The *Open Pluggable Edge Services (OPES)* [20] IETF working group is defining an architecture that allows services to operate on application data when they transit across an intermediate node (a proxy or a surrogate server). In some sense, OPES devices (intermediaries supporting the OPES ar-chitecture) are programmable by means of a rule language that may depend on some protocol properties such as HTTP headers.

Several content adaptation proxies have been developed for image or video transcoding for wireless clients [1,7,9,4,22]. However, most of them are fixed in the sense that their functionalities cannot be dynamically extended nor custom-ized—they are only configurable, but not programmable.

The programmable video gateway [19] uses a scripting language to program a video gateway. The focus here is on the video data only and not on the protocol data structures. By integrating a parser of a given protocol, *GateScript* can deal with data packets not only at the application layer.

7 Conclusion

In this paper, we have presented *GAG*, a generic active gateway that supports *GateScript*, a scripting language for easy programming of custom processing on data packets. Unlike other active networking platforms it is

- *generic and easy to use*: we automatically create a PDU parser and reassem-bler for the protocol that needs to be enhanced with custom processing, and provide useful functions to operate on the content of PDUs; in this way, the programmer may focus on PDU processing and not on cumbersome and error prone interpretation of incoming data packets.
- *reactive*: in addition to custom processing of packets, active applications are able to react to the state of the environment: they can receive events from monitors and test variables reflecting the state of the environment;
- *flexible*: *GateScript* allows processing at different protocol layers ranging from network to application levels.

GateScript makes the development of active applications fairly easy within the grasp of a user not familiar with expert network programming. Our ex-amples show that even complex problems such as snooping TCP can be easily programmed in *GateScript*.

GateScript can be especially useful for creating personal communication gate-ways on mobile computers. In this case, we place the active gateway on a mobile host so that standard applications may benefit from network customization of flows entering the host. The user can easily specify the behavior of the gateway by injecting scripts into the *GateScript* engine. In this way, we can handle con-figuration modifications while the host changes the point of attachment to the global network. We plan to experiment with *GateScript* to develop such personal communication gateways.

We also need to get more insight into the performance of our prototype and its ability to handle an increasing number of flows, packet filters, and active applications.

Acknowledgments

This work has been partially supported by France Telecom R&D.

References

1. E. Amir, S. McCanne, and R. Katz. An Active Service Framework and its Application to Real-time Multimedia Transcoding. *ACM Communication Review*, 28(4):178–189, Sep. 1998.
2. H. Balakrishnan, S. Seshan, and R. H. Katz. Improving Reliable Transport and Handoff Performance in Cellular Wireless Networks. *ACM Wireless Networks*, 1(4), December 1995.
3. J. F. Barnes and R. Pandey. CacheL: Language Support for Customizable Caching Policies. In *the 4th International Web Caching Workshop*, San Diego, California, 1999.
4. S. Chandra, C.S. Ellis, and A. Vahdat. Multimedia Web Services for Mobile Clients Using Quality Aware Transcoding. In *the 2nd ACM International Workshop on Wireless and Mobile Multimedia (WoWMoM'99)*, Seattle, Washington, USA, August 1999.
5. D. Decasper, Z. Dittia, G. Parulkar, and B. Plattner. Router Plugins: A Software Architecture for Next Generation Routers. *IEEE/ACM Transaction on Networking*, Feb. 2000.
6. A. Eleftheriadis and D. Hong. Flavor: A Language for Media Representation. In *the Fifth ACM International Conference on Multimedia*, Seattle, Washington, 1997.
7. A. Fox and E.A. Brewer. Reducing WWW Latency and Bandwidth Requirements by Real-Time Distillation. In *the 5th International WWW Conference*, Paris, France, May 1996.
8. M. Fry and A. Ghosh. Application Level Active Networking. *Computer Networks*, 1999.
9. R. Han et al. Dynamic Adaptation in an Image Transcoding Proxy for Mobile Web Browsing . *IEEE Personal Communications Magazine*, 5(6):8–17, December 1998.
10. M. Hicks et al. PLAN: A Programming Language for Active Networks. In *Proc. ICFP '98*, 1998.
11. ipqmpd - IP Queue Multiplex Daemon. http://gnumonks.org/projects/.
12. Java Compiler Compiler (JavaCC) - The Java Parser Generator. http://www.webgain.com/products/java_cc/.
13. R. Keller, L. Ruf, A. Guindehi, and B. Plattner. PromethOS: A Dynamically Extensible Router Architecture Supporting Explicit Routing. In *IWAN02 - Fourth Annual International Working Conference on Active Networks*, Zurich, Switzerland, December 4-6, 2002.
14. A. Kind, R. Pletka, and M. Waldvogel. The Role of Network Processors in Active Networks. In *IWAN03 - Fourth Annual International Working Conference on Active Networks*, Kyoto, Japan, Dec. 2003.
15. Muffin - a World Wide Web Filtering System. http://muffin.doit.org/.

16. The NETFILTER/IPTABLES project. http://netfilter.samba.org.
17. H-B. Nguyen and A. Duda. ProAN: an Active Node for Proactive Services in Pervasive Environments. In *The 2nd International Workshop on Active Network Technologies and Applications (ANTA 2003)*, Osaka, Japan, May 2003.
18. E. Nygren, S. Garland, and M. F. Kaashoek. PAN: A High-Performance Active Network Node Supporting Multiple Mobile Code Systems. In *The Second IEEE Conference on Open Architectures and Network Programming-OpenArch99*, New York, New York, March 1999.
19. W. T. Ooi, R. Renesse, and B. Smith. Design and Implementation of Programmable Media Gateways. In *the 10th International Workshop on Network and Operating System Support for Digital Audio and Video*, Chapel Hill, North Carolina, June 2000.
20. The Open Pluggable Edge Service (OPES). http://www.ietf-opes.org.
21. S. Schmid, T. Chart, M Sifalakis, and A. C. Scott. Flexible, Dynamic and Scalable Service Composition for Active Routers. In *IWAN02 - Fourth Annual International Working Conference on Active Networks*, Zurich, Switzerland, December 4-6, 2002.
22. J. Seitz, N. Davies, M. Ebner, and A. Friday. A CORBA-based Proxy Architecture for Mobile Multimedia Applications. In *MMNS'98 - 2nd IFIP/IEEE International Conference on Management of Multimedia Networks and Services*, Versailles, France, November 1998.
23. Y. Yemini and S. Silva. Towards Programmable Networks. In *IFIP/IEEE International Workshop on Distributed Systems: Operations and Management*, L'Aquila, Italy, October 1996.

Appendix

```
GateScriptProgram  = Statements
Statements = ([static] Statement ``;'')*
Statement = AssignStatement
        | IfStatement
        | FunctionStatement
AssignStatement = "set" Variable  Expression
IfStatement = ``if'' Expression ``then''
Statements  [ElseStatement] ``endif''
ElseStatement = ``else'' Statements
OnEventStatement =``onEvent'' Expression ``then''
Statements ``endEvent''
FunctionStatement = FunctionName (Expression)*
Expression  = ConstantValue
            | ``$``Variable
              | Expression BinOp Expression
              | UnOp Expression
              | ``[`` FunctionStatement ``]``
            | ``(`` Expression ``)''
Variable    = Identifier
FunctionName = Identifier
Identifier    = Letter (Letter | Digit)*
ConstantValue = Boolean | String | Integer |
              Real | Character
```

```
BinOp        = ``+'' | ``-'' | ``*'' | ``/''
             | ``<'' | ``<='' | ``='' | ``!=''
             | ``>'' | ``>=''
             | ``and'' | ``or'' | ``contains''
UnOp         = ``-'' | ``+'' | ``!''
Boolean      = ``true'' | ``false''
String       = ``"'' (~[``"'',``\'',``\n'',
               ``\r'',"[","]"])* ``"''
Integer      = Digit (Digit)*
Real         = Integer [Fraction] [Exponent]
Fraction     = ``.'' Integer
Exponent     = (``e'' | ``E'') [``+'' | ``-'']
               Integer
Digit        = ["0"-"9"]
Letter       = ["a"-"z", "A"-"Z"] | "_"
```

Management and Performance of Virtual and Execution Environments in FAIN

Thomas Becker[1], Lawrence Cheng[2], Spyros Denazis[3], Dusan Gabrijelcic[4], Alex Galis[2], George Karetsos[5], and Antonis Lazanakis[5]

[1] Fraunhofer Institute for Open Communication Systems FOKUS, Germany
becker@fokus.fhg.de
[2] University College London, United Kingdom
{l.cheng,a.galis}@ee.ucl.ac.uk
[3] Hitachi Europe Ltd., Hitachi Sophia Antipolis, France
spyros.denazis@hitachi-eu.com
[4] Jozef Stefan Institute, Laboratory for Open Systems and Networks, Slovenia
dusan@e5.ijs.si
[5] National Technical University of Athens, Greece
{laz,gkaret}@telecom.ntua.gr

Abstract. Next generation network nodes are required to function within heterogeneous network environments, where new services and protocols are rapidly deployed on demand. In such emerging environments, traditional node architectures that offer a predetermined and preloaded set of services, are increasingly incapable of coping with these new requirements. Accordingly, there is a need for new node architectures that offer higher degrees of flexibility measured by their capability to extend the functionality of the node and change its behaviour on demand. This paper makes use of programmable and active network technologies as developed during the FAIN project[1], to present a novel secure active node architecture, called the FAIN node architecture, capable of supporting virtual environments (VEs) for the allocation of the required amount of resources in which new services are dynamically deployed together with their entire execution environments (EEs). To this end, multiple VEs and services run simultaneously and interact securely with the node resources and mechanisms through open interfaces and the FAIN node management framework. We also present the implementation of the FAIN node architecture and two case studies that demonstrate its extensibility aspects and novel features.

1 Introduction

One of the biggest obstacles faced by the networking industry today is the difficulty traditional network nodes and management stations have, in coping with increasing degrees of heterogeneity. This heterogeneity is manifested in the form of different types of networks, i.e. access, edge or core, hardware and software technologies, and

---

[1] The FAIN project is partially funded by the Commission of the European Union as IST project 10561 (www.ist-fain.org).

G.J. Minden et al. (Eds.): IWAN 2004, LNCS 3912, pp. 21–34, 2007.
© IFIP International Federation for Information Processing 2007

protocols. Accordingly, the goal for rapid and autonomous service creation, deployment, activation and management becomes even more elusive, with detrimental effects on the operator's and service providers' revenues and on their willingness to upgrade their infrastructures and support innovation. Equally important is the type of heterogeneity generated by the different communities of users and their varying requirements. Services designed and engineered to address the needs of these communities place different and, most notably, conflicting demands on the use of network resources, the degree of quality of service, the levels of security etc. Furthermore, these services must coexist with each other and evolve as their corresponding user communities evolve.

Dealing with these different types of heterogeneity is a complex problem. Its solution calls for services that are free to choose the software technology that is best suited for the needs thereof and deployed at strategic places in the network for higher performance and scalability gains. In contrast, networks must be capable of hosting such technologies, sharing and allowing the open control of their resources by a multitude of services. They must also provide the means of extending and updating their functionality on demand, thereby adapting their behaviour according to real time service/application requirements in present and future. Similar solutions are advocated by emerging hardware technologies such as network processors [1], research initiatives such as active and programmable networks [2][3][4][5] and standardisation efforts such as IETF ForCES [6] and IEEE P1520 [7][8].

In this paper, we attempt to provide an elaborate answer to the question about the characteristics and features of the next generation network architectures that support the aforementioned network capabilities. Central to such network architectures is the network node architecture the detailed description of which is used in order to demonstrate how such design goals have been met. Section 2 starts with a summary of the main concepts of the FAIN project [19]. In section 3, we present the FAIN node architecture with its major architectural components, namely, the VE management framework, the Resource Control Framework, the Demultiplexing/Multiplexing system, and the Security system. In section 4, we describe the implementation of different types of EEs on FAIN nodes. Next, we outline two case studies built as part of the FAIN project with initial performance measurements. In section 6, we contrast FAIN concepts and innovation with related work from the state of the art. Finally, our conclusions and future work are given in section 7.

2 FAIN Overview

The FAIN node architecture heavily draws on the FAIN reference architecture and the two main concepts of the FAIN project, namely, the Virtual Environment (VE) and the component based EE (a particular type of EE). A detailed description may be found in [9][10]. The FAIN reference architecture proposes a node that supports the partitioning of its resources assigned to VEs. VEs act as containers in which multiple EEs may be deployed. In turn, EEs act as hosts to the services running in them, and consuming resources allocated to VEs. EEs also represent different implementations (technologies), implying that services must be implemented in the same technology as the EE, e.g. Java EE, in order to be deployed in the EE. Services may be distributed across different EEs, which, in turn, may be interconnected with each other. The interconnected EEs may reside in different operational planes, namely, control, management and transport. This approach has also been recently adopted by the ForCES model [11]. Finally, access to node resources and services is achieved through open interfaces [12], which act as an interoperability layer among the different implementations.

The FAIN node provides additional support for the component-based type of EE, being one of the most flexible programming environments for service deployment. Its existence implies that services must be designed and developed along the lines of the component-based approach in order to exploit the EE's capabilities. According to this approach, complex services are composed of simpler ones, which are then connected together to form specific structures representative of the service. In this way, services become extensible, their lifecycle management is simplified, and they can be readily introduced in the network. VEs are part of a virtual network owned by a provider. The provider uses the virtual network and consequently the VEs to deploy customer services and control the allocated resources according to its policies. As services may require the presence of specific EEs, these EEs must also be deployed. Each node must then make sure that the allocated resources are solely used by the owner of the virtual network and charged only to the appropriate services running in it. In other words, a VE provides a place where services together with their execution environments may be instantiated and used by a community of users or groups of applications while remaining isolated from others residing in different VEs. In the next section we describe the FAIN node architecture specified according to these design principles.

3 FAIN Node Architecture

Fig. 1 depicts the FAIN node architecture with its major components, and its interaction with the management node that includes the Active Service Provisioning (ASP) and Policy Based Management System (PBNM) [13]. When the FAIN node boots up, a Privileged VE (pVE), with its VE manager (VEM) component, is

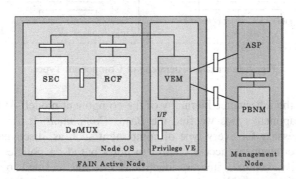

Fig. 1. FAIN active node architecture and its components

automatically instantiated. The VE manager implements the VE management framework that offers access to a number of node services necessary to configure, setup and manage the node. Four major operations may be carried out: a) deployment and instantiation of VEs, b) deployment and instantiation of a number of EEs, c) deployment, instantiation and interconnection of service components with an EE, and d) control and management of a service component or a resource by means of open interfaces, leading to the interconnection of EEs residing in different operational planes (see Fig. 1). The VEM interacts with the Security component that offers a set of security services and enforces node policies, the Resource control component responsible for implementing the FAIN resource control framework (RCF) and the demultiplexing/multiplexing component which is configured to deliver packets to the right VE and EE when the latter has been deployed. In the subsequent sections, we describe each one of these components.

3.1 The FAIN VE Management Framework

The purpose of the VE management framework is to manage virtual environments and their allocated resources as well as the services installed therein. According to this framework, services and resources are both represented as components, which all offer a specific set of ports. Ports are used to inter-connect components and to make a component's particular functionality available to the outside. In the case of a resource component, it also represents a certain share of the available computation, storage, or communication capacity of the node. Components may be combined in various formations creating in this way more complex resources and services from simpler ones.

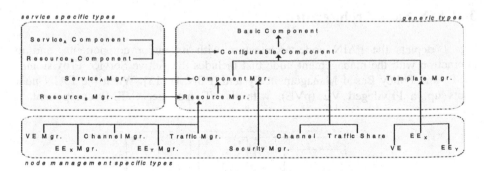

Fig. 2. Inheritance Hierarchy of Component Types

Fig. 2 depicts the inheritance hierarchy of the component model. At the root of the hierarchy of component types we find the *Basic Component*. It abstracts common functionality necessary for every type of component such as, discovery of the ports provided by the component, access control to ports based on policies defined in an individual security context, unique identification, and defined ownership. The *Configurable Component* adds to this the possibility to get and set the current internal configuration of the component in the form of a list of name-value pairs. It also offers operations to set up and manage connections between its own ports and the ports of other components. Using these operations of the Configurable Component, one can create services out of a set of available components by interconnecting and configuring them appropriately.

Components of a certain type need to be discovered, instantiated, linked with other components, and deleted when not in use. This is the job of the *Component Manager*. Since components may represent resources in the node we have extended the component manager with the *Resource Manager* that manages resources according to their allocated resource quotas. These resource instances represent a certain resource share for which the current usage can be monitored and callbacks can be registered for notifications when specific thresholds are reached.

As mentioned earlier, resources are allocated to specific VEs and services are deployed together with their entire EEs within VEs. Accordingly, the component model has been enhanced with a number of specific component types and managers in order to adhere to the FAIN design principles. They consist of management of VEs and EEs, security, traffic, and packet dispatching. More specifically, the *VE Manager* is acting as a factory and finder for VEs. It will allocate requested resource shares using other basic managers during the creation of a new VE and monitor the overall resource usage during its lifetime. Various technology specific *EE Managers* take care of the management of EEs providing the runtime environments for component instances, e.g. a Java virtual machine. The *Channel Manager* is used to create channels which forward packets from the network to connected component instances based on a set of rules and also send packets coming from component instances to the network. The *Traffic Manager* partitions the node's available bandwidth into shares and allows to assign packet flows to them. The *Security Manager* is used to set up and manage the individual security contexts which are assigned to each component instance during its creation and used to control the access to the instance's ports.

After the creation of the requested resource shares the VE Manager will attach them to the new VE so they are available to service components which will be installed and instantiated inside the VE later. In order to install components we introduced the notion of a *Template Manager*. A template is identified by a name and a version number and includes a particular implementation of a component type together with its corresponding component manager type. Both VEs and EEs are Template Managers and thus support the installation and management of component types. While an EE provides a concrete technology dependent runtime environment for component instances the VE abstracts from this. During the installation of a template the VE will try to find an appropriate EE in the list of attached EEs and forward the installation request to the EE. The EE is then responsible to carry out the technology dependent steps to make the new component type available.

The generic component framework serves as a starting point for new services or resource abstractions (see upper left part of Fig. 2). A developer would implement specific component types by deriving from the basic or configurable component types and simply add the implementation for the service specific ports, if any. For service components the developer would derive a manager type from the generic component manager type while for resource components the resource manager type would be used.

3.2 The FAIN Resource Control Framework (RCF), Demultiplexor (De/MUX), and Security

In the design of the FAIN node, major attention was given to the management of the node resources and their sharing among the various users of the node. The part of the node responsible for this task is called Resource Control Framework (RCF). An overview of the RCF is given here. Detail descriptions of the RCF can be found at [30][32]. The RCF is considered very important as it supports one of the major design goals of the FAIN project: the partitioning of resources (capacities) among VEs and their residing services. Through resource partitioning, supported by the RCF, the various VEs are kept isolated from each other and allowed to consume only the allocated amount of resources. In a similar manner, VEs are enabled to further allocate, manage and control their own (virtual) resources according to the VE's own policies and logic, customised according to the type of services that are running in them.

As a FAIN node supports multiple VEs with multiple EEs running in them, arriving packets must be delivered in a secure way to the right entity inside the node. The functional entity responsible for delivering packets is the Demultiplexing/Multiplexing (De/MUX) component. An overview of the De/MUX architecture is presented here. For details readers should refer to [30][31]. The design of the De/MUX is also influenced by and built according to the component model principles, thereby making use of the VE management framework and its abstractions. The main components of the De/MUX are the Channel Manager and the Channel components. The Channel Manager is responsible for creating and deleting the Channel object. The Channel object is created for each VE. The specific types of Channels correspond to different types of flow packets arriving at the node: namely active and non-active (data) packets but these may be extended to new types of packets by introducing new Channels and deploying them through the VE management framework mechanisms. Furthermore, the De/MUX also interfaces with the Security architecture, which provides a safety framework to protect against unauthorised active packet processing. When the Channel Manager receives the active packets, it calls a security interface to execute security check, the result of which determines whether the Channel Manager forwards or discards the active packets. For outgoing active packets, the Channel Manager calls the security interface to insert security information into them, used for executing the security checks at the next active node.

Active networking raises a number of different security issues, and FAIN designed and implemented a complete security architecture to address these issues. As this security architecture is thoroughly explained by another paper [27] we only discuss here the functionality and aspects relevant to the VE management framework. To this end, we distinguish between two different categories of facilities the security functionality offers: a) *Communication security facilities* are set of services, protocols and mechanisms that provide at system level data origin authentication and integrity services for packets exchanged in between nodes. Combination of per hop protection, which uses symmetric cryptography, and protection regarding the originator, which uses asymmetric cryptography, were used to protect active packets data tackling the issue that parts of the packets (i.e. the packets' payload) may be changed in the network, whilst certain parts of the packets (i.e. static executable codes) should remain unmodified; *b) System security facilities* are set of services and mechanisms that provide authorization and policy enforcement on a node, system integrity, code verification and accountability of system operation.

4 EE Implementation

The implementations of EEs may differ in the employed technology and the way deployed service components are executed. Two different types of EE were implemented in FAIN: a) the Java EE, and b) the Active SNMP EE. The Java EE type is used for the installation and execution of components implemented in Java. It also serves as the EE for the node's management layer described in section 3.1. For the management of templates (i.e. component types) a Java class loader is employed. At the operating system level, the Java EE is mapped as a separate process executing a Java virtual machine (JVM) charged to the VE it belongs to. The CPU and memory usage of all Java EE processes are monitored by the Java EE manager and will be temporarily suspended when the previously agreed resources are overused for a certain amount of time. Although the underlying component model allows connections between component ports using arbitrary protocols, the Java EE implements component ports as CORBA interfaces. Consequently, the communication inside the management layer is based on CORBA. The enforcement of access control policies for those ports is realised with CORBA portable object adaptors and interceptors interacting closely with the respective component's security context. The implementation of access control enforcement also supports delegation so that a chain of calls via a series of interfaces can be checked against policies. The Active SNMP EE [14][17][29] extends the functionality of Safe and Nimble Active Packet (SNAP) active packet protocol [15] through exploitation of the SNMP protocol. SNAP packets essential contain a series of byte code instructions. It is claimed to be light-weight, efficient, safe and practical. The discussion of SNAP is beyond the scope of this paper. For details of SNAP, readers should refer to [15]. It is a management EE we have built in FAIN and is used in the Diffserv scenario presented in the next section and in [30]. Other examples of management EE are for instance the Smart Environment for Network Control, Monitoring and Management (SENCOMM) [33]. The FAIN management EE consists of two components: a) the *SNAP Activator*: consisting of the SNAP Sender/Receiver and the snapd (snap daemon), and b) the *ANEP-SNAP Packet Engine* (ASPE). The SNAP Sender is responsible for generating SNAP packets and injecting them into the network. The snapd is extended to include SNMP functionalities and is responsible for the execution of SNAP active packets. The ASPE is responsible for providing ANEP encapsulation/de-encapsulation for SNAP packets, and co-ordinates Active SNMP EE operations with De/MUX and SEC for transmitting active packets and for securing active packets during-transit across the network, respectively [14][17].

5 Case Studies

The Diffserv scenario [16][30] demonstrates the deployment of *heterogeneous technologies* (EEs) on *different planes* (i.e. control / management planes) for enhancing flexibility and extensibility in the FAIN architecture; this is demonstrated through the co-existence of *multiple heterogeneous* EEs within a VE, and subsequently a generic approach for *inter-EE communications*. In addition, the *dynamic deployment of service components* (i.e. a DiffservController) within an EE to support new services through *interactions* between various FAIN components was also demonstrated. The full Diffserv scenario was presented in [30]. The WebTV scenario was proposed in order to demonstrate the deployment of a service component together with its corresponding EE. According to it, a WebTV Service Provider requests the creation of a VE in order to use the node resources for transmitting video to his customers. A new customer that wants to get this service is not capable of receiving the stream in the transmitting format. For this reason the Service Provider (SP) dynamically downloads to a nearby node a service component in the form of a transcoder that is compatible with the customer's system. This component adheres to the definition of the component model which makes it possible to seamlessly deploy it using the VEM. The service component is instantiated in a Java EE and the flow is rerouted to be processed by the new component [13] [16], which sends the TV stream in the correct format. In contrast with the Diffserv scenario, the WebTV scenario deploys an EE in the transport plane wherein packet receive additional processing through the newly deployed service component. This component may be further configured e.g. changing the value of the transcoder to a new one, by another EE that resides in the control or management plane.

5.1 Performance Trials

Performance trails for the Diffserv scenario were carried out with the objective of evaluating the viability of the features of the FAIN active node; namely the *VEM bootup time* (i.e. node instantiation time and manager installation time), and *service deployment time*. A PC with an Intel 746MHz Pentium III CPU and 512MB memory was used to measure the VEM bootup time. Note that the bootup sequence of VEM on a FAIN active node involves two steps: node initialisation and managers installation. The average total time for node initialisation is 313.8 ms. This is the average time to initialise an ORB (4.6 ms), a pEE (94.1 ms) and a pVE (165.2 ms). The average manager installation time for installing the VE manager is 389.6 ms, 72 ms for the Java EE manager, 2146.5 ms for the channel manager, 76.7 ms for SEC manager, 75.9 ms for traffic manager, 23.1 ms for Diffserv manager, 28 ms for Active SNMP EE manager. An addition 6.1 ms for finishing the boot sequence. Thus the average total time for booting up VEM on a FAIN active node is 3031.9 ms. Note that different times for installing different managers mainly depend on the individual size and numbers of classes to be loaded. The channel manager also has to load an external library for connecting to Linux netfilter. For service deployment performance measurement, a PC with an Intel 995MHz Pentium III CPU and 112MB RAM was used. The average active packet processing time in the Active SNMP EE is 19.3 ms.

Note that in a real-life scenario, the VEM is expected to be brought up once only when a FAIN active node boots up. Consequently, a service EE deployed in a VE is brought up only when there is a new service request. Thus neither node instantiation nor manager installation is frequent. Moreover, VEM will operate for a long period of time commensurate with the lifetime of the SP virtual network. Although service (i.e. EE) deployment is comparatively more frequent, it should be noted that dynamic service creation on networks through service EE deployment is much more efficient than manually configuring each node to enable new services. Given that the enhanced level of flexibility of the FAIN active node architecture, the results of these feasibility trials are encouraging, and are proving the feasibility of deploying FAIN active nodes in a real network.

Another test was run in order to get an assessment of the scalability of the Java based EE and thus the implementation of the FAIN active node's management layer. For this test a PC with an Intel 746MHz Pentium III CPU and 512MB was used. After the boot-up of the privileged VE eight separate VEs with attached Java EEs were created (average of 8 seconds per VE/Java EE). Using a local test client a Java based test service was installed in each of the eight VEs (average of 366 milliseconds per installation) and for each VE 1000 instances were created and configured. As an example for user-space packet processing the test service connects itself to the respective VE's packet dispatching channel during configuration which requires also interaction with the privileged VE where the dispatching channels are managed. For the test security was enabled, i.e. the communication between the test client, the privileged VE and the particular VE was secured and access to the involved components was controlled by the security manager. Fig. 3 shows the times in milliseconds for the creation and configuration of instances versus the number of instances for each VE. For the first few instances the minimal time is decreasing due to already loaded classes in the Java EEs. After that the average time is increasing constantly with the number of instances already created. The sporadic peaks are most probably due to garbage collection inside the Java EEs. The average time for service creation is still below 500 milliseconds for 1000 service instances per VE. Considering the non-trivial service configuration which requires interaction with the

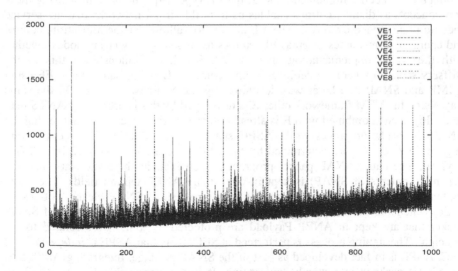

Fig. 3. Service creation in 8 VEs with attached Java EEs

packet dispatcher inside the privileged VE plus the control of all interactions by the security manager we argue that this figure is acceptable and the Java based implementation of the FAIN active node's management layer scales well.

6 Related Work

The definition of EEs was defined by DARPA. EEs can be treated as the runtime environment of a process or a process itself [20], or toolkits for building active applications (services) [18], or a programming environment characterised by the implementation language, like Java [4] [21]. EEs have also been proposed as extensions of the Node OS [22] whereas in [23] [24] EEs are characterised not by the choice of technologies but rather by the services they offer and the architectural plane they operate at, namely, control, management, and transport. In other cases, EEs are treated as VEs acting as the principal abstraction for authentication, authorisation and resource control [21] [22]. As a result the reference architecture proposed in [21] makes it very difficult to support inter-EE communication either within the same node or in different ones. All this ambiguity has an impact on defining a systematic approach around a consistent model that facilitates the dynamic deployment of new services taking into consideration the de-facto heterogeneity found in the network in the form of hardware and software technologies, protocols etc

In contrast, FAIN attempted to deal with the problem of service deployment in heterogeneous networks by defining a reference architecture [9] based on a clear separation between VEs and EEs. Another approach to isolating active services from each other was described in [34], [35], [36].To this end, we have used the same approach in defining and using VEs as in [12], while EEs are distinguished between *EE type* (the programming environment and programming methodology) and *EE instance* (the specific implementation of the EE type) [9]. The benefit of using these two concepts as distinct entities enables us to build virtual networks that are service specific (e.g. service overlays). The VE abstraction allows for the allocation, control and charging of resources whereas EEs allows us to deploy services in nodes together with the whole implementation environment. We have demonstrated this in the Diffserv scenario where we deployed a Java control EE and a management EE using SNMP and SNAP (the latter was developed by the Switchware team). In the same way, using the VEM framework other EEs developed by third parties, e.g. ANTS may be deployed and combined with EEs already present in the node. Note that during the ANEP encapsulation process at the ASPE, static contents of a SNAP packet program (e.g. the byte codes) are determined by the ASPE and are encapsulated into ANEP Payload. The entire SNAP packet program (which includes both the static and the dynamic contents of SNAP) is kept in one of the ANEP Option fields. The static contents of SNAP packet can be easily determined since SNAP clearly defines its static contents to be its byte codes stored on its stack. The static contents of SNAP packet that are kept in ANEP Payload are protected by a signature related to the principal. The signing process is performed at SEC. Note that ASPE is *independent* of SEC. ASPE is in fact developed as part of the SNAP package. Integrating ASPE into the SNAP package is currently undergoing. It is the responsible for the ASPE to recognised the packet format of SNAP and to determine which parts of the SNAP packet are static. Whereas the ANEP Option that keeps the SNAP packet program (which includes both the static and dynamic contents of SNAP) is protected by hop protection again at SEC. Symmetric cryptography techniques are used for hop-protection, a solution that is similar to deploying the Authentication Header in IPSec [16] [17] in a per-hop fashion. The advantage of keeping the *entire* SNAP packet in an ANEP Option is that no packet marshalling at the Active SNMP EE is needed: the entire SNAP packet is put into the ANEP Option. This is in contrast with existing authentication methods such as SANTS (Secure ANTS) [28] where static and dynamic contents of an active packet are actually *split* and encapsulated into corresponding ANEP fields. When encapsulating ANTS packets in ANEP in the SANTS approach, it was said that "The variable area of our (ANEP) packet includes the variable fields of the EE header (of ANTS) and the variable portions of the data payload (of ANTS)" [28]. This implies certain (variable) parts of ANTS packets must be extracted and placed in the variable area of ANEP packet. This incurs overhead on packet marshalling at each node. By avoiding packet splitting the overall efficiency of the security processing on FAIN architecture is improved. Also, unlike the SANTS approach in which a modified ANEP format is used to keep active packets, the standard ANEP format is used in FAIN to avoid interoperability problems. Full explanation on the functionalities of the ASPE can be found in [17] [29]. The process of integrating the ASPE functionalities into the SNAP package is currently undergoing.

The component-based approach heavily draws on the Netscript and the IEEE P1520. We have generalised it to treat also node resources as components that can dynamically be deployed upon request and accessed via open control interfaces. These control interfaces may be instantiated on demand in any EE irrespective of its implementation. In this way services are enabled to control their allocated resources from their specific implementation environment.

In FAIN we have also built a high-performance EE [25] residing in the Linux kernel-space in order to deploy service components with time restrictions. This EE is deployed using the same toolset offered by VEM and controlled by control EEs implemented in Java residing in the user-space. Furthermore, we have used the reference model of the architecture to automate the process of service provisioning in the network. This is achieved through the network Active Service Provisioning system [26] which uses VEM to enforce the deployment decisions taken at the network level.

7 Conclusion

In this paper we have presented the FAIN Active Node architecture, capable of combining and coordinating different Execution Environments that represent different technologies which are then used to host service components and interact with each other as part of the overall service operation. To this end, the FAIN node may change or extend its functionality and seamlessly operate in a heterogeneous network. This has been achieved through the definition of the VE management framework that combines EEs, VEs, and service components.

The VE management framework is realised through a number of classes with methods that allow EEs to be deployed in VEs, in turn, service components to be deployed and linked with existing services in EEs, and exports control interfaces of these components for their configuration. The operation of the EEs, and of the services running in them, is regulated by the FAIN resource control framework. This framework is based on the VE abstraction, which is used as a principal for accounting and resource allocation and partition. Moreover, all the operations take place in a secure environment founded on the flexible FAIN security architecture, which provides authentication, authorisation of the use of resources and verification of packets. The FAIN node architecture and its components have been implemented, and a number of different EEs residing in different operational planes and interworking with each other have been created. Their functionality and mechanisms achieve the design goals. The JavaEE, residing in the management plane, binds together all the FAIN node components as well as the other EEs. Finally, the flexibility of the FAIN node and its new features has been demonstrated through two case studies, namely, Diffserv and WebTV deployment.

Acknowledgments

This paper describes work undertaken and in progress in the context of the FAIN – IST 10561, a three year project (2000-2003), that is partially funded by the Commission of the European Union. The authors would like to acknowledge other members of the FAIN consortium.

References

[1] IEEE Network Magazine, Special Issue on Network Processors, Harrick Vin and Raj Yavatkar (eds), Vol. 17, No 4, July/August 2003.
[2] Open Signalling Working Group, http://www.comet.columbia.edu/opensig/.
[3] Campbell, A. T., H. De Meer, M. E. Kounavis, K. Miki, J. Vicente, and D. Villela "A Survey of Programmable Networks", ACM Computer Communications Review, April 1999
[4] Johnathan M. Smith, Kenneth Calvert, Sandy Murphy, Hilarie K. Orman, and Larry L. Peterson, "Activating Networks: A Progress Report", IEEE Computer 32(4):32–41, April 1999.
[5] Jonathan M. Smith, Scott M. Nettles, "Active Networking: One View of the Past, Present and Future", Special Issue of IEEE T-SMC on technologies promoting computational intelligence, openness and programmability in networks and Internet services, Autumn 2003 (in press)
[6] IETF ForCES, http://www.ietf.org/html.charters/forces-charter.html
[7] Biswas, J., et al., "The IEEE P1520 Standards Initiative for Programmable Network Interfaces", IEEE Communications, Special Issue on Programmable Networks, Vol. 36, No 10, October, 1998
[8] Vicente, J., S. Denazis, et al., "L-interface Building Block APIs", IEEE P1520.3, P1520.3TSIP016, 2001.
[9] S. Denazis, S. Karnouskos, T. Suzuki, S. Yoshizawa, "Component-based Execution Environments of Network Elements and a Protocol for their Configuration", IEEE - Transactions on Systems, Man and Cybernetics, Special Issue on Technologies that promote computational intelligence, openness and programmability in networks and Internet services, February 2004 (in press)

[10] "Overview FAIN Programmable Network and Management Architecture", FAIN Project Deliverable 14

[11] Yang, L., J. Halpern, R. Gopal, R. Dantu, "ForCES Forwarding Element Functional Model", March 2003.

[12] J.E. van der Merwe, S. Rooney, I.M. Leslie and S.A. Crosby, "The Tempest - A Practical Framework for Network Programmability", IEEE Network, Vol 12, Number 3, May/June 1998, pp.20-28.

[13] Christos Tsarouchis, Chiho Kitahara, Spyros Denazis, et. al., "A Policy-Based Management Architecture for Active and Programmable Networks", Special Issue on Network Management of Multi-service, Multimedia, IP-based Networks, IEEE Network Magazine, May/June 2003.

[14] Eaves, W., Cheng, L., Galis, A., "SNAP Based Resource Control for Active Networks", IEEEGLOBECOM 2002.

[15] Moore, J., Hicks, M., Nettles, S., "Practical Programmable Packets", Proceedings IEEE INFOCOM 2001.

[16] FAIN Project Deliverable D40 - FAIN Demonstrators and Scenarios, http://www.ist-fain.org/deliverables

[17] Cheng, L., Eaves, W., Galis, A., "Strong Authentication for Active Networks", IEEE-Softcom 2003.

[18] Wetherall, D.J., "ANTS: a toolkit for building and dynamically deploying network protocols", OpenArch 1998, San Francisco, CA, April 1998, pp.117-129, IEEE.

[19] A. Galis, S. Denazis, C. Brou, C. Klein, (ed) – " Programmable Networks and Programmable Network Management " ISBN 1-58053-745-6; contracted for publishing in Q4 2003 by Artech House Books, 46 Gillingham Street, London SW1V 1AH, UK; www.artechhouse.com

[20] Steven Berson, Bob Braden, and Livio Ricciulli, "Introduction to The ABone", June 15, 2000.

[21] "Architectural Framework for Active Networks", Draft version 1.0, K.L. Calvert, ed., July 27, 1999. http://protocols.netlab.uky.edu/~calvert/arch-latest.ps

[22] "Node OS Interface Specification", AN Node OS Working Group, Larry Peterson, ed., November 30, 2001.

[23] Bhattacharjee, S., "Active networks: Architectures, Composition, and Applications", Ph.D. Thesis, Georgia Tech, July 1999

[24] B. Braden, A. Cerpa, T. Faber, B. Lindell, G. Phillips, J. Kann and V. Shenoy, "Introduction to the ASP Execution Environment (Release 1.5)", Nov 30, 2001.

[25] R. Keller, L. Ruf, A. Guindehi, B. Plattner. PromethOS: A Dynamically Extensible Router Architecture Supporting Explicit Routing, Proceedings of the Fourth Annual International Working Conference on Active Networks IWAN, Zurich, Switzerland, December 2002. Lecture Notes in Computer Science 2546, Springer Verlag.

[26] Y. Nikolakis, E. Magana, M. Solarski, A. Tan, E. Salamanca, J. Serrat, "A Policy-Based Management Architecture for Flexible Service Deployment in Active Networks", IWAN 2003, Kyoto, Japan 2003

[27] D. Gabrijelčič, B. J. Blažič, J. Tasič, Future Active IP Networks Security architecture, Computer Communications Special Issue on Activated Internet, 2004, in revision.

[28] S. Murphy, "Strong Security for Active Network", IEEE OpenArch 2001.

[29] L. Cheng, "Active Networks Authentication", LCS 2003.

[30] T. Suzuki, S. Denazis, L. Cheng, T. Becker, D. Gabrijelcic, A. Lazanakis, "Dynamic Deployment & Configuration of Differentiated Services Using Active Networks", IWAN 2003.

[31] Chapter 4, FAIN Project Deliverable D7 – Final Active Node Architecture and Design, http://www.ist-fain.org/deliverables/del7/d7.pdf

[32] Chapter 3, FAIN Project Deliverable D7 – Final Active Node Architecture and Design, http://www.ist-fain.org/deliverables/del7/d7.pdf

[33] A. Jackson, "Active Monitoring and Control: The SENCOMM Architecture and Implementation', Proceedings of the DARPA Active Networks Conference and Exposition (DANCE), 2002 pp.379-393.

[34] M. Brunner, "Service Management in Multiparty Active Networks", IEEE Communications Magazine, 2000, p.144-151

[35] M. Brunner, B. Plattner, R. Stadler, "Service Creation and Management in Active Telecom Environments" Communications of the ACM, March 2001

[36] A. Galis, D. Griffin, W. Eaves, et. al - "Mobile Software in Active Virtual Pipes: Support for Virtual Enterprises" pp. 427-450 in "On The Way To Information Society," ed. Magedanz et. al., IOS Press, Amsterdam, The Netherlands, ISBN 1 58603 007 8, April 2000.

Secure, Customizable,
Many-to-One Communication

Kenneth L. Calvert, James Griffioen, Billy Mullins, Leon Poutievski,
and Amit Sehgal*

Laboratory for Advanced Networking, University of Kentucky, Lexington, KY

Abstract. Concast is a customizable many-to-one network-layer communication
service. Although programmable services like concast can improve the efficiency
of group applications, accompanying security concerns must be addressed before they are likely to be deployed. The problem of securing such services is
interesting because conventional end-to-end security mechanisms are not applicable when messages are processed inside the network, and also because of the
potential for interaction among the various policies involved. In this paper we
describe our implementation of a secure concast service, which leverages existing network-level security mechanisms (IPsec) to provide secure distribution of
program code (merge specifications) as well as authentication of participating
nodes. We describe the various policies supported, how they interact, and how
our approach provides security against various attacks.

1 Introduction

The design of the Internet protocols has produced a remarkably flexible, robust, and
scalable system. Perhaps nowhere is the end-to-end design principle more evident than
in the area of security, where the best services and solutions are universally considered
to be those that are closest to the application. Over time, however, a number of network
services have appeared that involve, in one way or another, processing that occurs in
the shared infrastructure, *away* from the end systems on which the applications reside.
Many of these services depend on the ability to look beyond the information needed for
traditional forwarding (i.e. the packet header), into the packet payload. In some cases,
this processing is performed on the application's behalf *during* forwarding [1,2,3,4,5,6].

The problem of securing applications that rely on this type of processing[1] is interesting because the conventional end-to-end security solutions preclude processing that
occurs apart from the endpoints, and thus are incompatible with such applications. In
addition, reliance on the infrastructure to perform processing on behalf of the application implies the existence of multiple policies that need to be enforced.

The *concast* service is a good example of a service that performs processing on
the applications behalf during forwarding. Concast is a many-to-one communication
service that can be viewed as a companion service to multicast (i.e., the inverse of one-
to-many communication). In concast, multiple senders transmit data packets towards

---

* Authors are listed in alphabetical order.
[1] As opposed to securing applications *against* involuntary processing in the infrastructure.

G.J. Minden et al. (Eds.): IWAN 2004, LNCS 3912, pp. 35–53, 2007.
© IFIP International Federation for Information Processing 2007

a single receiver which results in a single packet, containing the combined (merged) data from the multiple senders, being delivered to the receiver. Because the merging operation is application-dependent, concast allows end systems to define the merge processing that is applied at internal network nodes. The benefit of concast is in reducing the limiting factor on the scalability: from the total number of senders to the branching factor at any node.

In this paper we consider the problem of securing scalable infrastructure-based services, in particular the problem of creating a secure concast service. We outline a set of security requirements for such services, and identify the relevant policies and trust relationships involved. We then describe a new security approach based on the fundamental idea that the control plane can be secured using conventional point-to-point security techniques for authentication, confidentiality, and integrity. Given a secure control plane, the responsibility for end-to-end security can then be distributed among the participating nodes. We describe the application of our approach to implementing a secure concast service. We report performance measurements taken from our prototype implementation of the secure concast service.

2   Security Requirements

We assume a network environment in which network services are offered to users as a business proposition by *service providers*. We believe that a customizable service will only be deployed if it offers some benefit to the service provider. We assume this benefit takes the form of money paid to the provider in return for access to the enhanced service. Thus our first security requirement is:

> *Only authorized users can take advantage of the customizable service.*

We assume that users will pay for a service only if they are assured of receiving some benefit from it. In the case of concast, the main benefit to the user is *scalability through anonymity*: by moving application-specific processing into the network infrastructure, the service hides the details of where the data is coming from and how much processing is occurring. To put it another way: placing application-specific processing in the infrastructure hides scale and complexity from the users. This leads to an additional requirement:

> *The scale and complexity of the processing should not be exposed at any single point.*

As a consequence, the user must rely on the network to carry out processing according to user-supplied specifications. On one level, this is no different than any other network service. However, in terms of security there is of course a profound difference between relying on the network to *forward* data as opposed to examining and possibly *modifying* it. In the former case, end-to-end security mechanisms exist that can provide assurance that (under standard assumptions) user data is not disclosed or tampered with. In the latter case, the users not only have to trust the network to carry out the specified processing, but also to protect the confidentiality and integrity of the application's data. That is, the user/application has to rely on the network infrastructure to enforce its *security policies*. This brings us to the third security requirement:

Integrity and confidentiality of application data are protected according to user-supplied policies.

In other words, a user-supplied policy specifying the entities authorized to participate in that instance is associated with each instance of the service.

This requirement is nontrivial for two reasons. First, because the infrastructure is a key participant in the enhanced service, the application policy needs to cover not only users, but also components of the infrastructure (nodes). In other words, each participant must be able to identify nodes that are *not* trusted to carry out processing on its behalf, and the service provider must take steps to prevent such nodes from participating in providing service to that user. Second, and more importantly, the service is designed so that the set of participating nodes grows incrementally, hop-by-hop toward participating users. Participants are *only* aware of other participants (either users or infrastructure nodes) that are up to one hop away; this is a fundamental characteristic that is required for scalability and indeed, even for practical deployment. As a consequence, users cannot themselves ensure that only trusted nodes participate in the service; they must rely on the infrastructure to enforce their policies on participation.

Our approach to satisfying the last two requirements is to state an invariant that is to be maintained at all times by the service:

All participating nodes are trusted by the user to enforce user policies regarding (i) processing, confidentiality and integrity of user data; and (ii) which nodes are trusted to participate.

In other words, we rely on (an explicit form of) *transitive trust.* This seems to be an unavoidable requirement for *scalable* services that rely on third parties for key functionality.

3 Securing a Programmable Service

The first step in securing a programmable service is establishing trust relationships between the participating entities (senders, receivers, and network nodes).

Trust relationships can be represented as the set of principals (nodes) that are allowed to perform certain actions (e.g., join the concast group, receive the merge specification, or be given an encryption key). We say a *policy* defines the set of nodes that can perform a certain action. For example, a concast receiver will define the list of sender nodes that are allowed to join the group (called the *join policy*). At the same time, each local node in the provider's network will define the list of end-systems that are allowed to use the concast service (e.g., have paid for the service). Clearly, both policies must be met before a sender is allowed to join a concast group.

The most important policy is the one that defines the nodes that can be trusted to enforce the policies of others. This type of transitive trust is critical for network-level services where processing occurs hop-by-hop. Because the user's data does not remain encrypted end-to-end, intermediate nodes that handle the user's data must enforce the user's policies on the user's behalf. If a node cannot be trusted to enforce the user's policies, that node cannot be allowed to participate in the service. For example, a concast receiver must rely on routers in the network to enforce the receiver's join policy. If unauthorized senders were allowed to send data along the concast flow and the membership check did not occur until the merged packet reached the receiver, it would be too late. The damage (corruption of authorized sender data) would already have occurred at intermediate nodes in the network.

The key to achieving a scalable yet secure service is the ability to incrementally add nodes to the service such that the invariant is not violated. To initiate a secure service, the user's policies must be propagated, hop-by-hop through the network, checking the integrity of each node along the path before adding them to the flow.

Note the above description assumes that policies are themselves propagated securely. At each hop along the propagation path, the adjacent nodes must authenticate one another and verify policy compliance before proceeding. Once authenticity and authorization have been established, the policies can be sent over a confidential channel. Because the trust relationships are established hop-by-hop, existing point-to-point security techniques can be used. In particular, protocols such as IPsec can be used to perform both the authentication check and create the confidential tunnel over which policies can be sent.

Once a path of trusted network hops has been established, this path can be used for control plane messages; in particular, control messages that enable service-specific processing at each trusted node along the path. Given a secure (programmable) control plane, end-systems can take on the responsibility for security in the data plane, providing modules that offer as much or as little security as desired. In other words, by supporting a secure, authenticated, hop-by-hop signaling protocol in the control plane, applications can implement end-to-end security in the data plane, thereby maintaining the end-to-end principle.

In the next section, we present a specific approach for implementing a secure control plane, and show how it can be applied to the concast service. The approach is novel in the sense that it leverages existing point-to-point secure communication protocols (i.e., IPsec) to create a secure path and distribute policies and user-specified processing modules. Given this basic infrastructure, end-systems then define and control security in the data plane by programming the service appropriately.

3.1   The Concast Service

Before we describe how a secure concast service can be implemented using our approach, we need to take a moment and briefly review the basic (non-secure) concast service. Additional details of the concast service can be found in our earlier papers [7] and [1].

Concast is a many-to-one communication service that provides the symmetric inverse of multicast: a group of senders belonging to a *concast flow* transmit messages that are *merged* by the network en route to a common receiver R. Like multicast, concast provides a scalable abstraction: an arbitrary number of *group members* (senders) are treated as a single entity by R. A concast flow is identified by its receiver R and a group identifier G; senders "join" the flow before they begin sending.

The packets delivered to R on a concast flow are derived from the packets sent by the group members according to a *merge specification (MS)* supplied by the receiving application. The concast service allows a limited amount of network programmability, where the desired processing semantics are defined within the framework of a merge specification. The merge specification defines (1) how datagrams delivered to the receiver are derived from datagrams transmitted by different senders (2) the timing of datagram forwarding and delivery; and (3) which datagrams are combined with each other (e.g. only packets containing the same sequence number are merged with each other). The merge specification is supplied by the receiver at flow creation time (e.g. in the form of bytecodes for a collection of Java classes conforming to a certain type specification), and is executed by a merge daemon (*Merged*) at each network node.

Concast *merge specification* deployment is accomplished via the *Concast Signaling Protocol (CSP)*, implemented using a receiver-side CSP daemon (*RCSPd*) and a server-side CSP daemon (*SCSPd*). The CSP protocol creates the flow and establishes concast-related state, called the *flow state block (FSB)*, in network nodes (i.e. at all concast-capable nodes on the paths from group members to the receiver.) The *flow state block* records the *merge specification* describing how packets are to be merged, and an *upstream neighbor list (UNL)* that records the next concast-capable nodes "upstream" (towards the senders) for this flow. The UNL is maintained using soft-state techniques similar to RSVP [8].

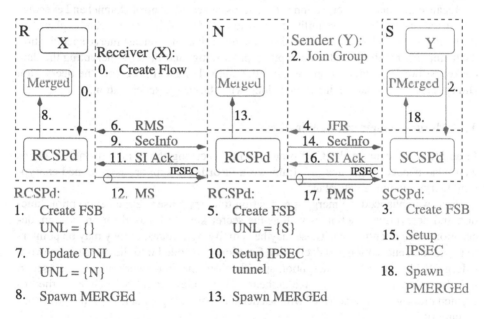

Fig. 1. The Secure Concast Signaling Protocol

Figure 1 shows the secure version of the CSP protocol, but the basic idea is the same as the original CSP protocol. First, the receiver initiates the flows (step 0,1). The senders then attempt to join the flow by *Join Flow Requests (JFR)* messages toward the receiver which CSP intercepts and propagates toward the receiver as *Request for Merge Spec (RMS)* messages (steps 2-8). The merge specification is then "pulled" from the receiver towards the senders (steps 9-18).

3.2 Securing Concast

Because the receiver is responsible for initiating the concast flow, the receiver should also be responsible for defining the flow's membership (i.e., join policy). As we saw earlier, the policy must propagate through the network toward the senders so that routers can decide whether a sender is allowed to join or not. Unfortunately, the concast receiver does not know (in fact never learns) the identity, or the location, of the senders. Obviously the join policy cannot be pushed into the network toward the senders until the location of the senders is known (i.e., the senders issue join requests).

Because senders must identify themselves before the policies can be sent out, the secure version of the CSP protocol begins just like the original CSP protocol (see Figure 1). A new sender issues a join request message that propagates (in the clear) to the receiver (steps 2-8). At this point the path from the sender to the receiver is known and the user's join policy can be "pulled" toward the sender. This is accomplished by creating a set of secure tunnels back to the sender (steps 9-18). The secure path is created hop-by-hop, each time authenticating the next hop (and verifying its integrity) and then passing it the user's join policy and merge specification across the secure tunnel (e.g., steps 9-12).

Because the merge specification is sent across a secure control channel and executes on trusted nodes, the responsibility for end-to-end data path security can be placed in the hands of the end-systems. To achieve this objective, the concast merge specification itself implements the code for decrypting, processing, and then re-encrypting the data packet before forwarding it on. Because the control channel is secure, the decryption and encryption key can be distributed along with the merge specification.

3.3 Merge Framework Modifications

In addition to securing the CSP protocol (i.e., securing the control plane), changes were also needed in the merging framework in order to support user-defined encryption/decryption in the data plane.

First, we enhanced the merge specification to carry a user-defined encryption function and decryption function as well as the secret keys to be used for encryption, decryption and authentication. These may be actually byte codes, or they may be pointers to predefined encryption and decryption functions we added into the merge framework (MergeD). As part of the encryption specification, the framework allows the user to specify whether a MAC (message authentication code) should be include in the encrypted message. If so, the MAC will be checked when the packet is decrypted to verify its integrity.

The second change to the framework creates different forms of the merge daemon (MergeD) to be deployed at senders, merging nodes, and the receiver. Merge daemons executing on sender nodes receive packets over a local socket. Because these incoming packets are unencrypted, the decryption function does not need to be invoked; only the encryption is called, on outgoing packets. On receiver nodes the situation is reversed: incoming packets need to be decrypted, but outgoing packets go straight to the receiver application and do not need to be encrypted. On intermediate nodes, all incoming packets are decrypted and all outoing packets are encrypted (as long as merging is occurring, i.e. there is more than one upstream neighbor—otherwise, the packets are simply forwarded). Because we trust sender nodes only to transmit data, not merge packets, the signalling protocol transfers only a *partial* merge specification to the sender, containing an encryption function and the secret key (that is, the merge routine is not passed).

4 Secure Concast Signaling Protocol

This section describes the Secure Concast Signaling Protocol, which is based on the original Concast Signaling Protocol [1]. Together with IPsec Secure CSP provides a foundation for the secure concast service. We begin by defining notational conventions, data types, and cryptographic primitives used. Next we describe the protocol messages and their contents. Finally, we give a high-level operational description of the (normal) process of setting up a concast flow.

4.1 Basic Types and Cryptographic Primitives

Our protocol uses the following types:

- **appident:** Identifier of an application-level principal, i.e. a participant in the concast flow (receiver or sender). E.g., if X.509 certificates are used, this could be an OSI Relative Distinguished Name (RDN).
- **nodeident:** Identifier of a network-level principal, i.e. a node. We use IP addresses as network identifiers.
- **flowspec:** A pair (R, G) identifying a concast flow, where R is the receiver's IP address (a **nodeident**) and G is the group identifier.
- **mergespec:** A collection of data and function definitions that defines the merge processing to be carried out by intermediate nodes, and that conforms to the requirements of the concast merging framework.
- **pmergespec:** A partial or "thinned" **mergespec**, containing only the security-related portions of the merge specification. End systems receive partial mergespecs because they need to do security-related processing but may not be trusted to apply policies or perform merging.
- **policy:** A specification of a set of principals that are authorized in some way. We consider a policy to be a predicate on identifiers (**appidents** or **nodeidents**) and credentials; if the predicate has the value "true" for a given identifier and credential, it means that (i) the identified principal is authorized, and (ii) the given credential is an acceptable witness for evaluating authenticity of information to be provided by the principal.
- **signature:** A digital signature, essentially a cryptographic digest of message data encrypted with some principal's private key, computed and formatted according to accepted cryptographic standards (e.g. SHA-1 [9] and PKCS #1 [10]). The notation $\{h(a|b|c)\}_k$ denotes the result of concatenating messages or fields a, b and c and signing the digest (created using a well-known cryptographic algorithm such as SHA-1) of the resulting bit string with private key k. Unless otherwise specified, **signature** fields in messages cover the entire contents of the message preceding the field.

- **cert:** A public-key certificate, which binds an identifier (of type **appident** or **nodeident**) to a public key.
- **ipsecinfo:** A structure containing IPsec information of a host needed by another host to create an IPsec tunnel to the former host.
- **timestamp:** A timestamp.
- **ccasthdr:** the first field of every secure CSP message. Indicates the version of the protocol and the type of the message.

The notation $verify(m, a, c)$ denotes the result of verifying the authenticity and integrity of (some part of) a message m using signature a and certificate c. This function returns true if digesting the information in m results in a value consistent with that obtained by decrypting a with the public key contained in c. For brevity, we sometimes abuse notation by indicating that the entire message m is being verified even though the authenticator covers only a portion of it.

The notation $p(u, c)$ denotes the result of applying policy p to identifier u with credential c. The value "true" means that u, presenting credential c, is authorized. The notation $time\text{-}check(t)$ denotes the result of verifying that a timestamp t is within some δ of the current time as known locally. We assume that δ is configured appropriately at every node for the degree of clock synchronization achievable in the network. (As usual when timestamps are used to ensure freshness, if δ is too small the protocol may fail between nodes whose clocks are not well-synchronized; setting δ too large increases the window of vulnerablility to replay attack.)

4.2 Policies and Principals

As described earler, the signaling protocol makes use of various policies. Per-flow policies are supplied by the receiver, and specify the principals—nodes and applications—that are allowed to participate in the flow. Per-node policies are supplied by service providers (ISPs), and specify the nodes that are allowed to perform various functions in a flow. Per-node policies are only applied to **nodeident**s.

The supported policies include:

- *fp.j:* per-flow join policy. Specifies application entities (**appident**s) authorized to join the flow. This policy is specified by the concast receiver along with the merge specification.
- *fp.u:* per-flow upstream node policy. Specifies nodes (**nodeident**s) that are authorized to participate in the flow either as host of an application-level sender or as a merging node. This policy is specified by the concast receiver along with the merge specification.
- *np.r:* per-node receiver policy. Specifies nodes (**nodeident**s) that are authorized to be the terminal points of concast flows. This implies that the node is authorized to supply merge specifications. This policy would typically characterize nodes that either have had a fee paid on their behalf, or are part of some trusted nonlocal domain.
- *np.d:* per-node downstream policy. Specifies nodes (**nodeident**s) that are authorized to relay a merge specification from a downstream receiver.

- *np.s:* per-node sender policy. Specifies the set of nodes (**nodeidents**) authorized to be the source of requests to join a concast flow. Again, typically characterizes the set of nodes in this domain that have paid for service, and nodes trusted by virtue of the other domain to which they belong.
- *np.u:* per-node upstream policy. Specifies the set of nodes authorized to be upstream of this node in a flow. Note that such nodes are trusted not only to handle (merge) user data, but also to apply this node's policies.

The protocol description involves the following principals and their associated information: X is the receiver (application), which has private key k_X and certificate C_X; it is running on node R, which has private key k_R and certificate C_R. Y is a sender (application), which has private key k_Y and certificate C_Y. Y is running on node S, which has k_S and C_S. Finally, N is a merging node with private key k_N and certificate C_N.

4.3 Protocol Messages

Message contents are given in terms of the structured types shown in Figure 2, which in turn use the basic types defined above. Note that the CREATEREQ structure contains two signatures; the first covers the MERGETOKEN, while the second covers the same data except that **mergespec** is replaced by the subset of its information that constitutes a **pmergespec**. Also, the PCREATEREQ structure contains only the fields of a CRE-ATEREQ that are relevant to the reduced mergespec, i.e. the subset of mt that constitutes a reduced mergespec, the pMTSig, and the userCert; given a valid CREATEREQ, a PCREATEREQ can be derived from it.

JOINREQ	
flowspec	flowID;
appident	user;
signature	userSig;
cert	userCert;

MERGETOKEN	
flowspec	flowID;
mergespec	ms;
policy	PFUpstreamP;
policy	PFJoinP;
appident	user;

CREATEREQ	
MERGETOKEN	mt;
signature	MTSig;
signature	pMTSig;
cert	userCert;

Fig. 2. Structures used in concast messages

The contents of the protocol messages are shown in Figure 3.

4.4 Protocol Operation

With the help of Figure 1 we describe the normal sequence of steps for a secure concast flow establishment. In the interest of clarity we omit steps related to error processing, and assume that the flow in question is not currently present on any node involved.

Step 0: To create a flow (R, G), the receiver application X generates the secure merge specification (ms) and per-flow policies (PFUpstreamP and PFJoinP), formats the requisite information as a MERGETO-KEN, and generates a signature (MTSig) using its private key k_X.

Join Flow Request (JFR)	
ccasthdr	flowInfo;
JOINREQ	userReq;
nodeident	sNode;
timestamp	ts;
ipsecinfo	sinfo;
signature	msgSig;
cert	sNodeCert;

Request for Merge Specification (RMS)	
ccasthdr	flowInfo;
JOINREQ	userReq;
nodeident	upNode;
timestamp	ts;
ipsecinfo	sinfo;
signature	msgSig;
cert	upNodeCert;

Security Information (SecInfo)	
ccasthdr	flowInfo;
JOINREQ	userReq;
nodeident	downNode;
timestamp	ts;
ipsecinfo	sinfo;
signature	msgSig;
cert	downNodeCert;

Sec. Info. Acknowledgement (SIAck)	
ccasthdr	flowInfo;
JOINREQ	userReq;
nodeident	upNode;
timestamp	ts;
signature	msgSig;
cert	upNodeCert;

Merge Specification (MS)	
ccasthdr	flowInfo;
CREATEREQ	userSpec;
nodeident	downNode;
timestamp	ts;
policy	nodeP;
signature	msgSig;
cert	downNodeCert;

Concast Join Succeeded (CJS)	
ccasthdr	flowInfo;
PCREATEREQ	pUserSpec;
nodeident	downNode;
timestamp	ts;
signature	msgSig;
cert	downNodeCert;

Fig. 3. Secure CSP Messages

It also generates a signature (pMTSig) for the partial MERGETO-KEN(the MERGETOKEN minus ms). X finally bundles the MERGETO-KEN, the signatures MTSig an pMTSig, and its certificate userCert=C_X into a CREATEREQ and hands it over to the local CSP module.

Step 1: Upon receiving the CREATEREQ cr, the CSP at R verifies the signatures[2] cr.MTSig and cr.pMTSig using the public key in the certificate

---

[2] While the channel between the receiver application and the local CSP is probably trusted, this verification is a good idea because other nodes are going to perform it. If there is a problem, it is better to detect it locally. (Similarly for the JOINREQ passed by Y.)

cr.userCert; that the principal of certificate cr.userCert matches identity cr.user; and that cr.userCert is a valid certificate generated by a trusted certificate authority. If the verification succeeds then the CSP creates the local flow state for the flow (R, G) and returns a success indication to X.

Step 2: To join the flow (R, G), the sending application Y creates a JOINREQ by including its identity user=Y, certificate userCert=C_Y, and a signature userSig generated by signing the request using its private key k_Y. The JOINREQ is then passed to the local CSP.

Step 3,4: Upon receiving JOINREQ jr from Y, the CSP at S verifies (i) the join request signature jr.userSig using the public key in certificate jr.userCert, (ii) that the principal of certificate jr.userCert matches application identifier jr.user and (iii) that jr.userCert is a valid certificate. The CSP at S next checks (i) if Y is allowed by local policy to act as a concast sender, and (ii) if R is an acceptable concast receiver node according to local policy, i.e. that $S{:}np.r(R, \perp)$ is true[3]. If so, a flow state block is created for the flow (R, G) and its state is marked "pending". A JFR message containing the user's join request userReq, the current timestamp ts, S's identifier sNode=S and certificate sNodeCert=C_S, ipsec information sinfo to connect to S and a signature msgSig obtained by signing the JFR message using k_S is generated and forwarded toward R.

Step 5,6: Upon intercepting a JFR message jm on its way to R, the CSP at N first verifies the signatures jm.userReq.userSig and jm.msgSig to ensure the authenticity and integrity of the user request and the JFR message respectively. It also checks the validity of the timestamp $time\text{-}check(jm.ts)$. Next, the CSP verifies that $N{:}np.r(jm.userReq.user, \perp)$, and $N{:}np.u(jm.sNode, m.sNodeCert)$ are all true. If so, it creates a temporary flow state block for the flow (R, G), adds the pair $(m.sNode, m.sNodeCert)$ to the upstream neighbor list, and marks the flow "pending". It also constructs a RMS message containing the user's join request userReq, a fresh timestamp ts, N's identifier upNode=N and certificate upNodeCert=C_N, IPsec information sinfo needed to connect to node N and a signature msgSig obtained by signing the RMS message using k_N. It forwards the RMS message toward R.

(This process will be repeated at each concast-capable node along the path to R: the node intercepts the RMS message, validates the signatures, checks that the message sender is acceptable to its local upstream node policy, and then constructs and forwards toward R a signed RMS message containing the original JOINREQ and its own

---

[3] Note that this check should "tentatively succeed" at this stage without a certificate for R. The purpose is to prevent wasted effort in case R is unacceptable regardless of what credentials are presented.

identifier and certificate. For brevity, we assume here that N is the last concast-capable node on the path toward R.)

Step 7,8: Upon receiving an RMS message rm, the CSP at R, the destination node, the CSP verifies the signatures rm.userReq.userSig and rm.msgSig. It also checks that *time-check*(rm.ts) $\wedge$ *fp.j*(rm.req.user, rm.req.userCert) $\wedge$ *fp.u*(rm.sNode, rm.sNodeCert) $\wedge$ R:*np.u*(rm.sNode, rm.sNodeCert) are true, i.e. the flow policy admits the joining sender Y and both flow and node policies admit the upstream neighbor who sent the message. If so then it spawns the Merge daemon for the flow, if not, it sends a signed error message upstream, indicating that the connection failed for policy reasons.

Step 9: Before the CSP can send the merge specification to the upstream node it must create an IPsec tunnel to the upstream node. To do this the CSP first sets up all necessary IPsec connection information using rm.sinfo at its own end. It then creates a SECINFO (Security Information) message that contains the userReq=rm., a fresh timestamp ts, R's identifier downNode and certificate downNodeCert, R's IPsec information sinfo and a signature obtined by signing SECINFO with k_R. It then sends the SECINFO message to the upstream node.

Step 10,11: Upon receiving the SECINFO message sm, the CSP at the upstream node N checks that the flow identifier sm.userReq.flowID referes to a legitimate pending flow, and verifies (i) the sigatures sm.userReq.userSig and sm.msgSig, (ii) and also verifies that certificate sm.downNodeCert is valid. Next the CSP checks if *time-check*(sm.ts) is true. It then applies its local downstream node policy, i.e. verifies that N:*np.d*(sm.downNode, sm.downNodeCert) is true. If so, it sets up its local IPsec connection files using sm.sinfo and establishes a security association with sm.downNode. Upon successful creation of the IPsec tunnel the CSP creates a SIACK message that includes the userReq=sm.userReq, the node's identity upNode=N and certificate upNodeCert=C_N, a timestamp ts and a signature msgSig obtained by signing the SIACK message with k_S. CSP then sends the SIACK message downstream toward R.

Step 12: When the tunnel is established, the CSP at R adds the pair (N, C_N) to the flow's upstream neighbor list (UNL) and then constructs a MERGE-SPEC (Merge Specification) message containing the flow's create request userSpec, a fresh timestamp ts, its identity downNode=R and certificate downNodeCert=C_R. R also adds its upstream policy *np.u* to nodeP in the MERGESPEC message, signs the message with k_R and sends it to N.

Step 13,14: Upon receiving an MS message mm (through the tunnel), the upstream node N verifies signatures mm.userSpec.MTSig, mm.userSpec.pMTSig and mm.msgSig, checks the timestamp mm.ts (allowing for travel and processing time to get to the receiver node and back), unpacks and installs the merge specification and policies, and then performs the following steps for each node q (with certificate C_q) in the flow's upstream neighbor list.[4]

1. Verify that q is acceptable according to the node upstream policy received in the merge specification: $mm.\text{nodeP}(q, C_q)$.
2. Verify that q is acceptable according to the flow's upstream neighbor policy: $fp.u(q, C_q)$.
3. Spawn a MERGEd and send the MERGEd an update of the upstream neighbor list. (Note that this step happens once for all upstream neighbors at intermediate and receiver nodes. At senders, however, for technical reasons a separate MERGEd is spawned for each sending application program.)

Step 14,15,16: N checks whether an IPsec tunnel to q already exists. If not, it sets up IPsec to establish a tunnel, and constructs, signs and sends to q a SECINFO message. SECINFO contains the original JOINREQ for the flow, its identity downNode=N and certificate downNodeCert=C_N, and IPsec information sinfo to enable establishing a tunnel. The upstream node, similar to the previous steps, prepares its end for the creation of an IPsec tunnel and if successful sends a SIACK message to the downstream node.

Step 17: The downstream node after receiving the SIACK message from S sends the merge specification to the upstream node. But since the upstream node S was added after the receipt of a JFR message and not a RMS message, a partial merge specification instead of a full merge specification is sent upstream. N thus creates a pms message that includes the original userSpec=$mm.$userSpec, the partial merge specification **pmergespec**, a timestamp ts, N's identity downNode=N and certificate downNodeCert=C_N, and a signature msgSig obtained by signing the pms message using k_N. The CSP then sends the pms message upstream to S.

Step 18: Upon receiving a PMS message pm, the CSP at the sender node S verifies (i) the signatures $pm.$userSpec.pMTSig and $pm.$msgSig, (ii) the timestamp $pm.$ts, and (iii) the certificate $pm.$downNodeCert. If the verification is successful S spwans a partial merge daemon and notifies Y that the join operation has completed, and data transfer can begin.

5   Security Analysis

The *Security Architecture for Active Networks* [11] enumerates the various attacks that can be mounted against an active network framework. Given this threat model, we briefly describe how our secure concast service fares under these various attack scenarios.

---

[4] Note that at this point it has already been established that the originating user satisfies $fp.j$, and that the downstream node satisfies $N{:}np.d$, the local downstream node policy.

Attacks resulting in usurpation: *Theft of service* attacks are prevented by concast's authentication mechanisms. As described earlier, the concast service is based on well-defined trust relationships that must be met before any node, sender or intermediate merge node, will be added to the flow. Because the flow is established hop-by-hop, each node's authenticity and integrity can be verified individually and compared against the receiver's and provider's security policies before being included in the flow. As a result, only nodes with the proper certification are allowed to access the service.

Attacks resulting in unauthorized disclosure: Outside of breaking into an end-system or router, packet snooping is the most common technique for obtaining access to content. In secure concast, all traffic is encrypted. Merge specification are exchanged via encrypted IPsec tunnels and the data packets are exchanged using a shared key that is only disclosed to authenticated group members.

Attacks resulting in deception: Secure concast prevents *masquerading by spoofing* attacks via two methods. First, all control messages are sent over IPsec tunnels whose endpoints have been authenticated. The only exception are the initial JFR and RMS messages which are transmitted in the clear. However, these message carry a digital signature that can help identify spoofed addresses. Even if these messages are not identified as spoofed messages, they are simply used to trigger the initiation of fully authenticated IPsec tunnel where their identity will be checked. Second, all data packets are encrypted and carry a message authentication code. Packets can be spoofed, but without the correct encryption key, the merge daemon will discard them. At best, such packets result in a denial of service attack (see below).

Replay attacks are another form of deception. Because all control packets are carried over the IPsec tunnel, replay attacks are automatically detected by IPsec. Only the initial JFR and RMS travel outside the tunnel. Both carry an authenticated timestamp that is used to detect packets that are outside the acceptable delivery time window. Packets replayed during the window while the tunnel exists are automatically discarded. In regards to the data channel, all packets are encrypted and can carry a sequence number that can be used to detect duplicates if the user desires.

Substitution attacks, which represent another form of deception, are prevented via the use of cryptographic integrity checks. All packets are digitally signed to guarantee the packets integrity.

Attacks resulting in disruption/Denial of Service: These types of attacks present the biggest problem for the secure concast service. Although secure concast prevents some of the attacks, there are several different attacks that could be launched to consume packet processing cycles at network nodes, the receiver, or senders.

An example of a disruption attack that secure concast prevents is the *join circumvention attack*. In this case a malicious node circumvents the join process and simply sends data to a merge daemon for merging. Because the data cannot be decrypted, the merge daemon does not merge the packet into the stream, thereby preventing disruption of the stream with bogus data. However, the time spent processing the packet still represents a DoS attack that is difficult to prevent.

Fig. 4. Concast video application containing four merged streams

DoS attacks can also be mounted via false requests. Every time a bogus join request is received, the network nodes expends resources trying to setup the IPsec tunnel, only to find that the sender is not responding.

6   Performance Evaluation

In order to measure the performance of our secured concast service, we used a concast video-merging application[12]. Some video applications require the ability to receive video feeds from multiple sources simultaneously; examples include distance learning and video monitoring/surveillance. The objective is to receive the best possible video quality from all sources. For our concast video merging application, a concast session is established that transcodes the incoming streams into lower-quality streams, thereby reducing the network bandwidth requirements. The idea is to replace uncontrolled loss due to congestion with *controlled* loss due to transcoding. To support this type of application, we designed a simple merge function that scales the incoming video stream by down-sampling the pixels that comprise each frame of the video, and combining all incoming streams into a single outgoing stream. In other words, each network link should carry no more than one video steam. To achieve this, the merge specification keeps track of the number of incoming video streams and the number of original video streams encoded in each incoming stream. It then assigns a region of each outgoing frame to each incoming video stream and down-samples the stream appropriately to fit in the assigned region. The assignment of streams to regions takes into account the relative sizes of the (possibly already down-sampled) incoming streams. As new streams "join" the concast session, the existing images are adjusted to make room for the stream. Each composite stream carries information about how many original streams it contains and how they have last been combined so that each node can determine how to combine its incoming streams. This ensures that even if an unbalanced merge tree was built by all the concast senders, the final video stream delivered to the concast receiver will have a roughly proportional display area for each of the constituent video streams.

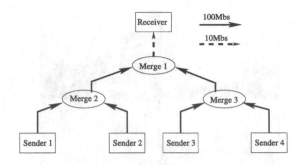

Fig. 5. Experimental Network - Secure Concast Video Merging

Our test topology is shown in Figure 5. We used four video senders, each transmitting an uncompressed black-and-white 320x240 video stream at a given frame rate. At each merging hop in the network the frames were merged into a single sub-sampled image. Figure 4 is a resulting frame captured at the receiver node. We ran with both a 'NULL' cipher specification as well as using AES (128-bit) encryption with a SHA1 message digest for 4, 6, and 8 frames per second (fps). In each case, we measured the total system and user level CPU utilization. The data was taken from merge node 3 in the experimental topology. All nodes in the network were 1.5Ghz Pentiums with 128MB of RAM, resulting in similar results for the remaining merge nodes. Our concast merge specification was written in Java and runs in a user-level JVM, which accounts for the majority of the load. The results of our experiments are presented in figure 6. As can be seen from the graphs, in each case encryption/decryption of the video streams imposed an overhead of roughly 20 percent. We found 8 frames per second to be the maximum speed we could attain while maintaining video quality. As can be seen from the results for AES/SHA1 with 8 fps, the merge nodes were running at maximum CPU utilization (system + user). When trying to go beyond 8 fps the nodes were overloaded which resulted in packet loss. The initial high load in each case is measurement taken during JVM startup.

Our results demonstrate that the presented security mechanism (in particular, per packet data security) is feasible and can be implemented with a reasonable overhead. Note that our implementation of the secure merge specification has been done in Java only with the intention to show feasibility and not optimality.

7   Related Work

The DARPA Active Network community has defined an architecture for an active nodes [13] that comprises a NodeOS and one or more Execution Environments (EE). A security architecture has been proposed for the architectural framework, with particular attention paid to capsule-based EEs (i.e. those that expect code to be included in each packet). An important observation by the authors is that some part of the active packet is dynamic (changes at intermediate hops) and the rest of it is static. Digital signatures are used to provide end-to-end authentication and integrity protection to the static part of

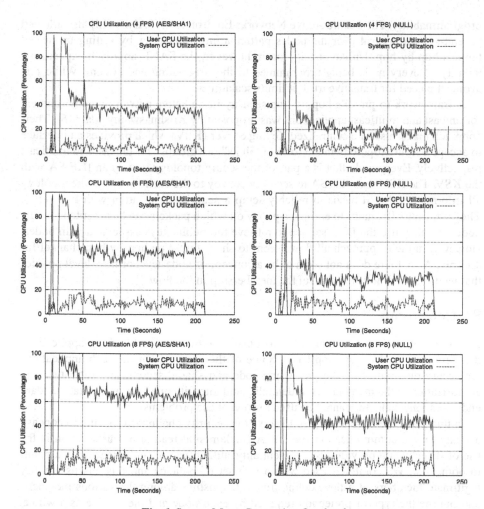

Fig. 6. Secure Merge Processing Overhead

the packet. HMAC-SHA-1 integrity protection is used between two neighboring nodes to provide integrity protection. Certificates are stored in DNS CERT records and every packet carries references to the appropriate certificates. Authorization to execute code is based on the Java 2 security architecture with modifications to support multiple policies, a feature often needed in active networks.

Like the AN security architecture, SANTS [11] differs from the approach described in this paper mainly in its focus on a capsule-based processing model. Every packet is singly responsible from its own authentication, integrity and authorization. In our approach, however, packets belong to a flow. Initial efforts are required to authorize all the members belonging to the flow. But once achieved, the problem of confidentiality and integrity is simplified due to the use of a shared secret by all members of the flow.

The Switchware project [14] included one of the first attempts to deal with security in active networks. Like concast, the Switchware architecture allowed for flow-based programmability. The Secure Active Networks Environment (SANE) [15] also allowed an end-system control over the nodes participating in its flow, by setting up nested tunnels hop-by-hop. Unlike our approach, however, the SANE approach exposes the identity of every node being programmed to the originating end system. While this avoids the need for transitive trust, it limits scalability.

A framework to provide hop-by-hop security in an active networking environment for unicast and multicast applications was proposed by Krishnaswamy et.al [16]. Their approach makes use of a centralized Keying Server (KSV) which provides an interface to accept a secure topology in the form of "links" or "groups" for unicast and multicast respectively. Every node that is a part of the secure topology sets up an IKE SA with the KSV. The KSV uses this SA to securely convey to the each "node" in the topology all information that it needs to reliably setup a security association with its peer(s). They use Linux IPChains to enforce a policy on which packets can be accepted into the node, and they use the DNS service to retrieve the public keys associated with nodes. However, in their approach all flows seem to share the same hop-by-hop channel for security. Also, there does not seem to be a concept of node-level or flow-level policies that would enable nodes to control the membership in the flow.

8 Conclusion

A number of security challenges are associated with active networking applications that process data on a per hop basis. Some of the requirements of such applications are secure distribution of the processing code and shared secrets, authentication and authorization of the members, confidentiality and integrity of application data. Standard end-to-end mechanisms cannot be used to solve these problems.

In this paper we have attempted to solve the security challenges specific to concast, a many-to-one communication service. A fundamental feature of our solution is the use of IPsec which provides us confidentiality, authentication and integrity on a point-to-point link. We combine IPsec with a rich set of policies and this lets us identify legitimate members of a flow, define trust relationships among the various members, and outline the type of protection required by each node and the service as a whole. The availability of a secure control plane helps us provide a platform to applications to securely distribute shared secrets and thereby achieve confidentiality and integrity of application data.

References

1. Kenneth L. Calvert, James Griffioen, Billy C. Mullins, Amit Sehgal, and Su Wen, "Concast: Design and implementaion of an active network service," *IEEE Journal on Selected Areas in Communications (2001)*, pages 19(3):426–437, March 2001.
2. Sneha Kumar Kasera, Supratik Bhattacharyya, Mark Keaton, Diane Kiwior, Jim Kurose, Don Towsley, and Steve Zabele, "Scalable Fair Reliable Multicast Using Active Services," *IEEE Network Magazine*, February 2000.
3. I. Kouvelas, V. Hardman, and J. Crowcroft, "Network Adaptive Continuous-Media Applications Through Self Organised Transcoding," in *the Proceedings of the Network and Operating Systems Support for Digital Audio and Video Conference (NOSSDAV 98)*, July 1998.

4. E. Amir, W. McCanne, and H. Zhang, "An application level video gateway," in *ACM Multimedia '95*, 1995.
5. D. Wetherall, J. Guttag, and D. L. Tennenhouse, "ANTS: A toolkit for building and dynamically deploying network protocols," in *IEEE OPENARCH'98*, San Francisco, CA, April 1998.
6. S. Merugu, S. Bhattacharjee, Y. Chae, M. Sanders, K. Calvert, and E. Zegura, "Bowman and canes: Implementation of an active network," 1999.
7. K. Calvert, J. Griffioen, A. Sehgal, and S. Wen, "Concast: Design and implementation of a new network service," in *Proceedings of 1999 International Conference on Network Protocols, Toronto, Ontario*, November 1999.
8. Bob Braden, Lixia Zhang, Steve Berson, and Shai Herzog Sugih Jamin, "Resource ReSerVation Protocol (RSVP)," September 1997, RFC 2205.
9. Donald E. Eastlake 3rd and Paul E. Jones, "US Secure Hash Algorithm 1 (SHA1)," September 2001, RFC 3174.
10. Burt Kaliski and Jessica Staddon, "PKCS #1: RSA Cryptography Specifications. Version 2.0," October 1998, RFC 2437.
11. S. Murphy, E. Lewis, R. Puga, R. Watson, and R. Yee, "Strong security for active networks," in *The Fourth IEEE Conference on Open Architectures and Network Programming*, April 2001.
12. Kenneth L. Calvert, James Griffioen, Billy Mullins, Swaminathan Natarajan, Leon Poutievski, Amit Sehgal, and Su Wen, "Leveraging emerging network services to scale multimedia applications," *Software - Practice and Experience (SPE)*, vol. 33, no. 14, pp. 1377–1397, November 2003.
13. AN Architecture Working Group, "Architectural framework for active networks ver 1.0," July 1999.
14. D. Alexander, W. Arbaugh, M. Hicks, P. Kakkar, A. Keromytis, J. Moore, C. Gunder, S. Nettles, and J. Smith, "The switchware active network architecture," *IEEE Network*, May 1998.
15. D. Alexander, W. Arbaugh, A. Keromytis, and J. Smith, "Safety and security of programmable network infrastructures," *IEEE Communications Magazine, Special issue on Programmable Networks*, 1998.
16. Suresh Krishnamswamy, Joseph B. Evans, and Gary J. Minden, "A prototype framework for providing hop-by-hop security in an experimentally deployed active network," in *DANCE: Darpa Active Networks Conference and Exposition*, 2002.

Distributed Instrusion Prevention in Active and Extensible Networks

Todd Sproull and John Lockwood*

Applied Research Laboratory
Department of Computer Science and Engineering:
Washington University in Saint Louis
1 Brookings Drive, Campus Box 1045
St. Louis, MO 63130 USA
http://www.arl.wustl.edu/arl/projects/fpx/reconfig.htm

Abstract. The proliferation of computer viruses and Internet worms has had a major impact on the Internet Community. Cleanup and control of malicious software (malware) has become a key problem for network administrators. Effective techniques are now needed to protect networks against outbreaks of malware. Wire-speed firewalls have been widely deployed to limit the flow of traffic from untrusted domains. But these devices weakness resides in a limited ability to protect networks from infected machines on otherwise trusted networks.

Progressive network administrators have been using an Intrusion Prevention System (IPS) to actively block the flow of malicious traffic. New types of active and extensible network systems that use both microprocessors and reconfigurable logic can perform wire-speed services in order to protect networks against computer virus and Internet worm propagation. This paper discusses a scalable system that makes use of automated worm detection and intrusion prevention to stop the spread of computer viruses and Internet worms using extensible hardware components distributed throughout a network. The contribution of this work is to present how to manage and configure large numbers of distributed and extensible IPSs.

1 Introduction

Security has become a daunting task for network administrators. There are numerous vulnerabilities that affect the millions of computers attached to the Internet. Network administrators are overwhelmed by the task of securing their networks against operating system flaws, poorly written network applications, and end-system misconfigurations. Security devices integrated within the network have become a necessity for networks that need to be safe and reliable.

Network administrators currently use several types of devices to secure their networks. The first line of defense is typically a firewall. Firewalls provide some

---

* This research was supported by a grant from Global Velocity. The authors of this paper have received equity from the license of technology to Global Velocity, and have served as consultants to the company.

G.J. Minden et al. (Eds.): IWAN 2004, LNCS 3912, pp. 54–65, 2007.

protection by limiting how packets destined to and from machines on the Internet send traffic through a network node. While firewalls are useful, they lack the features needed to filter malicious content that passes between Internet hosts that have become infected with an Internet worm or computer virus. To detect a worm or virus activity, intrusion detection systems (IDSs) are needed. IDSs help administrators detect when exploits pass over a network and they log which machines were targeted. The most advanced type of network security device is called an Intrusion Prevention System (IPS). An IPS scans the content of traffic flowing through a network and actively drops the traffic flows which are detected to be malicious. Unfortunately, there are several problems with the way that firewall, IDS, and IPS devices are deployed throughout the Internet today.

In recent years, Internet worms generally entered a network only at the edge. Today, malware is *multi-modal* meaning that it uses multiple techniques to propagate and infect machines. Multi-modal malware can spread both over the network as a worm and via removable media as a virus. Multi-modal worms provide several mechanisms for an infected machine to infect other machines using other modes independent of the original mode of infection. With *Sasser*, for example, a laptop user could have their machine infected by network traffic while it was connected to a Digital Subscriber Line (DSL) at home. When that same user takes the machine to work, that laptop infects the rest of the hosts on the internal network by using a port scan. To be effective against this type of threat, network security devices need to distributed throughout the network, not just used at the edge.

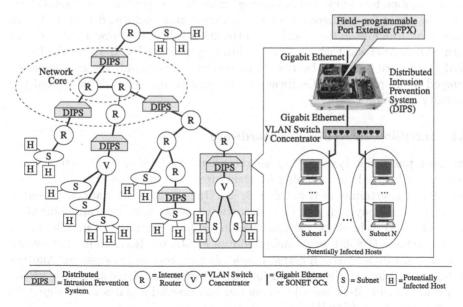

Fig. 1. High level view of potential threats

A problem with network security devices is that they can be hard to manage. Many IPS and IDS devices lack the ability to automatically download patches that allow them to protect networks against new threats. As the number of network security devices increase, so does the time spent by an administrator to push out the latest rules and virus signatures to remote devices. Methods are needed to automatically distribute information regarding new virus signatures to all of the IPS devices on a network. Better security for entire networks can be achieved with a Distributed Intrusion Prevention System (DIPS). Figure 1 depicts an example network containing DIPS spread throughout a network. Hosts (H) attach to Subnets (S). Routers (R) forward traffic between subnets. DIPS nodes placed in-line with high-speed links actively measure and filter malicious traffic attempting to flow between subnets, routers, or virtual local area networks (V). We believe that active and extensible networks can be used as the foundation to implement highly scalable distributed intrusion prevention devices and that active network technology can be used to implement the control and configuration software for a network of DIPS.

2   Intrusion Detection

One of the first widely used intrusion detection systems is called *SNORT* [1]. SNORT enabled network administrators to promiscuously scan a network link to see what type of exploits were passing over the network and being used to attack their hosts. HOGWASH [2] expanded upon SNORT to implement intrusion prevention functions. Traffic passing through a PC that ran the HOGWASH software would be sanitized to remove malware and malformed packets before the exploit could reach the machines on the other side of the network. A problem with HOGWASH was that the limited throughput of the PC that ran the HOGWASH software became a bottleneck to network throughput. Packets would be delayed or dropped as the software that executed on the node saturated the capacity of the processor.

2.1   Intrusion Prevention in Hardware

Intrusion prevention systems that use reconfigurable hardware can detect signatures at high speeds by scanning for signatures in traffic that contain malware and blocking certain data transmissions [3]. One system that scanned for signatures in packets payloads and blocked malware using Field Programmable Gate Array (FPGA) technology was described in [4]. Large numbers of parallel Finite State Machines (FSMs) were configured into FPGA hardware to implement the computationally intensive function of scanning for regular expressions. Another system used Bloom filters to scan for large numbers of signatures with FPGA hardware. Bloom filters had allowed for fast incremental updates to the signature list with nearly no delay [5].

2.2 Distributed Firewalls and IDS Control

Distributed control is needed to manage large numbers of firewalls or IDSs. The distributed firewall described in [6] allows for a centralized access control policy that could be enforced at multiple remote locations. In [7], the implementation of a distributed firewall using the *KeyNote* trust management system was described in order to ensure secure transmission of credentials and distribution of network policies.

In other work, Huang introduced a framework for large scale intrusion detection using strategic decision making [8]. The model analyzes a sequence of events and uses global knowledge to make an informed decision regarding an intrusion. This approach relies on local agents to monitor and announce events, while a global agent predicts trends and makes strategic decisions. Here the sensor nodes do not actively block traffic until receiving an order from a global command node.

2.3 Real-Time Anomaly and Worm Detection

A system which discovers worms on a network in real-time has been developed using reconfigurable hardware [9]. Network content is monitored to discover frequently occurring signatures that appear in packet payloads. The system uses FPGAs to scan packets for patterns of similar content at Gigabit per second link rates. This system can be used to automatically detect signatures of new Internet worms just as an outbreak begins. Another system has been developed that uses anomaly detection to contain a worm to a small subsection of the network [10]. This approach allows for cooperation among multiple containment devices to respond an attack more effectively.

2.4 Peer-to-Peer Control and Management

In order for a DIPS to be scalable, there needs to be a way to control and configure thousands to tens of thousands of remote devices. It is not necessary to implement a centralized control of all DIPS devices. Peer-to-peer strategies can and should be used to distribute information in large-scale networks.

A software system called *Scribe* [11] provides a scalable, self-organizing Peer-to-Peer (P2P) location and routing substrate. Scribe was built on top of *Pastry* [12] and added functionality to perform large-scale, decentralized, application-level multicast. In the Scribe model, nodes participate as equal participants in groups. These nodes are joined together using routes provided by the Pastry software to form a multicast tree. Scribe provides an API for nodes joining groups and takes advantage of the robustness and reliability provided by Pastry. The effectiveness of a coordinated approach as compared to other types of P2P communication models has been proven in [13].

Janakiraman [14] proposed a scalable IDS/IPS solution that distributed a firewall and placed IDS systems throughout a P2P network. In this work, nodes share information on network intrusion attacks that occur throughout the network. The prototype system classified intrusions such as failed login attempts or port scans. A framework called DShield provides a platform for firewalls to share intrusion information [15]. By sharing information about new exploits among multiple machines, better protection can be provided than if information was only collected locally. DShield interacts with network administrators by providing graphs in real-time that include the identification of the top attacker and most prevalent port being targeted. Other work in network management for security devices includes the model proposed by Hyland and Sandhu [16]. In this work, security devices on the network are described as managed objects that interact through SNMP. A new protocol is also introduced to propagate security information throughout a network similar to the mechanism used by Internet routing protocols.

2.5   Security

In order to protect the network of DIPS, the infrastructure that provides protection must be secure itself. The system must ensure that only trusted systems can control the operation of remote DIPS. Some work has been done to secure the control and configuration of reconfigurable hardware platforms [17]. But as noted there are challenges with the implementation of a public key exchange using hardware alone. Key generation functions can be better handled by a general purpose processor in software. There are now FPGAs, like the Xilinx Virtex II Pro, that embed a full-feature PowerPC core within the FPGA logic array to allow use of both hardware and software on a single integrated circuit [18].

Distributed security techniques have also been proposed in Centaurus2 [20] and SHOMAR [21]. These projects demonstrated how decentralized services throughout an enterprise could provide authentication, anti-replay prevention, and non-repudiation. The security model employed is based around a simplified public-key infrastructure (PKI) [22]. This allows nodes to communicate and authenticate themselves throughout an untrusted network. Centaurus2 describes the framework for supporting this secure infrastructure, while SHOMAR demonstrates a distributed intrusion detection system (DIDS) using the aforementioned security techniques.

3   Distributed Intrusion Prevention Design Framework

To protect entire networks from rapid outbreaks of worms, computer viruses, and other malware; next generation networks should actively scan data passing through the network and provide an automated response in a coordinated fashion to stop the spread of malware. We feel that the active networking community is well positioned to develop the technologies which can provide automated protection of networks. In fact, data security appears to be a killer application that will drive the use of active and extensible networks in the Global Internet.

Several issues must be considered in order to design effective distributed intrusion prevention systems. One goal is to detect and block large numbers of Internet worms and viruses. Another goal is to enable large numbers of DIPS to organize themselves into an overlay network and securely communicate with each other. To address these challenges, a framework has been developed that describes how multiple sensors and actuator nodes communicate to perform intrusion detection and prevention in a secure distributed system.

3.1 Sensor and Actuator Nodes

We envision that each active network node in the intrusion prevention system contains six primary modules in order to detect and block worms and viruses. The first module in each node reconstructs Transmission Control Protocol (TCP) flows passing through the network node [27]. The second module processes headers and payloads to match rules that are specified using a syntax like the one used by SNORT [26]. The third module drops packets or flows containing known virus signatures. The fourth module performs anomaly detection. Unusual network activities cause the node to generate an alert, unusual activity includes port scans or a particular host opening a large number of TCP connections in a small period of time [10]. The fifth module monitors network traffic looking for a large increase in commonly occurring content. The sixth module decides what traffic flows to filter based on clues from the content scanning and anomaly detector modules.

3.2 Management Nodes

System administrators do not have the ability to monitor all of the IPSs distributed throughout a network, nor can they react quickly enough to stop an outbreak the moment that a new virus is discovered. Active intrusion prevention systems are needed that automatically reprogram IPS devices to stop rapid worm outbreaks. To be effective, entire networks of DIPS should be reconfigured within seconds of a new worm outbreak.

Scalable mechanisms are needed to control and configure large numbers (thousands to tens of thousands) of distributed intrusion prevention systems, in large scale, self-organizing networks. We propose use of a P2P solution based on the Scribe model [11].

To deploy active protection in the Internet, we propose that nodes be managed as small and large groups. Small groups consist of hundreds to thousands of hosts attached to tens to hundreds of active IPS nodes. Large groups encompass multiple small groups, and are managed by individual network providers with different levels of trust established between them.

3.3 Security for Group Membership

Care must be taken to decide whether or not to trust a node when it attempts to join a group. Access Control Lists (ACLs) restrict communication among a group of nodes. In order for a new DIPS to join the group, the DIPS must be authenticated by a node already trusted on the network. If a node lies outside of the trust domain, other techniques are needed to verify its credentials.

Communication among DIPS nodes in a secure manner is critical. Public Key Infrastructure (PKI) uses digital certificates, public-key cryptography, and certificate authorities to implement trust relationships and secure communication between network nodes [23]. To secure the entire distributed network of intrusion prevention systems, we propose using a secure communication model based on SHOMAR [21].

In this model, communication occurs between a DIPS, the Certificate Authority (CA), and the DIPS Manager (DM). The CA generates and signs x.509 certificates [24] for each DIPS in the network. The CA also verifies certificate queries from DIPS. The DM holds an ACL of all the nodes and their group membership capabilities.

As with [21], certificates are initially generated for each DIPS. That information is placed into the DIPS through an out-of-band mechanism. Certificates are stored on each DIPS in a secure manner, using a mechanism such as a PKCS#11 container [25].

4   Distributed Intrusion Prevention System Model

Distributed intrusion prevention can be implemented in a way that both provides high performance and is cost effective. The model uses both extensible hardware to process large volumes of data and active network software to manage and control the distributed system.

4.1   Extensible Hardware

Extensible hardware enables network traffic to be processed at the full line rate of Gigabit/second networks. As described in [3], an IPS was built using the Field Programmable Port Extender (FPX) platform. The FPX is equipped with a Virtex 2000E FPGA that can be dynamically reconfigured over a network to perform data processing functions. Several functions have been implemented on the FPX that perform IPS functions as modules. A TCP processor was implemented that can reconstruct traffic in 8 million active flows at 2.5 Gigabits/second [27]. A Bloom Filter was implemented on the FPX to scan for 10000 virus signatures at a data rate of 2.4Gbits/sec [5]. An Internet Security module was implemented that performs a subset of the SNORT functionality by processing headers and performing full packet scanning in hardware [26]. A worm detection module was also prototyped on the FPX platform [9].

The FPX platform has been integrated into a chassis that allows multiple FPX cards to be stacked and includes an embedded Single Board Computer (SBC). This SBC contains an Intel Celeron Processor that runs Linux from a flash memory device. The Celeron processor is only used to perform control functions. All of the core packet processing is done on one or more FPX cards. Figure 2 shows a photo of this new system, called the GVS 1500, with the cover open. As can be seen in the figure, FPX cards are stacked in the front of the chassis below two Gigabit Ethernet line cards. The SBC can be seen in the back of the chassis. When the system is powered on, the SBC boots into Linux and programs FPX cards using a program called NCHARGE [28].

4.2 Active Network Management

We propose to execute management and control services of the distributed system using the Scribe communication protocol. Each IPS would automatically discover other IPS in the distributed network using a communication protocol defined by Pastry. The entire DIPS would then self-organize into a tree structure as a single group.

The FreePastry tool provides an open-source Java implementation of Pastry including Scribe [29]. This software serves as framework for the P2P substrate with security extensions to allow for encrypted communication.

4.3 Detection and Reaction to New Malware

There are many characteristics of computer activity that indicate an end host has been infected with malware. Each IPS sensor has a local view of the traffic passing to and from hosts on a local subnet. The activity may be observed as a port scan, worm propagation, high volumes of traffic, or other types of anomalous behavior. Observed behavior might be malware, or it could instead be a false positive triggered by a valid use of the host.

By fusing data collected by multiple sensors, then coordinating the efforts of multiple IPS, effective security against worm attacks can be implemented.

Fig. 2. Distributed Intrusion Prevent System (DIPS)

We envision that three phases are needed in order to block malware and avoid programming the network to block legitimate traffic, as shown in figure 3. To be effective against a worst case worm, all of these activities must be performed within a few seconds to a minute.

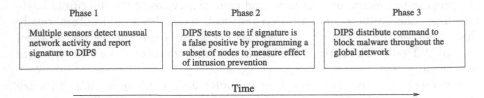

Phase 1

| Multiple sensors detect unusual network activity and report signature to DIPS |

Phase 2

| DIPS tests to see if signature is a false positive by programming a subset of nodes to measure effect of intrusion prevention |

Phase 3

| DIPS distribute command to block malware throughout the global network |

Time

Fig. 3. Phases of the DIPS during a worst-case worm outbreak

4.4   Adding a New IPS to the Trusted DIPS

To build a large network of trusted IPS nodes, nodes must assemble in a secure and scalable way. Several steps are required for an IPS to join an DIPS group, as shown in figure 4.

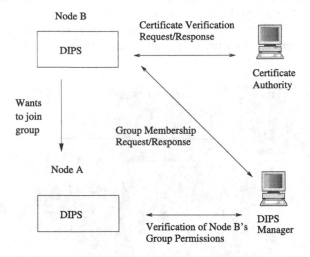

Fig. 4. DIPS joining a group

The example shows how DIPS B would join the group for which A is already a member. B first verifies the digital certificate it holds for the CA by issuing a certificate request. The CA then issues a signed response for the request, assuming it is valid. B next sends a message to the DM for a certificate request and to register itself to join the group. The DM responds with an acknowledgment indicating that it is eligible to join the groups predetermined for B by a network administrator. B then sends a request to A indicating it wishes to join the group.

A issues a request to the DM to verify B's membership criteria, once validated B is allowed to become a part of the group and is able to communicate with A.

This verification process is only needed when nodes join a group. The number of requests received by the CA and the DM will be fairly small in comparison to the communication between nodes implementing the SCRIBE multicast overlay.

The model works well with the Scribe infrastructure, as the only nodes allowed to join require the proper credentials to participate in the overlay network. In this example, each DIPS maintains a table of the nodes that it has authenticated as belonging to the group.

Since the time scale in which a DIPS joins or leaves a group is slow, the amount of overhead associated with introducing a new DIPS to the network is relatively small. Software can perform the authentication task and establish a secure connection via a digital certificate.

Trust between the networks can be established using properties similar to that of the Web-of-Trust model used for PGP communication [30]. For networks not under the control of a single authority, an administrator of one domain can choose to receive updates from other domains. In order for this model to scale with larger networks, a decentralized CA model can be implemented. An example of one such system was described by Koga [31].

5 Conclusion

The spread of worms and viruses throughout the Internet has had a devastating impact on end users who suffer when their computers become infected with malware and on system administrators who deal with the burden of protecting entire networks of hosts. Active and extensible networks can be used to implement a distributed intrusion prevention system that decreases the rate at which worms and viruses spread. By stopping or slowing a worm outbreak, data can be saved and machines can be patched before they would otherwise become infected. Passive systems for intrusion detection have been used in the past to alert when a machine is compromised or a network is under attack. Active systems can be used to stop an attack and prevent a worm from spreading. By using extensible hardware, this type of protection can be provided with minimal impact on overall network performance.

Distributed network intrusion prevention systems can be used to protect large numbers of system globally. This paper described how active network management software and extensible hardware can work together in order to protect high speed networks from fast outbreaks of new Internet worms and viruses. A prototype implementation of the system is being developed at Washington University in Saint Louis and being deployed by Global Velocity.

6 Future Work

Large test beds should be built in order to evaluate the effectiveness of the distributed system. The circuits that implement the hardware functionality of the system are already in place. Anomaly detection modules can be developed as reconfigurable modules then deployed using active network technology. Time and effort is needed to port the Pastry/Scribe architecture to the DIPS platform. Measurements of the system should be performed to determine how quickly the system can deploy protection against new virus signatures. We plan to deploy this infrastructure on large scale networks to determine how quickly it can quarantine a network from the spread of viruses as the system reacts to various changes in the network.

References

1. Roesch, M.: SNORT - lightweight intrusion detection for networks. In: LISA '99: USENIX 13th Systems Administration Conference, Seattle, Washington (1999)
2. Hogwash Homepage `http://hogwash.sourceforge.net/docs/overview.html` (1999)
3. Lockwood, J.W., Moscola, J., Reddick, D., Kulig, M., Brooks, T.: Application of hardware accelerated extensible network nodes for internet worm and virus protection. In: International Working Conference on Active Networks (IWAN), Kyoto, Japan (2003)
4. Lockwood, J.W., Moscola, J., Kulig, M., Reddick, D., Brooks, T.: Internet worm and virus protection in dynamically reconfigurable hardware. In: Military and Aerospace Programmable Logic Device (MAPLD), Washington DC (2003) E10
5. Dharmapurikar, S., Krishnamurthy, P., Sproull, T., Lockwood, J.W.: Deep packet inspection using parallel Bloom filters. In: Hot Interconnects, Stanford, CA (2003) 44–51
6. Bellovin, S.M.: Distributed firewalls. ;login: magazine, special issue on security (1999) 37–39
7. Ioannidis, S., Keromytis, A.D., Bellovin, S.M., Smith, J.M.: Implementing a distributed firewall. In: ACM Conference on Computer and Communications Security. (2000) 190–199
8. Huang, M.Y., Wicks, T.M.: A large-scale distributed intrusion detection framework based on attack strategy analysis. In: Proceedings of the First International Symposium on Recent Advances in Intrusion Detection, Louvain-la-Neuve, Belgium (1998)
9. Madhusudan, B., Lockwood, J.: Design of a system for real-time worm detection. In: Hot Interconnects, Stanford, CA (2004) 77–83
10. Weaver, N., Staniford, S., Paxson, V.: Very fast containment of scanning worms. In: Proceedings of the 13th Usenix Security Symposium. (2004)
11. Castro, M., Druschel, P., Kermarrec, A., Rowstron, A.: SCRIBE: A large-scale and decentralized application-level multicast infrastructure. IEEE Journal on Selected Areas in communications (JSAC) (2002) To appear.
12. Rowstron, A., Druschel, P.: Pastry: Scalable, decentralized object location, and routing for large-scale peer-to-peer systems. Lecture Notes in Computer Science **2218** (2001) 329–350
13. Castro, M., Jones, M.B., Kermarrec, A., Rowstron, A., Theimer, Wang, H., Wolman, A.: An evaluation of scalable application-level multicast built using peer-to-peer overlays. In: INFOCOM, San Francisco, CA (2003)

14. Janakiraman, R., Waldvogel, M., Zhang, Q.: Indra: A peer-to-peer approach to network intrusion detection and prevention. In: Proceedings of IEEE WETICE 2003. (2003)
15. Dshield homepage. http://www.dshield.org (1995)
16. Philip C. Hyland et al.: Management of network security applications. In: Proceedings of the 21st NIST-NCSC National Information Systems Security Conference, Arlington, Virginia (1998)
17. Song, H., Lu, J., Lockwood, J., Moscola, J.: Secure remote control of field-programmable network devices. In: FCCM, Napa, CA (2004)
18. Xilinx Virtex 2 Pro product webpage. http://www.xilinx.com/virtex2pro (2004)
19. Bagnulo, M., Alarcos, B., Caldern, M., Sedano, M.: Rosa: Realistic open security architecture for active networks. In: International Working Conference on Active Networks (IWAN), Zurich, Switzerland (2002)
20. Cedilnik, A., Kagal, L., Perich, F., Undercoffer, J.L., Joshi, A.: A Secure Infrastructure for Service Discovery and Access in Pervasive Computing. Technical report, University of Maryland, Baltimore County (2001)
21. Undercoffer, J.L., Perich, F., Nicholas, C.: SHOMAR: An Open Architecture for Distributed Intrusion Detection Services. Technical report, University of Maryland, Baltimore County (2002)
22. IETF Simple public key infrastructure (spki) charter http://www.ietf.org/html.charters/spki-charter.html (1994)
23. Maurer, U.: Modelling a public-key infrastructure. In Bertino, E., ed.: Proceedings of 1996 European Symposium on Research in Computer Security (ESORICS' 96). Volume 1146 of Lecture Notes in Computer Science., Springer-Verlag (1996) 325–350
24. Housley, R., Ford, W., Solo, D.: RFC 2459 Internet X.509 Public Key Infrastructure Certificate and CRL Profile (1999)
25. RSA Laboratories PKCS 11 Cryptograhic Token Interface Standard. http://www.rsasecurity.com/rsalabs/pkcs/pkcs-11
26. Attig, M., Dharmapurikar, S., Lockwood, J.: Implementation results of bloom filters for string matchings. In: FCCM, Napa, CA (2004)
27. Schuehler, D.V., Lockwood, J.: A modular system for fpga-based tcp flow processing in high-speed networks. In: Field Programmable Logic and Applications (FPL), Antwerp, Belgium (2004) 301–310
28. Sproull, T., Lockwood, J.W., Taylor, D.E.: Control and configuration software for a reconfigurable networking hardware platform. In: IEEE Symposium on Field-Programmable Custom Computing Machines, (FCCM), Napa, CA (2002)
29. Freepastry webpage. http://www.cs.rice.edu/CS/Systems/Pastry/FreePastry (2004)
30. Zimmermann, P.: The official PGP user's guide. MIT Press, Cambridge, MA (1995)
31. Koga, S., Sakurai, K.: Decentralized Methods of Certification Authority Using the Digital Signature Schemes. In: 2nd Anual PKI Research Workshop Proceedings. (2003)

Secure Service Signaling and Fast Authorization in Programmable Networks

Michael Conrad, Thomas Fuhrmann, Marcus Schöller,
and Martina Zitterbart

Institut für Telematik
Universität Karlsruhe, Germany

Abstract. Programmable networks aim at the fast and flexible creation of services within a network. Often cited examples are audio and video transcoding, application layer multicast, or mobility and resilience support. In order to become commercially viable, programmable networks must provide authentication, authorization and accounting functionality. The mechanisms used to achieve these functionalities must be secure, reliable, and scalable, to be used in production scale programmable networks. Additionally programmable nodes must resist various kinds of attacks, such as denial of service or replay attacks. Fraudulent use by individual users must also be prohibited.

This paper describes the design and implementation of a *secure, reliable, and scalable* signaling mechanism clients can use to initiate service startup and to manage services running on the nodes of a programmable network. This mechanism is designed for production scale networks with AAA-functionality.

Keywords: Programmable Networks, Flexible Service Platforms, Secure Signaling.

1 Introduction

Programmable and active networks extend programmability of network components from the network's edge into the network itself. (See [2,3] for an overview of the basic concepts). Among its key motivations is the idea to quickly and flexibly create new services within a network. This could overcome the long deployment-cycles usually experienced in this area. In such programmable networks, services are created by so-called *service modules*. These are executed in an *execution environment* on the *programmable nodes* of the system (e.g., [8]). The user can start such service on demand to support its already running application.

Varying from approach to approach, programmable nodes are expected to be deployed densely or sparsely. The FlexiNet project (www.flexinet.de), in the context of which this work has been performed, assumes that the programmable nodes are placed near the network edge, e.g. as gateway of a (small) sub-network or as additional programmable nodes within such a sub-network. Typical locations might thus be the access routers of wireless networks, small offices, home offices, or off-path programmable nodes at the Internet service provider or customer premises. These off-path nodes provide supplementary resources for services the on-path routers provide. The service

G.J. Minden et al. (Eds.): IWAN 2004, LNCS 3912, pp. 66–77, 2007.

startup process in general is as follows: first access rights of the client to start the service must be checked and then an evaluation process [8] selects the node where the service gets executed. The access rights of a client are checked by an authorization server which can be found dynamically by the client through a indirect signalling scheme using any one programmable node on path between client and content server (see section 2). After successful authorization the evaluation process determine the programmable node on which the service gets executed – depending on the service this can be the on path node or any off path node. For this paper we will assume that the service gets executed at the programmable node which is involved in the authentication process.

In todays networks it must be assumed that the traffic between the clients, the programmable nodes, and the service providers could be intercepted and spoofed by malicious devices at will. Since programmable network nodes are enhanced routers, their availability is critical for the overall connectivity of clients in the sub-network behind such a node. A programmable node usually handles data streams for multiple receivers. This makes a programmable network node an attractive target for any kind of attack. Hence, special care has to be taken to assure robustness and stability.

The second goal to be achieved is user authentication, authorization, and accounting (AAA). A service provider might want to offer different kinds of services to different user groups. Some of the services should be accessible only by local users, other services may be used by roaming users, too. Services might require a fee, and therefore accounting information must reliably be collected by the provider. This means that an attacker must not be able to forge its identity in order to charge the costs to another user or to start services he does not have access permissions to.

Scalability of the signaling scheme is the third goal of the design. The mechanisms used must cope with multiple signaling messages from many users in parallel. The scalability of the system depends on the resources that handle requests and how these can be duplicated and distributed over the network. The presented design will show on the one hand that only little resources will be needed at the programmable node's side to handle requests and on the other hand that we are willing to overwhelm the authentication and authorization server to preserve the robustness and stability of the programmable node.

This paper presents a secure service signaling mechanism that allows the reliable operation of a programmable network under regular conditions and attacks. Section 2 presents the design of our approach and a threat analysis, followed by implementation details of the proposed mechanisms in section 3, and section 5 finally concludes with the summary.

2 A Flexible Signaling Concept

Generally, there are four types of entities in the programmable network scenario we examine. Without loss of generality we assume that there is a client, a server, a programmable node, and a service module repository (see fig. 1). The client receives a data stream from the server and wants to use a special service provided by the programmable network. The service modules that provide this service are stored in the service module repository. From there they are loaded onto the programmable node. To start the service the user sends a so-called *service start request* to the programmable network. This can be done either directly or indirectly.

Direct signaling can only be used if the client knows one or more programmable nodes, e.g. by using a dynamic configuration protocol like DHCP. Static configuration of clients might also be a solution in some scenarios. With direct signaling the service start request can then be sent directly to one of the programmable nodes.

Indirect signaling applies when the client has no knowledge about any programmable node. In this case, the client simply sends its service start request towards the server's address. Any programmable node that supports indirect signaling must filter transiting packets to discover service start requests. In this way a indirect signalling packet is filtered by the first programmable node on the path between client and server. Such a filter is easily implemented as a programmable network service as shown in section 3.

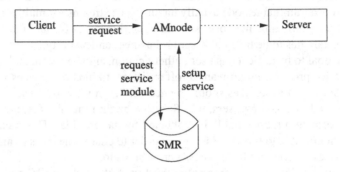

Fig. 1. Service deployment

The minimum of information that must be contained in a service start request is a service identifier. How these identifiers are assigned to the services, is outside the scope of this paper, but we assume that the client knows the identifier, which is associated with the service it is about to start. Furthermore, we assume that the client's address is included in the service start request, too. It is used to notify the client of the success or failure of its request.

This simple and flexible approach suffices for a client to set up a service. Beyond the basic signaling exist several issues of the network provider concern e.g. to allow accounting: *Who is requesting a service in the network? Is that person authorized to do so?* And to secure its network infrastructure: *How can the programmable nodes be protected from spoofed service start requests? How can replay attacks be prevented?* These questions will be addressed in the following sections:

2.1 A Secure Approach

To design a secure system, some assumptions about trust relationships of the involved parties must be clarified. The service provider runs the programmable network nodes, the service module repositories, an authentication server, and an authorization server. Both servers are fully trusted by the programmable nodes and the repositories.

The trust relationships of the client are more complicated, especially if clients can roam between multiple domains. To trust a repository, the client must be able to authenticate the repository. After a successful authentication, the client will bind a session key and other temporal data to the proven identity of the repository, and only messages authenticated with that session key are accepted. Since repository and programmable node implement a full trust relationship, the client extends its trust of the repository to all programmable nodes in the domain of this repository. A programmable node proves its domain membership by authenticating its messages to the client through the knowledge of the session key. After terminating the session, all temporarily data gets deleted, and no further messages authenticated with that key are accepted any more.

On the other hand, the repository needs to authenticate the client to grant or deny access to its services. Since clients may roam to the domain of the repository, a long term secret between these two entities can not be assumed. A PKI-based authentication scheme provides secure authentication with good scalability. For free services, such a scheme is sufficient but not for services that require a fee. Depending on the economic relationship between the service provider and the client, accounting information must be available to the repository. This might imply secure communication between the repository and an accounting server in the home network of the client. The client must provide information about its accounting server to the repository during authentication to allow online checking of e.g. available credit.

The protection of the programmable nodes from attacks is the top priority. To this end, we propose the paradigm that a programmable node only handles authenticated requests and does *not establish any state for unauthenticated requests* on the node. On the other hand, for administrative reasons, user authentication and authorization data should not have to be distributed to every programmable node. We accomplish these two fundamental requirements by combining both the authentication scheme (used for initial client contacts) with a special request redirection mechanism. This mechanism scales very well with the number of clients since a programmable node can redirect messages up to 100 MBit/s in real-time.

Basic Constraints. As described above, we do not assume any pre-shared secret between the client and the programmable network provider. However, since a pure certificate-based approach suffers from the much greater computational overhead of public key cryptography, as compared to a hash function or secret key cryptography, the use of asymmetric cryptographic algorithms should be limited as much as possible. Experiments on hand-held devices like a Palm (20 MHz - Dragonball) were presented in [5]. They show that only 0.14 RSA sign operations can be performed per second, rendering a application based on such operations unusable.

2.2 Authentication Scheme

Our proposed authentication scheme uses public key algorithms to prove the client's identity to the network provider, to prove the identity of the service provider to the client, and – at the same time – to distribute the keys for the HMAC algorithm that is later used for the authorization scheme and client to service communication. The process is as follows:

The client generates an authentication request containing its identity together with its certificate and the socket (IP-address and UDP port number), at which he will listen for the response. Before sending this request to the programmable node the client creates a MAC (message authentication code) for the message. This is a digitally signed hash value of the message, and is appended to it. Thereafter, the request is sent to a programmable node by direct or indirect signaling.

The programmable node forwards the request to the authentication server using the request redirection mechanism, where the identity of the client is checked. If the authentication fails, no error message is sent to the client, to prevent the system from responding to flooding attacks. Otherwise the authentication server adds the session key, a key lifetime, two sequence numbers, its certificate, and the IP-address of the authorization server to the client message to create the response. The session key is encrypted with the client's public key and the complete authentication reply is digitally signed by the authentication server. The response is sent to the IP address and the port number of the client contained in the request.

If the authorization server is not collocated with the authentication server the session dependent data must be transferred to the authorization server, too. Therefore, the authentication server sends the session key and the two sequence numbers to the authorization server in an additional message. This message must be integrity protected and confidentially transferred to the authorization server.

The client validates the server's certificate first, either on its own or by an online protocols like OCSP [11]. Then it checks the signature and finally decrypts the session key and stores the sequence numbers.

Message (1), (2) and (3) in fig. 2 are the message of the authentication scheme.

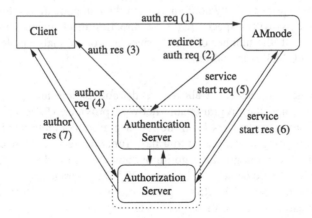

Fig. 2. The secure signaling scheme

Threat Analysis. If an implementor uses state-of-the-art encryption (e.g. RSA) and hash function (e.g. SHA1) it is reasonable to assume that attacks on these will not be successful. Other kinds of attacks must be analyzed in more detail: DoS attacks and replay attacks.

Since the programmable node only forwards authentication requests to the authentication server without establishing any local state, the resistance against DoS attacks solely depends on the address rewriting functionality. As shown in [4] our system can handle simple UDP header manipulations in real time up to 100 Mbit/s. Therefore, the authentication server might become a bottleneck if DoS attacks are launched at the system. Since the authentication server checks the authenticity of any request, a flooding attack might lead to CPU exhaustion of the server. No further real requests can be handled at the authentication server, thus preventing the authentication of new users. It is the intention of the design to sacrifice the authentication server in favor of the programmable nodes. To limit DoS attacks during authentication, an additional cookie exchange or installment of filters at the programmable node might further reduce the impact of DoS attacks. Such filter installment and configuration is still a subject of our research and is not further covered here.

The second type of attack is the replay attack. The attacker monitors the messages exchanged between client and programmable node, and replays these messages sometime in the future. This attack can be prevented if the authentication server creates different session keys for every request. An attacker gets a positive authentication response from the authentication server but can not replay any further sniffed messages, because these messages can not be authenticated. To prevent the attacker from replaying the authentication request infinitely until the authentication server picks the same session key by chance, a monitoring facility at the authentication server should log all authentications, and might disable the authentication of users in case of such an attack for a limited time.

Authentication Result. All further communication between the client and the programmable network can be protected with the now established shared secret. During further communication, the sequence numbers are incremented by the sender and checked by the respective recipient to be in increasing order. Any message with a smaller sequence number is silently discarded. Afterwards the recipient checks the authenticity of the message. If this check succeeds, the receiver stores the sequence number of this message as the new lower boundary; otherwise the message is silently discarded. This mechanism prevents replay attacks of sniffed messages. (We accept that messages are discarded and have to be retransmitted with a new sequence number if messages sent with correct sequence numbers got reordered during transmission.)

2.3 Authorization Scheme

After a successful authentication the client can request one or more services to be started on the programmable net. The authorization server checks the access rights of the user with respect to the requested service. As with the authentication server, the authorization server can be a stand-alone server or be collocated with the service module repository.

The client creates an authorization request, uses the session key to generate a MAC and appends the MAC to the message. Besides the user ID and the sequence number, this request contains the service ID and the service parameters (if necessary). The message is then sent to the authorization server indicated in the authentication response (message (3) in fig. 2). This server first checks the sequence number, then the MAC, and finally processes the request, if all checks have succeeded.

If the user is not allowed to start this service, an error notification is sent to the client, indicating why the access was denied. Otherwise the authorization server informs the programmable node that the service can be started (message (5) and (6) in fig. 2). After a successful service startup on the programmable node, an authorization response is sent to the client (message (7) in fig. 2). This response carries any necessary information to allow client to service communication: IP address of programmable node, id of the service on that node, and two sequence numbers.

The client derives a new service session key for this service by using a hash function with the authorization session key and the two new sequence numbers from the server as arguments. To allow secure client to service communication, the corresponding session state containing this session key, and the sequence numbers have to be transfered to the programmable node, too. The server derives the service session key in the same way and sends the key to the programmable node in an extra message, which can be piggybacked to message (5). The client to service communication is protected using the service session key and the sequence numbers. Section 2.4 shows how the keep-alive messages are protected by this key.

Rekeying. The introduction of sequence numbers, to protect the communication between client and programmable node against replay attacks, makes a mechanism to handle the wrapping of these sequence numbers necessary. As soon as a sequence number cannot be increased, new session keys must be requested from the authorization server. Either the client sends an authorization request to the authorization server, as described above, containing additionally the service dependent data to inform the server for which service new session keys are requested or the programmable node sends a rekey request containing the same data. The authorization server generates a new session key and transfers this key plus the two new sequence numbers for this security association to the client and the programmable node.

Threat Analysis. The authorization scheme is resistant against replay attacks through the usage of sequence numbers. During authentication two sequence numbers have been transferred to the client. The client uses the first one to authenticate messages sent to the server, the other one to receive message from the server. As long as the session key is known only to client and server, it is reasonable to assume that no attacker can create a valid MAC for a message with a valid sequence number.

Including the IP address of the authorization in the authentication response informs the client reliably to which authorization server the security association has been established. This information assures the address of the authorization server to the client, even if an attacker manipulated the unprotected IP header of the authentication response.

Third, the scheme has a good resistance against DoS attacks. Using the first message of the authorization scheme, the client must prove that it has access to the session key. The authorization server first checks the authorization request, and only in case of a valid request is the programmable node involved in the process. Again a DoS attack on the system might bring down the server, but the programmable node is not disrupted.

The creation of session state on the programmable nodes is delayed, until the client has proven access to the session key. This implies that session state on the programmable node is only created for actual running services on that node. As soon as the service is stopped, the node can purge any service dependent data.

Authorization Result. The requested service has been set up on the programmable node, and the user is informed that he can use the service. If client to service communication is supported by this service, all address information of the service is transferred to the client. Depending on the service, reconfiguration requests and keep-alive messages can be sent directly from client to the service instance.

2.4 Service Lifetime

To explicitly support roaming users, we propose a soft state approach for services on programmable nodes. Since client to node communication can break down suddenly, the client cannot always send a service stop request to the node. Service execution and accounting of service usage must be stopped by other means. A service execution based on a soft state approach enables the desired behavior, but requires the client to refresh the state periodically. If no refreshment message reaches the node for a configured amount of time, the service is stopped automatically.

The message to refresh the state of the service must be protected against manipulation and replay attacks, too. The client uses the session key and sequence numbers to generate this request and sends the request directly to the programmable node the service is executed at. The mechanisms to check the message authenticity are performed, as during the authorization.

3 Implementation

Within the FlexiNet project we have implemented an exemplary client signaling GUI, the active node, and the service module repository. The authentication server and the authorization server are both collocated with the service module repository. Every programmable node creates a TLS tunnel [6] to its configured service module repositories during system startup. In contrast to the ordinary use of TLS, we demand mutual authentication of the communication peers. A programmable node uses the TLS tunnel to securely download service modules from the service module repository. Additionally, we will use this tunnel to exchange service start request and response messages between programmable nodes and the authorization server.

For user and machine identification we are using X.509 certificates, which carry RSA keys for the signature generation and validation. As cryptographic hash functions, HMAC/SHA1 are used in our extended signaling scheme.

This section details implementation issues of the message redirection mechanism, which is followed by an example of our message format.

3.1 Redirection Mechanism

To filter signaling messages at a programmable node, a special service module – called signaling filter module – must be installed. It is started during system startup and runs in a special environment – the so called framework execution environment. This environment, and thereby the signaling filter service, cannot be stopped by normal means. The service is active as long as the programmable node is working. Furthermore, the signaling filter service is the only service allowed to forward messages to the programmable node's framework. The main task of the framework is node management, which includes service setup and termination. The framework instantiates a new execution environment every time a new service gets started on the programmable node, and the required service modules are loaded into this environment. If the required module is not stored in the local module cache, the framework has to download that module from the service module repository, via the established TLS tunnel.

The signaling filter service installs three network hooks during startup, in order to filter UDP ports 5000, 5001, and 5002. While the hook on port 5000 is accepting all bypassing traffic for any destination, the two other ports only accept messages directly addressed to the node. In our implementation the client uses port 5000 to indirectly send the authentication request to the programmable network. This allows for clients to discover a programmable node without knowledge about the network topology. The client sends its signaling request towards the server, and if a programmable node is located on the path between client and server, it will filter this signaling message. Additionally, port 5001 is used by clients to directly signal the authentication request. All other messages, like keep-alive requests, have to be sent to port 5002.

The messages, which a programmable node filters on port 5000 or 5001, will be redirected, without any processing, to a connected service module repository. To achieve this, the signaling filter service just has to replace the destination address in the UDP packet and to recalculate the UDP checksum, if used. Thereby, no state has to be established, and the node is protected against flooding attacks.

Any message filtered on port 5002 must be forwarded from the signaling service to the local framework of the programmable node. Here the message gets re-instantiated, and its signature is verified. Only messages authenticated with the session key are accepted at port 5002. All other messages get immediately discarded.

3.2   Signaling Message Format

In an abstract signaling class, three types of messages – request, response for synchronous communication, and trap for asynchronous communication – and the basic attributes of these signaling messages are defined. The basic attributes are : command, group, msg-id, user-id, client and node sequence number. Every implementation of a message must be derived from this abstract class and can add message dependent attributes. Therefore, the implementation must assign a name and a type to the attribute, and provide methods to get and set the attribute values.

Authentication Request. Fig. 3 shows a serialized authentication request, which always consists of two parts: a message part (line 02-07) and a signature part (line 08-10).

The command `authenticate` within the group `Access` denotes that a client wants to authenticate itself to the system. The ID of the client is stated in attribute user-id. The two sequence numbers are not used during authentication and are set to zero.

```
01 <flexinet version="2.6"> <signaling>
02    <request client-seq="0" command="authenticate" group="access"
03           msg-id="42" node-seq="0" user-id="client@flexinet.de">
04      <scalar name="ip-protocol" type="string"><string>udp</string></scalar>
05      <scalar name="udp-port" type="int"><int>5000</int></scalar>
06      <scalar name="ip-address" type="string"><string>192.168.0.1</string></scalar>
07    </request>
08    <signature algorithm="SHA1withRSA" msg-id="42" user="client@flexinet.de">
09      U1Qe1z/9drf75zFA7JH18AWalz/VTzaFmsFJX6g1WQYAEAWPtoXTM1d...
10    </signature>
11  </signaling> </flexinet>
```

Fig. 3. Authentication request message

The id attribute is used to bind a signature to a request. This binding is necessary if multiple request, response, and trap messages are sent within a single signaling message. Besides these basic attributes, an authentication request contains attributes like the client's IP address, port number, and the type of the transport protocol.

The signature part states the algorithm used to generate the signature, which is bound to the message part with the same id. The signature is computed using the key of the denoted user. In the example above, SHA1withRSA is used as the signature algorithm. Since the object representation is unsuitable for signature generation, we have chosen the canonical XML serialization as input to the signature algorithm.

```
01 <flexinet version="2.6"> <signaling>
02    <request client-seq="3749" command="start" group="service"
03           id="46" node-seq="63953" user="client@flexinet.de">
04      <scalar name="ip-protocol" type="string"><string>udp</string></scalar>
05      <scalar name="udp-port" type="int"><int>5000</int></scalar>
06      <scalar name="ip-address" type="string"><string>192.168.0.1</string></scalar>
07      <scalar name="service-id" type="int"><int>23</int></scalar>
08      <scalar name="private-service-option" type="int"><int>3</int></scalar>
09    </request>
10    <signature algorithm="HMACSHA1" id="46" user="client@flexinet.de">
11      cvXzFkm6m2uc2NypaQ8Tbsai5RE=
12    </signature>
13  </signaling> </flexinet>
```

Fig. 4. Authorization request message

Authorization Request. To start a service, the client sends an authorization request (see fig. 4 to the authorization server. The message part denotes the command start within the service group (line 02). Sequence numbers and message id are set according to the current client state (line 02-03). In addition to these basic attributes, the client specifies the desired service using the service-id attribute (line 07) and service parameters using the private-service-option attribute (line 08). To receive an authorization response the attributes ip-address, ip-protocol, and udp-port (line 04-06) are set as in the authentication request.

The signature is generated using the HMAC-SHA1 algorithm and the shared secret. Again the id binds this signature to the corresponding message part.

4   Related Work

The related work can be divided into three categories: signaling protocols, general authentication and authorization protocols, and authentication and authorization in programmable networking.

GIMPS [12] is a draft of a general signaling protocol. The authentication schemes incorporated assume that the client knows his communication peer, which is not always true for programmable networks.

In the area of general authentication and authorization protocols, many solutions for different scenarios have been proposed. EAP [7] is an extensible authentication protocol used for network access control. The protocol was designed to authenticate a dial-in user to the network access server. A prerequisite of the protocol is that the user authenticates himself towards the next hop, since EAP is a layer 2 protocol. This behavior is not applicable to programmable networking, since the programmable node might be multiple hops away from the user.

Kerberos [10] provides user authentication based on symmetric key algorithms. A user authenticates himself via user name and password, and uses tickets to authenticate himself towards the resources of the network. The drawback of Kerberos is that it cannot support roaming users moving into a Kerberos domain. In our opinion, support of wireless clients is essential for programmable networking.

Key exchange protocols always implement an authentication scheme, and additionally solve the key distribution problem. TLS [6] is a TCP-based security protocol including a key exchange. The modifications to the protocol, which would be necessary to support indirect signaling, are non-trivial. Nonetheless, some basic mechanisms of TLS, like server based key generation, are reused in our design. IKE [9] is another key exchange protocol. It is based on UDP and fits many needs outlined, but the key generation mechanism can only use the Diffie-Hellmann algorithm. Furthermore, the complexity of the protocol is a known drawback of IKEv1, but might improve with IKEv2, whose standardization should be completed in the near future.

Within the active and programmable networking area, only little research on secure signaling has been introduced. Like in SARA [1] an analysis of security aspects and possible solutions are provided, but some forms of attacks have been neglected, like DoS attacks on the active router. To verify a request in SARA, the active router must first download the module from the code server and then verify the authenticity of the request. An attacker can easily mount an DoS attack on the active router by requesting different modules each time.

5   Conclusion and Future Work

We have presented a secure and scalable signaling scheme for user authentication, service startup, and service management. The authentication scheme can be used for direct and indirect signaling in the case, that the nearest programmable node is not known to the client. The usage of asymmetric cryptographic algorithms is thereby limited to the authentication process and all further messages are protected by cryptographic hash functions. The presented signaling scheme resists active attackers and stems the threats of denial of service attacks.

A secure evaluation scheme and a secure service relocation scheme will be available shortly and presented in the near future. These schemes will be build from the same building blocks as the presented authentication and authorization scheme, keeping the protocol complexity modest, and thereby lighten the analysis of the protocol.

References

1. M Bagnulo, B. Alarcos, M. Calderón, and M. Sedano. ROSA: Realistic Open Security Architecture for active networks. In *Fourth Annual International Working Conference on Active Networks (IWAN)*, 2002.
2. Kenneth L. Calvert, Samrat Bhattacharjee, Ellen Zegura, and James Sterbenz. Directions in active networks. *IEEE Communications Magazine*, 36(10):72–78, October 1998.
3. Andrew T. Campbell, Herman G. De Meer, Michael E. Kounavis, Kazuho Miki, John B. Vicente, and Daniel Villela. A survey of programmable networks. *ACM SIGCOMM Computer Communication Review*, 29(2), April 1999.
4. M. Conrad, M. Schöller, T. Fuhrmann, G. Bocksch, and M. Zitterbart. Multiple language family support for programmable network systems. In *Proceedings of the 5th Annual International Working Conference on Active Networks (IWAN)*, 2003.
5. Neil Daswani and Dan Boneh. Experimenting with Electronic Commerce on the PalmPilot. *Lecture Notes in Computer Science*, 1648:1–16, 1999.
6. T. Dierks and C. Allen. The TLS protocol version 1.0. RFC 2246, Internet Engineering Task Force, January 1999.
7. N. Freed and S. E. Kille. Network services monitoring MIB. RFC 2248, Internet Engineering Task Force, January 1998.
8. T. Fuhrmann, M. Schöller, C. Schmidt, and M. Zitterbart. A Node Evaluation Mechanism for Service Setup in AMnet. In *Proceedings of the 13th ITG/GI-Fachtagung Kommunikation in Verteilten Systemen (KiVS'2003), Kurzbeiträge, Praxisberichte und Workshop*, 2003.
9. D. Harkins and D. Carrel. The Internet key exchange (IKE). RFC 2409, Internet Engineering Task Force, November 1998.
10. J. Kohl and C. Neuman. The kerberos network authentication service (V5). RFC 1510, Internet Engineering Task Force, September 1993.
11. M. Myers, R. Ankney, A. Malpani, S. Galperin, and C. J. Adams. X.509 Internet public key infrastructure online certificate status protocol - OCSP. RFC 2560, Internet Engineering Task Force, June 1999.
12. Henning Schulzrinne. GIMPS: General Internet Messaging Protocol for Signaling, June 2003.

Tackling the Complexity of Future Networks

Takashi Egawa, Yoshiaki Kiriha, and Akira Arutaki

System Platforms Research Laboratories, NEC Corporation,
Shimonumabe 1753, Nakahara-ku, Kawasaki, Kanagawa, 211-8666 Japan
{t-egawa@ct,y-kiriha@ay,aarutaki@bp}.jp.nec.com

Abstract. Though the Internet succeeded to converge data and voice networks, it itself is diverging now. The authors believe this derives from two facts; one is the end of universal service era thanks to abundant communication services, and the other the fusion of computers and communications because the speed of networks is catching up that of computer's internal bus. These facts allow us to build networks proprietary for specific purposes such as sensor networks or web services for e-commerce where computer and communication technologies are tightly integrated. As a result, networks are becoming enormously complicated and heterogeneous, and without our effort they will become uncontrollable. The authors believe active network technologies were a good try, but it was not enough. Theories build on solid mathematical basis is indispensable for the analysis of huge systems, and we should try to build such theory. Complex systems theory provides various mathematical formulas such as 'scale-free', and it can be a good starting point. We show as an example that by using self-organization theory ubiquitous networks are considered indispensable for system stability in future business network environment.

1 Introduction

The network is diverging again.

Convergence of various networks, data and voice networks in particular was a dream of network engineers for many years. Huge amount of efforts such as ISDN or ATM were made, and finally IP succeeded to grasp the Holy Grail. It succeeded to integrate voice and data traffic. Layer three function, a function to identify a node in network-wide manner and to deliver data to the node, has been unified with IP in most important wired networks, and wireless networks will join when 4G mobile communication service starts.

However, dividing and diverging of IP network itself are under way. As shown in the end-to-end argument [1], IP networks was originally designed so that IP layer functions would deliver packets from end to end, and each end host controls data delivery by doing flow controls, retransmissions, or encryptions/decryptions. This is not the case any more. Network Address Translators (NATs) and virtual IP/virtual server technologies used in load balancers have destroyed the uniform address space. Firewalls have introduced application layer controls into IP packet flows, which make it possible to interfere policies or intentions of organizations in data delivery. IETF OPES WG enumerates various boxes possible to insert as an intermediary in the

G.J. Minden et al. (Eds.): IWAN 2004, LNCS 3912, pp. 78–87, 2007.

end-to-end loop [2]. One of them, TCP performance enhancement box [3], cuts off the feedback loop of TCP flow control and tries to increase the performance without the modification of end hosts. This is convenient for novice users, but this also means that the performance of TCP/IP communications with my PC does not increase even if I update the protocol stack of my PC.

Divergence of overlay networks on IP networks is even larger. There are many application specific networks such as P2Ps, x-bones, intranets, extranets, and the web. They have their proprietary address space and routing mechanisms. Some of them are unicast, and some of them are multicast. Even the property of connections may differ: connections between web sites, i.e., links, are unidirectional. Convergence of these various networks seems impossible in the near future. And active network technologies have been trying to make divergence easier.

Why such things happened? We believe this derives from the abundance of excellent networks. The abundance ended our desire for universal service, and we are now on a new stage where differentiation is more important. The excellence of communication service is accelerating the fusion of computer world and communication world, especially through the fact that the bandwidth of Ethernet is catching up with that of computers' internal bus.

The problem is, without our enormous effort this divergence would lead us to chaotic world where security breaches are common, root causes of failures or QoS degradation are unresolved, and routing tables never converge.

This paper is organized as follows. We discuss the cause of the divergence, abundance, in details in chapter 2, and excellence in chapter 3. Then in chapter 4 we propose to introduce knowledge from other areas to solve these issues. The theory of scale-free from complexity system theory is introduced, and why ubiquitous network is indispensable in future business network environment is explained using self-organization theory. Chapter 5 concludes this paper.

2 Abundance of Communication Services

People believed for many years that telecommunication services were different from other goods. Telecommunication carriers were considered as natural monopolies, and in compensation of monopoly status they had the obligation to provide, and they proudly provided, communication services universally [12]. The phrase 'anytime, anywhere, with anybody' well speaks the ideal.

However, as communication technologies evolve, it became easier to provide communication services. The precious service became common, and then abundant. The carrier's special status gradually diminished. Telecommunication carriers were privatized, and market mechanism was introduced in many countries. The initial cost to enter into the market decreased drastically. Startups provide public Wi-Fi infrastructure in some cities today. A person who installs LAN in his house is not very rare.

The necessity and the desire for universal service also diminished. Basic POTS service is available at anywhere in many countries. Best-effort IP service can easily be obtained, and it is not the target of universal service policy.

Abundance brings us to a new stage of economy where important properties of the industry differ, as Rostow claimed in [4]. The driving force of telecommunication services, and network technologies as well, changed from public sectors to private sectors. This changed the core competence from standardization and universality to differentiation and customization.

In business sector communication services are tools to do business. They must be optimized for business processes, and as long as the business requirements are satisfied the service must be cheap as much as possible. This leads us to various customizations. How a call should be transferred to the right personnel (is it OK for an executive to answer a phone call to another executive if all secretaries are out of office)? Reliability is always preferable, but the acceptable cost differs. Authentication for multicast clients is indispensable for applications of some companies, but is not for others.

In consumer sector various customization also exists. 'What sort of phone you carry and how you customize it says a great deal about you, just as the choice of car did for a previous generation', wrote the Economist [5]. The market size of customizing ring tones was Y85b ($770m) in Japan in 2002, which occupies 0.8% of the all IT sectors, and it will become Y150b ($1.4b) in 2007 [6]. In early days of short mails, the sales of a mobile phone was three times larger than others, because it could use heart mark [7]. The features of cameras (how many seconds of movies this mobile phone can take and send?) are the current target of differentiation. These differentiation and customization never ends because many people, young people in particular, tries hard to single them out.

These differentiation and customization leads to a complex, diverged network system.

3 Fusion of Computer World and Communication World

Link speed of networks is catching up that of computer's internal bus. Such excellent communication technologies are accelerating the fusion of computer world and communication world, which is another driving force that makes networks complicated and diverged.

Figure 1 shows the link speed of core telecommunication networks, networks that connect supercomputer nodes, and Ethernet. We can see that the link speed increase of networks is faster than that of supercomputers', and today the difference between supercomputer's internal bus and Ethernet is only one digit.

This is also true for common PCs. Gigabit Ethernet has the same speed with ordinary 32-bit PCI bus, and 10G-Ethernet is the same speed with PCI-X bus. Such high-speed WAN links are expensive, but a little bit modest one, 100Mbps FTTH is available at around $50/month in Japan and more than 1.4m customers are enjoying them.

This will make distributed computing into reality where communication functions and computer functions are tightly integrated. Technological reasons to distinguish RPC and ordinary system calls are diminishing.

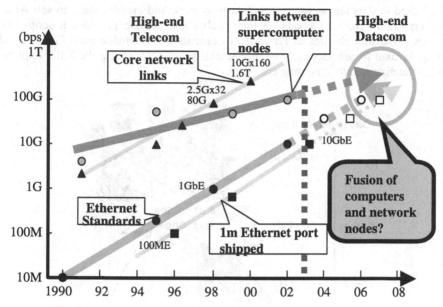

Fig. 1. Trends of link speed used in computers and telecommunications

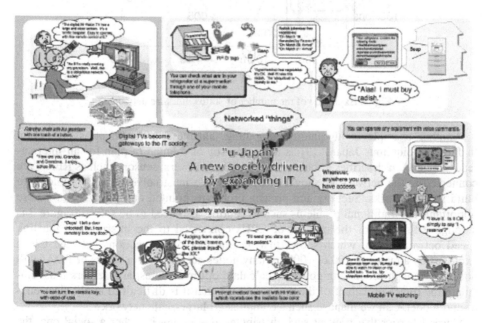

Fig. 2. U-Japan plan (cited from Japanese Government's white paper [4])

One example of distributed computing is various web services such as Amazon Web Services (AWS) [8]. AWS provides an API to search Amazon's bestsellers, prices, customer reviews and related items by using SOAP or XML. The search result can be used to decorate ordinary people's web sites, and enables them to sell Amazon's enormous kinds of goods on their web sites. Google provides a script that searches personal web sites as far as their contents are reachable from Google, and enables layman to use Google's mighty search power. These are the killer applications in the distributed computing era.

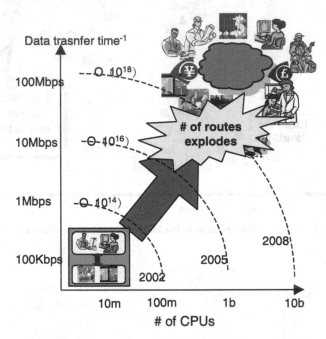

Fig. 3. Explosion of the number of status in future networks

Another example is ubiquitous computing. Japanese government is promoting 'u-Japan (Ubiquitous Japan)' [9] as the successor of e-Japan (a plan for an Internet-ready society). It describes a society where various servers, sensors such as RFIDs are connected to the network as shown in figure 2. We must solve various problems to build such networks. Security and privacy problems pointed out in [9] are of course important, but traditional problems such as routing also need to be solved. Figure 3 is a rough estimation of the number of CPUs connected to the Internet and the link speed between them, which shows that the number of connections between CPUs explodes by a factor of 100 or 10000. Many nodes such as sensor nodes or PDAs will not have enough processing power to calculate optimal routes, and servers must calculate the routes on behalf of them. This means that it is difficult to apply clear end-to-end model. Can we manage such a complicated large-scale network?

Current barrier that prevent such distributed computing is rather a social one, the right of ownership. Network operators cannot use customer's computing resources, vice versa. Management policy differs among different organizations. However, security threats are undermining this barrier. Cisco and IBM are cooperating to make security policies interoperable to protect systems from raging malwares, which means that 100% ownership is disappearing.

4 Tackling the Complexity

Active network technologies have been trying to make network functions easier to customize and to arrange by enabling dynamic program installation, by making management system more sophisticated and by introducing security mechanisms against various threats. This matches the technological trends described above.

However, the authors fear that current active network technologies for solving complexity and dynamically changing nature of future networks might not be enough. We have developed various management systems, but were they enough if the number of nodes increased 10000 times because we had to consider sensor nodes and user terminals? Can we track the route of a sensor data to check its integrity? Can we detect the occurrence of security breaches in the network?

This is a challenging goal, and we believe theories build on solid mathematical basis, an approach that traditional active network research did not focus on, is indispensable for solving such issues of huge systems. Toward this end, mathematical methods and formulas developed in different areas will help us. Complex systems theory has a long history of research, and it provides various mathematical formulas such as self-organization and 'scale-free' [10][11]. As an example to show the potential power of such mathematical formula, we show that if we apply self-organization theories to future business environment, ubiquitous network is a must for system stability [13].

4.1 The Theory of Scale-Free Networks

Scale means a typical number that characterizes the system (e.g., mean). Scale-free systems such as fractal do not have such characteristic numbers (the mean becomes zero or infinity). The theory of scale-free claims that we can find scale-free networks in various areas, and it tries to explain the structure of World Wide Web, biochemical reaction chains of proteins in cells, and even the social network that propagates AIDS.

Let us take WWW as an example. In the World Wide Web network, there are few nodes such as Google or Yahoo that are linked from huge amount of nodes, while most nodes are linked from only a few links. Nodes such as Google and Yahoo are called 'hubs' or 'connectors', and play an important role in the networks. Figure 4 shows a typical image of such a network. You can see beautiful pictures of scale-free networks in various areas at [15].

To be more precise, it is known that the distribution of the number of links that a node has in the WWW network becomes power law distribution. If we denote the number of links node v has as d_v, and the rank of node v as r_v, we can describe the relationship between these two values as

$$d_v \propto r_v^{\alpha}$$

where α is a constant specific to the system.

This means that very few www nodes are linked from huge amount of nodes (i.e. hubs), but most nodes are linked from only a few nodes.

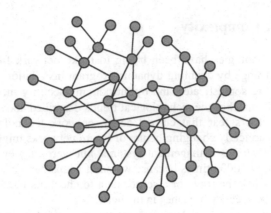

Fig. 4. A typical scale-free network (inspired by a figure in [16])

Barabasi [10] showed analytically that such network appears if we assume two simple rules.

1. [Growth] a network grows by adding nodes one by one (the network does not appear at a time as a result of careful planning).

2. [Preferential attachment] the probability that a new node connect to an existing node is proportional to the number of links the existing node has (a famous node becomes even more famous).

Figure 5 shows the concept of such growth.

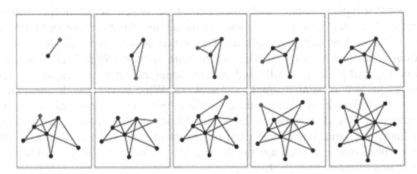

Fig. 5. Growth of a scale-free network (inspired by a figure in [11])

It has been proved that scale-free networks have many interesting properties. Scale-free networks are very robust against random failures, but fragile to intentional attacks [16]. They are also fragile to virus infection. According to percolation theory there is a minimum size of infected nodes to occur an epidemic in random networks, but in scale-free networks such threshold size does not exist [17]. Slight modification of the two rules, i.e. by adding the initial attractiveness of each web sites, changes the exponent a of the Zipf's law [18]. This shows a possibility to control networks by the modification of 'attractiveness' of each nodes.

There is an objection to this theory. Willinger [19] and Li [20] claim that preferential attachment is not the reason of IP networks' power-law distribution. They claim that the distribution is very common in complex systems because they are very 'robust' against various operations such as merging two groups, and it cannot be the proof of preferential attachment. Moreover, IP network is carefully designed considering various technological constraints, e.g., core routers cannot have many links. They conclude that Web network might be scale-free, but IP network is not. It is an open issue to find which claim (or still other claim) is true, and to build a formula for controlling networks on the findings.

4.2 Self-organization in the Future Business Environment

Now we would like to show that complex system theory such as self-organization can be used to describe the condition of complicated network stability, using networks for supply chain management (SCM) systems as an example.

SCM system builds a network among trade connections and by exchanging information on stocks it optimizes the stock of each company as a whole. Such business relations were stable and did not change very often in old days, but thanks to the Internet it becomes possible to establish relations with companies all over the world and change the trade connections for each trade.

Is this dynamically changing system stable?

Of course not, control theory tells us. The potential function of a system composed of many nodes becomes very complicated, and a little perturbation can shift the system to a new state, which often causes oscillation. We can see it as route flapping in the Internet.

However, there are many complex, still stable systems. Why?

Complex system theory claims that self-organization mechanisms reduce the number of dominant nodes in the system, and thanks to this degeneracy the potential function becomes simple, and the system becomes stable. If Yahoo and Google, or 'leader' or 'dominator' dominates the system, it becomes stable.

This phenomenon can be explained as follows [14]. System behavior can be described as a function of many parameters, each of which corresponds to each node. The time constant of each parameter differs. If some time constants are much larger than the others, the global behavior of the system can be described with these parameters. The parameters with large time constants are called 'order parameters'. This occurs because the behavior of nodes with small time constants changes before it affects the whole system, and its effect disperses. The behavior of these nodes can be described as a function of that of large time constants.

This means that if the time constants of the order parameters decrease, all other time constants must decrease to keep the system stable. If we would like to change a system more frequently every node must respond faster to various changes. Nodes require more sophisticated sensing system and communication tools to integrate the collected information.

And yes, this is the current trend in business world. To keep SCM systems every company are seriously working to respond more quickly to the changes of supply, stock, the environment, etc. To achieve this goal companies give their employee smart communication devices, and install various sensors in various places. The authors believe this is the reason why we need ubiquitous networks.

5 Conclusion

We showed that the requirements that active network technologies tried to solve, the adaptation to network complexity and diversity, would become even more important in the future networking environment. They derive from the abundance of communication devices and the fusion of computer and communication technologies, and currently we do not see any sign that this trend would end in the near future. We then proposed to import knowledge from different areas, in particular complex systems theory to obtain mathematical basis to solve complicated network problem, and explained the necessity of ubiquitous networks.

There are huge amount of things to do for network engineers. The theory of scale-free is still in its infancy. It succeeded to describe and to explain various phenomena, but it does not say anything on what we can, and how we can control them. The explanation we made for ubiquitous networks is just a qualitative, introductory one, and more precise description is necessary to construct stable networks. We must go a long way to describe, explain and control various features of the Internet with this framework.

References

1. Jerome H. Saltzer, David P. Reed, and David D. Clark. End-to-end arguments in system design. *ACM Transactions on Computer Systems 2*, 4 (November 1984) pages 277-288. An earlier version appeared in the *Second International Conference on Distributed Computing Systems* (April, 1981) pages 509-512.
2. A. Barbir, E. Burger, R. Chen, S. McHenry, H. Orman, R. Penno, 'Open Pluggable Edge Services (OPES) Use Cases and Deployment Scenarios,' RFC3752, April 2004.
3. Border, J., Kojo, M., Griner, J., Montenegro, G. and Z. Shelby, "Performance Enhancing Proxies Intended to Mitigate Link-Related Degradations", RFC 3135, June 2001.
4. Walt W. Rostow, *The Stages of Economic Growth: A non-communist manifesto,* 1960.
5. 'Why phones are replacing cars,' the Economist, April 29, 2004.
6. M report, "Trends and forecasts of ring tone market", July 2003 (in Japanese).
7. Howard Rheingold, *Smart Mobs: The Next Social Revolution,* Perseus Books Group, October 2002.
8. http://www.amazon.com/gp/aws/sdk/main.html
9. Ministry of Public Management, Home Affairs, Posts and Telecommunications, Japan, 'Information and Communications in Japan', 2004 White Paper, 2004.
10. A.-L. Barabási, and R. Albert, 'Emergence of scaling in random networks,' Science,286, 509-512 (1999)
11. Albert-Laszlo Barabasi, *Linked: How Everything Is Connected to Everything Else and What It Means,* Plume Books; April 2003.
12. Koichiro Hayashi and Yoshihiro Tagawa, *Universal service—fairness in multimedia era,* Chuko-shinsho, March 1994 (in Japanese).
13. Takashi EGAWA, Masayoshi KOBAYASHI, Kenji YAMANISHI, Akira ARUTAKI and Junji NAMIKI, 'Dynamic Collaboration" from Scientists' Eyes,' NEC Journal of Advanced Technology, Vol.1, No.1 Winter 2004.
14. Hermann Haken, *Synergetics: An Introduction,* Springer-Verlag, June 1977.
15. http://www.nd.edu/~networks/gallery.htm

16. R. Albert, H. Jeong, and A.-L. Barabási, 'Attack and error tolerance in complex networks,' Nature, 406, 387-482 (2000).
17. R. Pastor-Satorras and A. Vespignani, 'Epidemic dynamics and endemic states in complex networks,' Physical Review E 63, 066117, 2001.
18. S.N. Dorogovtsev, J.F.F. Mendes and A.N. Samukhin, 'Structure of Growing Networks: Exact Solution of the Barab´asi–Albert's Model,' Phys. Rev. Lett. 85, 4633, 2000.
19. W. Willinger, D. Alderson, J. Doyle, and L. Li, 'More "Normal" Than Normal: Scaling Distributions and Complex Systems,' in Proceedings of the 2004 Winter Simulation Conference, 2004.
20. L. Li, D. Alderson, W. Willinger, and J. Doyle, 'A First-Principles Approach to Understanding the Internet's Router-Level Topology,' in Proceedings ACM SIGCOMM 2004, 2004.

Evaluation of Integration Effect of Content Location and Request Routing in Content Distribution Networks

Hirokazu Miura[1] and Miki Yamamoto[2]

[1] Fuculty of Systems Engineering, Wakayama University
930 Sakaedani, Wakayama, 640-8510 Japan
miurah@sys.wakayama-u.ac.jp
[2] Graduate School of Engineering, Osaka University
2-1 Yamadaoka, Suita-shi, Osaka, 565-0871 Japan
yamamoto@comm.eng.osaka-u.ac.jp

Abstract. Recently the content distribution networks (CDNs) are highlighted as the new network paradigm which can improve latency for Web access. In CDNs, the content location strategy and request routing techniques are important technical issues. Both of them should be used in an integrated manner in general, but CDN performance applying both these technologies has not been evaluated in detail. In this paper, we investigate effect of integration of these techniques. For request routing, we focus on a request routing technique applied active network technology, *Active Anycast*, which improves both network delay and server processing delay. For content distribution technology, we propose a new strategy, *Popularity-Probability*, whose aim corresponds with that of *Active Anycast*. Performance evaluation results show that integration of *Active Anycast* and *Popularity-Probability* provides robust CDNs.

Keywords: Content distribution networks, content location strategy, request routing.

1   Introduction

In the Internet, several types of services use replicated servers which are geographically dispersed across the whole network. One typical example of this type of service is content distribution network (CDN)[1]. The aim of this approach is to prevent too many accesses from concentrating at a particular server, which causes degradation of response time of a server itself and congestion in the network around that server. In content distribution networks, the request routing [2][3] and content location techniques[4]-[7] are important technical problems. Both technologies should be used in an integrated manner in general, but CDN performance applying both of these technologies has not been evaluated in detail. In this paper, we investigate effect of integration of these techniques.

When a client would like to select a good (replication) server to obtain a object, one transparent way is making use of DNS[8][9]. In this approach, a DNS

G.J. Minden et al. (Eds.): IWAN 2004, LNCS 3912, pp. 88–100, 2007.

server has a list of servers and returns a selected server's IP address. Round robin selection is generally used, which cannot take account of server's location and load. An Anycast server selection is more sophisticated way of guiding a client's request to one of many hosts[10][11][12]. A packet destined for an Anycast address will be delivered to one of the hosts with Anycast address, ideally the closest one from the client. This Anycast technology only takes the distance between client and server into consideration. To select the optimal server which gives the smallest response time, server load is also an important factor to be considered. As one of possible way to resolve these server selection problems, we have proposed *"Active Anycast"*[13]. In *Active Anycast*, when a user request arrives at an active router, this active router selects an adequate server and directs this request to the selected server.

In content location strategy, the optimization problem is defined as replicating objects so that the average number of hops traversed is minimized when clients fetch objects from the nearest content server containing the requested object. This optimization problem is NP-complete[4]. Kangasharju et.al.[4] propose three heuristics (*Popularity, Greedy-Single, Greedy-Global*) for this optimization problem. These algorithms are designed for the object to be replicated so that the average number of hops traversed is minimized in the base of the assumption that Anycast is used for request routing.

In this paper, we claim that there is significant difference between aims of content location strategy and request routing. And we claim that these aims should be correspond. When *Active Anycast* is used for request routing, a user request has a tendency to be guided so that servers inside a network are effectively used. Thus, when request routing guides a user request intelligently so that load of servers to be balanced, content location strategy should work well together with this strategy. From these observation, we propose a new content location strategy, *Popularity-Probability*. In *Popularity-Probability*, objects are randomly located in replicated servers inside a network according to its popularity. It has a quite simple operation, i.e. a specific object is located in a content server with the probability which are given from its relative popularity. By this simple operation, objects are randomly located inside a network and an object with high popularity has larger number of copies inside a network than lower-popularity objects. With *Active Anycast* strategy, this content location strategy will provide good performance to CDNs. Performance evaluation in the paper will show that our proposed integration of request routing and content location strategy in CDN will open a new possible network design, the *robust CDN*.

Remainder of the paper is structured as follows. Section 2 describes about request routing technology and introduces Anycast and *Active Anycast*. Section 3 explains about previously published content location strategies in detail. Section 4 claims necessity of robust CDN and proposes a new integration of request routing and content location strategy, i.e. *Active Anycast* and *Popularity-Probability*. Section 5 shows simulation results which investigate effectiveness of our proposed integration. Section 6 concludes the paper.

2   Request Routing

In the content distribution networks, to effectively respond to requests in a reasonable amount of time, the load must be distributed across multiple servers. Request routing is the technique which directs user requests to an adequate server from the viewpoint of improving latency in obtaining objects. URL approach is the simplest one and some modifications of them have been proposed[3]. This approach assumes request routing decision is made at client side, so it can be categorized into end-to-end approach. In the paper, we focus on network support approach which makes use of active network technology. As a network support approach, we explain about Anycast and Active Anycast, in detail.

2.1   Anycast

In Anycast technology, an Anycast address can indicate a group of servers offering the same service[10][11][12]. A router which receives an IP datagram whose destination address field includes an Anycast address forwards this datagram to an output link on the path to the nearest server. The Anycast technology can be used for selection of the closest server without an end-user's knowing where it is.

2.2   Active Anycast

As a request routing, we have proposed *Active Anycast*[13]. In *Active Anycast*, a router in the network autonomously distributes accesses from clients adequately to geographically dispersed servers. The *Active Anycast* is based on Anycast[10][11][12] and active network technology[15][16].

In *Active Anycast*, a TCP connection which is initiated by the client is autonomously set up to an adequate server by an active router. When the client has a request to the server, it sends a name resolution query to the Domain Name System (DNS) and gets a resolved Anycast address (Step 1. in Fig.1). This Anycast address indicates a group of replicated servers (including an original server) which offer the same service. The initiating host sends a SYN packet whose destination address field indicates Anycast address (Step 2). The SYN packet is forwarded to an output link on the path to the closest server when it arrives at a conventional Anycast router (Step 3). When the SYN packet with the Anycast address arrives at an active router, it chooses an adequate server from all the candidate servers of the corresponding service based on the information and the policy of server selection. And this router changes the destination address of this SYN packet to the unicast address of the selected server (Step 4). Subsequently, the SYN packet is forwarded to the selected server as conventional unicast forwarding (Step 5). When the server receives this SYN packet, it replies an ACK+SYN packet (Step 7). And the client sends an ACK packet after it receives an ACK+SYN packet, which means establishment of the TCP connection (Step 8). After that, the ordinary information exchange phase is started between the server and the initiating client (Step 9).

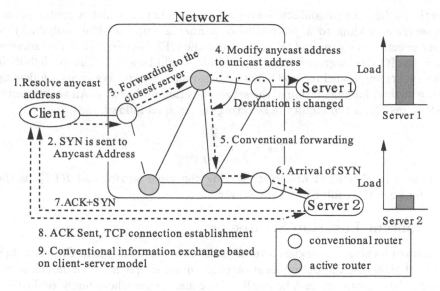

Fig. 1. Active Anycast

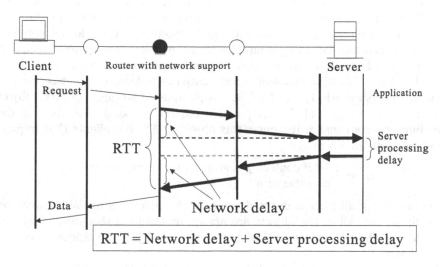

Fig. 2. RTT measurement

2.3 Active Anycast Server Selection

In [14], the way that an active router collects information necessary for server selection has been proposed. An active router is assumed to measure round trip time (RTT) of a request packet and its response packet as shown in Fig.2 and use this RTT for server selection. This measured RTT includes both of the network delay and the server processing delay, so an active router can select a good server from the viewpoint of both of network delay and server load. For the server selection policy, a probabilistic server selection policy in which a router selects the server according to a probabilistic manner is applied. The probability of server selection is calculated taking account the RTT between client and servers. When the RTT is large, selection probability should be small. This probabilistic selection prevents synchronized behavior of server selection. We apply a following simple method for calculation of the server selection probability. An active router i calculates P_{ij}, a probability of selecting server j, as follows.

$$P_{ij} = \frac{\frac{1}{RTT_j}}{\sum_{m=1}^{n} \frac{1}{RTT_m}}, \tag{1}$$

where n is total number of servers serving the same service and RTT_m is the RTT between the router i and the server m.

3   Content Location Strategies

For content location strategies, several works have been published. Cidon et al.[5] and Li et al.[6] discuss content location problem for simple network model, a tree model. These results cannot be applied for general case where many replication servers are located in the whole network and their decision affects each other, i.e. their decision of which objects to be located affects total performance. Qui et al.[7] evaluates several content location strategies by simulation. In their evaluation, replication server is assumed to be complete and they do not consider behavior of each content. In [4], content location problem is well formulated and they analyze which object to be located in each replication server.

In [4], content location problem is formulated as follows. Content server i in autonomous system $i(i=1,2,\ldots,I)$, ASi, has S_i bytes of storage capacity. Object j has a size of $b_{ji}, j \in \{1, 2, \ldots, J\}$ and a request probability p_j which is the probability that a client will request this object j. ASi has clients that request objects at aggregate rate λ_i.

$$x_{ij} = \begin{cases} 1 & \text{if content } j \text{ is stored at content server } i \\ 0 & \text{otherwise} \end{cases}$$

The matrix of all x_{ij}'s is denoted by $\mathbf{x}$. Each object j is initially placed on an origin server. All of the objects are always available in their origin servers, regardless of the placement $\mathbf{x}$. The placement of objects to origin servers is denoted as $\mathbf{x}_o$.

The storage is constrained by the space available at ASi, that is

$$\sum_{j=1}^{J} b_j x_{ij} \leq S_i \qquad i = 1, \cdots, I. \tag{2}$$

The average number of hops that a request must traverse from ASi is

$$C_i(\mathbf{x}) = \sum_{j=1}^{J} p_j d_{ij}(\mathbf{x}) \tag{3}$$

where $d_{ij}(\mathbf{x})$ is the shortest distance to a copy of object j from AS i under the placement $\mathbf{x}$.

Let $\Lambda(=\sum_{i=1}^{I}\lambda_i)$ be the total request rate of all ASs. The average number of hops from all ASs is then

$$C(\mathbf{x}) = \frac{1}{\Lambda}\sum_{i=1}^{I}\lambda_i C_i(\mathbf{x}) = \frac{1}{\Lambda}\sum_{i=1}^{I}\sum_{j=1}^{J}\lambda_i p_j d_{ij}(\mathbf{x}). \qquad (4)$$

The goal is to choose the $\mathbf{x}$ so that the cost function $C(\mathbf{x})$ is minimized. This means that the goal is to minimize the average number of inter-AS hops that a request must traverse. It is not feasible to solve this problem optimally for a large number of objects and ASs. This problem is NP-complete[4]. They proposed several heuristics to solve this problem as follows[4].

3.1 Popularity

Content server in the each AS stores the most popular objects. The content server sorts the objects in decreasing order of popularity and stores as many copies in this order as the storage constraint allows. The content server can estimate the popularities by observing the requests it receives from the clients. This heuristic does not require the node to get any information from outside of the AS.

3.2 Greedy-Single

Each ΛSi calculates

$$C_{ij} = p_j d_{ij}(\mathbf{x}_0) \quad (i \in 1,2,\cdots,I, j \in 1,2,\cdots,J) \qquad (5)$$

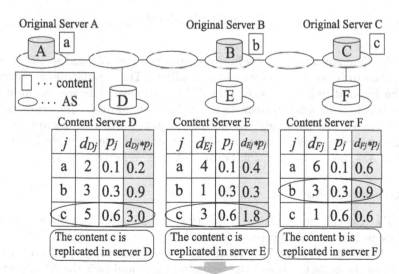

Content Server D

j	d_{Dj}	p_j	$d_{Dj}*p_j$
a	2	0.1	0.2
b	3	0.3	0.9
c	5	0.6	3.0

The content c is replicated in server D

Content Server E

j	d_{Ej}	p_j	$d_{Ej}*p_j$
a	4	0.1	0.4
b	1	0.3	0.3
c	3	0.6	1.8

The content c is replicated in server E

Content Server F

j	d_{Fj}	p_j	$d_{Fj}*p_j$
a	6	0.1	0.6
b	3	0.3	0.9
c	1	0.6	0.6

The content b is replicated in server F

This operation is iterated until each storage has been filled

Fig. 3. Greedy-Single

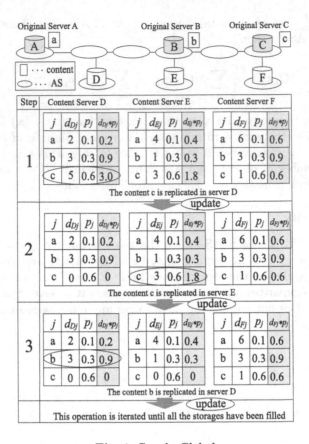

Fig. 4. Greedy-Global

The AS then sorts the objects in decreasing order of C_{ij} and stores as many copies in this order as the storage constraint allows. The popularities are obtained as in the Popularity heuristics, but the CDN also needs information about the network topology in order to estimate the d_{ij}'s. Note that the C_{ij}'s are calculated only once under the placement $\mathbf{x_0}$ and not adjusted when copies are stored in the content server. This means that every AS stores copies independently of all the other ASs and no cooperation between ASs is required (Fig.3).

3.3 Greedy-Global

The CDN first calculates $C_{ij} = \lambda_i p_j d_{ij}(\mathbf{x_o})$ for all AS i and objects j. Then the CDN picks the AS-object-pair which has the highest C_{ij} and stores that copy in that content server. This results in a new placement $\mathbf{x_1}$. Then the CDN recalculates the costs C_{ij} under the new placement and pick the AS-object-pair that has the highest cost. The copy of that object is stored in the content server in that AS and a new placement $\mathbf{x_2}$ is obtained. This operation is iterated until all the storages have been filled (Fig.4).

$$C_{ij} = \lambda_i p_j d_{ij}(\mathbf{x}) \quad (i \in 1, 2, \cdots, I, j \in 1, 2, \cdots, J) \tag{6}$$

4   Popularity-Probability

Popularity, Greedy-Single and Greedy-Global have the goal that objects are distributed to the content servers so that the total delay from each AS is minimized. These content location strategy is designed for a request routing which directs a users request to the closest server. So, they are designed for Anycast routing. When more sophisticated request routing technique, such as *Active Anycast*, is used, content location strategy for Anycast, e.g. Greedy-Global, may not work well. This is because of difference between aims of content location strategy and request routing. Aim of request routing of *Active Anycast* is to find a good server which gives optimal response time. This means *Active Anycast* can direct a user's access to a good server of light load even though this server is not the closest one. Thus, for content location strategy, it is not the most important requirement that requested objects are located close to users (of course, this does not mean it is not important). It is rather important that network has adequate amount of (the same) objects for a popular one. From these observation, we propose a new content location strategy which is applicable to *Active Anycast*-type request routing, i.e. request routing taking care both of network delay and server load, *Popularity-Probability*.

In *Popularity-Probability* content location strategy, each content server decides its storing objects according to object popularity. From the meaning that object popularity is a key factor of content location, Popularity and *Popularity-Probability* has the similar concept. However, in *Popularity-Probability*, content server decides whether it stores a specific object or not with probability which is predefined by its popularity. When the total number of content servers in a network is N and request probability of object i is p_i, expected number of content servers which store content i is Np_i. This means content are distributed randomly in a network so that the number of replicated content in a network is linear to its popularity. In *Popularity-Probability*, each content server can decide its storing objects independently and there is no necessity to exchange any information among servers. So, *Popularity-Probability* is very easy to be implemented.

5   Performance Evaluation

In this section, we evaluate the performance of the combination of the content location strategy and request routing technologies by computer simulation, and investigate the environment where each technology works effectively. In that evaluation, Popularity, Greedy-Single, Greedy-Global and *Popularity-Probability* are applied as a content location technology. For request routing technology, Anycast and *Active Anycast* is applied.

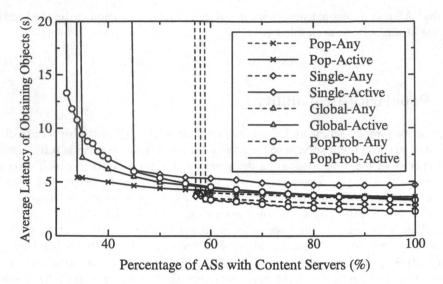

Fig. 5. Average latency characteristics

5.1 Performance of Request Routing and Content Location

To investigate territory where each content location and request routing technology works effectively, we investigate the average delay of obtaining objects with various percentage of ASs where the content servers are located. We make the following assumptions.

- The network model of the random graph with 100 ASs is used. Each AS has a router and at most one content server.
- The link capacity between any nodes is 25.0 requests/sec.
- The server is modeled as M/M/1 queueing model with capacity of 1.0 requests/sec.
- Accesses to servers are generated by Poisson process. The access arrival rate indicates aggregate access arrival rate to each router from users connected directly to it and is 30.0 requests/sec.
- The number of contents stored in the content server is 10% of all 100 objects, i.e. capacity of each server is 10 copies.

Figure 5 shows the average latency of obtaining objects vs. the percentage of the number of ASs which have a content server in the network. A solid line and a dotted line show latency of obtaining objects with Anycast and Active Anycast, respectively. As shown in this figure, with any combination of request routing technology and content location strategy there is some area that delay characteristics diverges. This is because utilization of servers inside a network becomes larger than 1, i.e. servers are in overload status when sufficient number of content servers are not prepared in a network. However, the percentile of AS's, i.e. the number of content servers, which gives delay divergence is varied for each combination. *Popularity-Probability* and *Active Anycast* combination gives the smallest value of this divergence point. This means this combination needs the smallest number of content servers in order to stabilize delay characteristics. Thus, combination of *Popularity-Probability* and *Active Anycast* can distribute adequate number of contents inside a network and guide users request with satisfying server load balance.

We also evaluated the performance in the case where the server capacity is 30%. Simulation results for this case show that there is no significant difference between the results for 10% case. As the server capacity becomes larger, the total performance of CDN is improved, of course. However, tendency that combination of *Popularity-Probability* and *Active Anycast* needs the smallest number of content servers in order stabilize delay characteristics.

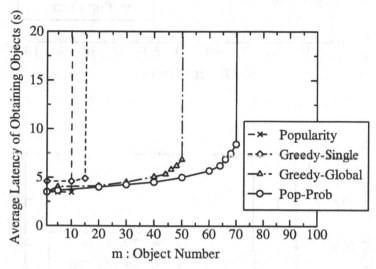

Fig. 6. Performance in the case where the popularity changes in 10 ASs

5.2 Simulation Results: Robustness

Another important performance for CDN is robustness. For content location strategy, e.g. Popularity and *Popularity-Probability*, measured or predefined information about popularity of object is necessary. When there is some error on its estimation or temporal change of popularity, there may be some performance degradation in CDN. We evaluate robustness from the viewpoint that how average latency characteristics are degraded with these errors. In this paper, we investigate the effect on the integration of request routing and content location in the case where the request probability of the objects p_j change from the original design. It is modeled as the situation where the request probability of most popular object is replaced with the request probability of m'th ($m \geq 2$) popular object. When the contents are sorted in decreasing order of popularity, it

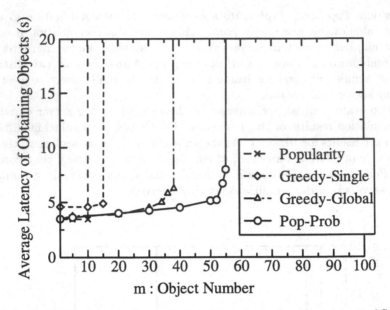

Fig. 7. Performance in the case where the popularity changes in 50 ASs

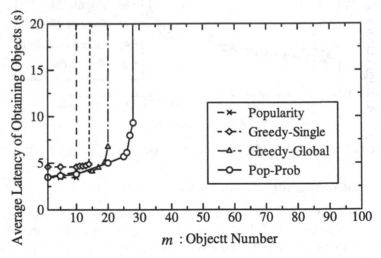

Fig. 8. Performance in the case where the popularity changes in 100 ASs

is assumed that the request probability of most popular object is $\hat{p}_1$ and m'th popular object is $\hat{p}_m$ originally. Each request probability p_1, p_m become as follows after change.

$$p_1 = \hat{p}_m, \quad p_m = \hat{p}_1$$

The x-axis shows the object number m to be replaced and y-axis shows the latency of obtaining objects in Fig.6, 7 and 8. Figures 6, 7 and 8 show the performance in the case where the popularity of objects changes in 10%, 50% and 100% of all ASs in the network, respectively. *Active Anycast* is used as request routing in above all figures.

As shown in these figures, combination of *Popularity-Probability* and *Active Anycast* gives the best performance from the viewpoint of robustness because it can hold stable delay characteristics even with large error happens in popularity pre-estimation.

6   Conclusion

In this paper, we have claimed that there is significant difference between aims of content location strategy and request routing. Aim of request routing of *Active Anycast* is to find a good server which gives optimal response time. Thus, for content location strategy, it is not the most important requirement that requested objects are located close to users. We thought that request routing and content location strategy works well together when content location strategy is aim to manage the number of objects according to their popularity. From these observation, we have proposed a new content location strategy, *Popularity-Probability*. In *Popularity-Probability*, objects are randomly located in content servers inside a network according to its popularity. In *Popularity-Probability*, each content server can decide its storing copies independently and there is no necessity to exchange any information among servers.

We have evaluated our proposed integration of request routing and content location strategy, i.e. combination of *Active Anycast* and *Popularity-Probability*. We compare the average latency of obtaining objects in our proposed integration with the various combinations of previously proposed request routing techniques: Anycast and *Active Anycast*, and content location strategies, Popularity, Greedy-Single and Greedy-Global. Our simulation results show that our proposed integration gives robust CDN in the meaning that CDN is tolerable to change of user request tendency. Our proposed integration of request routing and content location strategy in CDN will open a new possible network design, the *robust CDN*.

In our evaluation in this paper, we assume link capacities of all links are homogeneous. For content servers, we think their network situation should be good, i.e. their available bandwidth should be large. This is because these content servers will be prepared by network carriers or service providers. Thus, we believe that insights obtained in the paper can be applied to general CDNs. In the case that link capacity of each content server is different, content location strategy should take into account not only popularity of contents but also server's network situation. For example, popular contents should be located at a server with good network situation. We would like to leave this issue for our further research.

References

1. M. Day, B. Cain, G. Tomlinson, and P. Rzewski, "A model for content Internetworking(CDI)," draft-day-cdnp-model-09.txt(work in progress), Nov. 2001.
2. A. Barbir, B. Cain, F. Douglis, M. Green, M. Hofmann, R. Nair, D. Potter, and O. Spatscheck, "Known CN request-routing mechanisms," draft-cain-cdnp-known-request-routing-04.txt(work in progress), Nov. 2001.
3. L. Wang, V. Pai and L. Peterson, "The Effectiveness of Request Redirectionon CDN Robustness," in Proc. of the Fifth Symposium on Operating Systems Design and Implementation (OSDI'02), Boston, MA, December 2002.
4. Jussi Kangasharju, James Roberts, and Keith W. Ross, "Object Replication Strategies in Content Distribution Networks," Sixth International Workshop on Web Caching and Content Distribution, Boston, Massachusetts, USA, June 2001.
5. I. Cidon, S. Kutten and R. Soffer, "Optimal Allocation of Electronic Content," in Proc. of IEEE INFOCOM, Anchorage, USA, April 2001.
6. B. Li, M. Golin, G. Giuseppe, F. Italiano, X. Deng and K. Sohraby, "On the Optical Placement of Web Proxies in the Internet," in Proc. of IEEE INFOCOM, New York, USA, March 1999.
7. L. Qui, V. Padmanabhan and G. Voelker, "On the Placement of Web Server Replicas," in Proc. of IEEE INFOCOM, Anchorage, USA, April 2001.
8. T.P. Brisco, "DNS support for load balancing," Internet Request for Comments (RFC 1794), April 1995.
9. E.D. Katz, M. Butler, and R. McGrath, "A scalable HTTP server: The NCSA prototype," Computer Networks and ISDN syst., vol.27, pp.155-164, 1994.
10. R. Engel, V. Peris and D. Saha, "Using IP anycast for load distribution and server location," Proc. of IEEE Globecom Global Internet Mini Conference, pp.27-35, Nov. 1998.
11. C. Partidge, T. Mendez, and W. Milliken, "Host anycasting service," Internet Request for Comments (RFC 1546), 1993.
12. S. Weber and L. Cheng, "A Survey of Anycast in IPv6 Networks," IEEE Communications Magazine, vol.42, no.1, pp.127-132, January 2004.
13. H. Miura, M. Yamamoto, K. Nishimura, H. Ikeda, "Server load balancing with network support: Active anycast," The Second International Working Conference on Active Networks(IWAN2000), pp.371-384, 2000.
14. H. Miura and M. Yamamoto, "Content Routing with Network Support Using Passive Measurement in Content Distribution Networks", IEICE Transactions on Communications, Special Issue on Content Delivery Networks, Vol.E86-B, No.6, pp.1805-1811, June 2003.
15. D. Tennenhouse, J. Smith, W. Sincoskie, D. Wetherall, and G. Minden, "A survey of active network research," IEEE Communications Magazine, vol.35, no.1, pp.80-86, January 1997.
16. D. Tennenhouse and D. Wetherall, "Towards an active network architecture," ACM Computer Communication Review, vol.26, no.2, pp.5-18, April 1996.

Building a Reliable Multicast Service Based on Composite Protocols for Active Networks

S. Subramaniam, E. Komp, M. Kannan, and G. Minden*

Information and Telecommunication Technology Center
Department of Electrical Engineering and Computer Science
University of Kansas
2335 Irving Hill Road
Lawrence, KS 66045-7612 USA
gminden@ittc.ku.edu

Abstract. Active Networking embodies rapid development and deployment of new services. A network service typically consists of two or more cooperating protocols. In this paper, we describe a case study applying a composite protocol framework to developing a multicast network service. The composite protocol framework provides a rigorous mechanism to check protocol behavior before deployment. Our multicast serviced incorporates protocols for multicast routing, creation of spanning trees, reliable replication of multicast data and joining/leaving multicast groups. These protocols are built from re-usable components and communicate by means of global memory.

Keywords: Active networks, protocol components, composite protocols, composable services.

1 Introduction

In an active network [1], routers and switches in the network are programmable by the user and are capable of performing customized computations on packets passing through them. This allows easy injection of customized and innovative protocols and services into the network without the need for network-wide standardization. Several active networking architectures have been developed to deploy services need by an application on intermediate nodes of the network.

Active networking is built on the concept that many people will design, build, and deploy new protocols and services in the network. There is valid concern that network reliability is a risk if just anyone can place code in the network. One part of the effort to protect the network is insuring that new services are well thought-out, reasoned about, and tested before deployment. Composite Protocols [2] is a modular approach for specifying and implementing network protocols and services. In this paper, we present a case study of applying Composite Protocols to a multicast service.

* This research was supported by the Defense Advanced Research Projects Agency and the U.S. Air Force Research Laboratory under contract F30602-99-2-0516.

G.J. Minden et al. (Eds.): IWAN 2004, LNCS 3912, pp. 101–113, 2007.
© IFIP International Federation for Information Processing 2007

Reliable-delivery, sequential delivery, error checking, some form of routing, authentication, and request/reply are some of the common functions used in protocols. Any new protocol may also use of some of these functions. We call such single-functional protocol modules, *protocol components*. A group of such protocol components collected and connected together by means of a composition operator constitutes a *protocol*. For example, Time-To-Live (TTL), Fragmentation, Header Checksum, Forwarding, and Addressing are protocol components, which contribute to the IP protocol. Though many forms of composition exist, the most common form of composition and the one used in our implementation is a linear composition.

A collection of two or more cooperating protocols is called a *service*. Multicast is an example of such a service. Multicast consists of protocols for group membership and management, multicast routing and spanning trees, tunneling and reliable replication of multicast data. Our composite protocol framework [2] describes how protocol components are specified and how these protocol components are composed to form a composite protocol.

1.1   Multicast Service

Traditional IP-based multicast network services typically consist of multicast routing protocols like DVMRP, MOSPF or PIM and group-management protocols like IGMP in operation. In this paper, we describe how a component based multicast service is built by stacking protocol components into three different protocol stacks: (1) a DVMRP like multicast routing stack for creating and managing multicast routing tables and spanning trees, (2) an IGMP like group-management stack for managing group-memberships and (3) a multicast-traffic delivery stack for reliable and secure transmission of application data. We then describe how these protocols communicate among themselves using a global memory object.

The rest of this paper is organized as follows. Section 2 describes the various steps involved in building a composable service using our framework with multicast service as a case study. Section 3 briefly discusses the functionality of all the protocol components that constitute the service and illustrates how the stacks cooperate together to render the multicast service. Section 4 focuses on Inter-stack communication, its need and forms of representation. Section 5 summarizes the results and presents the conclusion.

2   Building a Composite Multicast Service

Multicast is an excellent example of a network service which is made up of several cooperating protocols. IP Multicast is a collection of multicast routing protocols like DVMRP, MOSPF, PIM and group management protocols like IGMP working in tandem with IP for best-effort multicast delivery. The reason for studying multicast service is that it combines data and control-oriented protocols. TCP and IP are data-oriented protocols, while routing protocols like RIP, OSPF,

DVMRP and group-management protocols like IGMP are control oriented (belong to the control-plane). It should be noted that protocol components that we specify and implement are not complete implementations of Internet standards for DVRMP [3], IGMPv1 [4], and IGMPv2 [5]. We are interested is the basic functionality in these protocols and evaluation of the composite protocol framework. Only a sub-set of the standard functionality is specified and implemented. We assume that the reader has a basic understanding how IP multicast and other protocols like DVMRP and IGMP work in general.

2.1 Building a Composite Service

Step 1: Decomposition - Identify components from the monolithic protocols in the service.
For multicast service, we decomposed the monolithic DVMRP [4] protocol into the following protocol components: *Neighbor Discovery, Route Exchange, Spanning Tree, Pruning* and *Grafting*. The IGMP [5] protocol is decomposed into the following components: *Join/Leave* and *Query/Report*. Other components include *Multicast Forwarding, Reliable Multicast (ACK/NACK based), Security (Authentication / Encryption)*. Figure 1 illustrates these stacks.

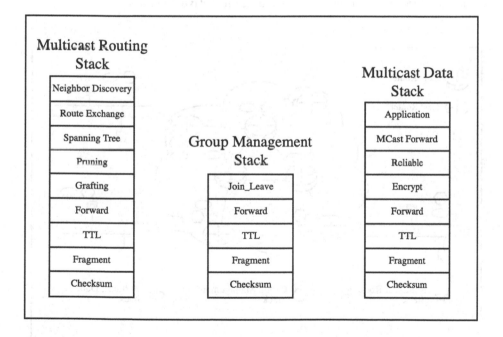

Fig. 1. Multicast service is a collection of three stacks viz. Multicast routing stack, Group Management stack and Multicast data/traffic stack. Multicast service is a collection of three stacks viz. Multicast routing stack, Group Management stack and Multicast data/traffic stack.

Step 2: Specification of protocol components.
Once the individual components are identified, the next step is to specify each
of these components using Asynchronous Finite State Machines (AFSM) [6]
as described in [2]. Each component is represented by a Transmit State Machine (TSM) and a Receiver State Machine (RSM), the set of events (data and
control) that can invoke this component, its memory requirements: local, stack-
local, global and packet memory along with its properties and assumptions. The
individual functionality of each protocol component is described later. While
specifying these components, care should be taken to ensure that each protocol
component performs only a single-function and is totally independent of other
components. Achieving total independence is only an ideal case. In practice, some
minor amount of dependence on other protocol components may be required.
We shall describe on the individual functionality of each protocol component in
section 3.

Step 3: Building Protocol Stacks.
Once all the individual protocol components are specified, these are grouped into
protocol stacks. The multicast service is the collection of these stacks.

Step 4: Deployment - Placing the stacks in the network.
Composite-protocol stacks are deployed in an Active Network.

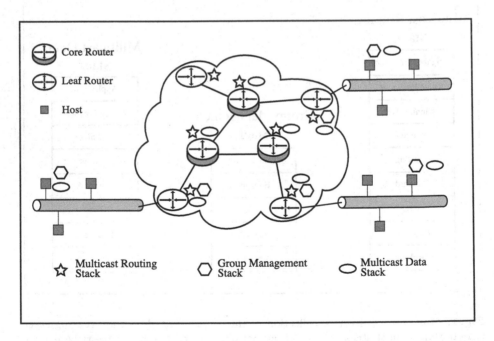

Fig. 2. An example multicast network showing core routers, leaf routers, and hosts.
The shapes indicate where each protocol stack is deployed in the network.

Figure 2 shows an example multicast network with the following types of nodes:

- Multicast Sender: sends multicast data destined for a particular group. Need not be a part of a multicast group to send a multicast packet. Typically attached to a multicast core-router.
- Multicast Core Router: present in the core of the multicast network. They are responsible for creating and managing multicast routing tables and setting up per source, group multicast delivery trees.
- Multicast Leaf Router: these are nodes that do not have downstream neighbors and are directly attached to multicast receivers (end-hosts).
- Multicast Receivers: these are end-hosts that have joined a particular group and are entitled to receive multicast traffic destined to that particular group.

Note that both Multicast core routers and Multicast Leaf routers can also be Multicast Receivers and Multicast Senders.

3   Component Description

This section contains a brief description of each component in the multicast service. Detailed state machine specifications for each component are beyond the scope of this paper [8]. For each component, its sender (TSM) and receiver (RSM) functionality, access to global memory data structures and dependencies on other components are briefly discussed. We start with components from the multicast routing stack first.

3.1   Neighbor Discovery

This component forms a part of the multicast routing stack deployed at multicast core and leaf routers. The main functionality of this component is to dynamically discover neighbors (multicast routers) on all its interfaces. The sender side of this component periodically broadcasts *probe packets* (hello packets) on all multicast-enabled interfaces. Each probe packet sent on a particular interface contains a list of neighbors for which neighbor probe messages have been received on that interface. The receiver side of this component first checks if the neighbor probe packet is received on one of its locally defined interfaces and if yes, updates in its local memory: the neighbor address and the interface on which it is received. It then checks for 2-way adjacency i.e. if the local interface address is present in the neighbor list of the probe packet. If present, then a 2-way adjacency is established and neighbor is discovered on that interface. This information is written into and maintained in a global data structure called *Neighbor Table*, which is part of Global Memory. It also provides a keep-alive function in order to quickly detect neighbor loss. Timers are used for sending probe packets and also for detecting dead neighbors. This component can be used in other protocols where there is a need for neighbor discovery e.g. in unicast routing protocols like RIP and OSPF.

3.2 Route Exchange

This component forms a part of the multicast routing stack deployed at all multicast core and leaf routers. The main functionality of this component is to dynamically create and maintain the routing tables at the multicast routers through periodic exchange of route exchange packets with neighbors. This is a RIP-like protocol component, with metric based on hop-counts. The sender side of this component periodically sends *route exchange* packets to all its neighbors. The list of neighbors is read from the global memory *Neighbor Table*. Each route exchange packet contains a list of routes with each route comprised of a network prefix, mask and metric. For each route exchange packet received, the receiver first checks with its local route cache if the received route is a new route or not. If new then the route is stored in the local route cache. If not, then the received metric for the route is compared with the existing metric after adding the cost of the incoming interface to the received metric. If the resultant metric is better than the existing one, then the local route cache is updated. After all the received routes are processed, the contents of the local route cache are written to a global data structure *Routing Table* in global memory. The *Routing Table* contains entries of the form *prefix, mask, metric, next-hop*. Timers are used for the periodic transmission of *route exchange packets*. This component can be re-used in other distance vector-based unicast routing protocols like RIP.

3.3 Spanning Tree

In DVMRP, the poison reverse functionality and creation of spanning trees is embedded as part of the route exchange process itself. Here the functionality is built into a separate component. This component enables each upstream router to form a list of dependent downstream routers for a particular multicast source. Each downstream router informs its upstream router that it depends on it to receive multicast packets from a particular source. This is done through periodic exchange of *Poison Reverse* packets. The sender side of this component needs access to the global *Neighbor Table and Routing Table*. The entries in the *Routing Table* are grouped based on next-hop information. All prefixes having the same next-hop are grouped together in different lists called *poison reverse lists*. Each of these lists is sent to their corresponding next-hops (which are actually upstream neighbors for the source networks in the list). The receiver side (the upstream neighbor) uses all the poison reverse lists it receives to form a *spanning tree* for each source. Thus, this component builds a list of downstream dependent neighbors for each source network. The tree is stored as global data structure *Spanning Tree*.

3.4 Group Membership/Join Leave

This component forms a part of the *group management stack* deployed at multicast leaf routers and end-hosts. Initially, the IGMP protocol was decomposed into two separate components: *Join Leave* and *Query Report*. But the *Join Leave* component did not fully satisfy our definition of a protocol component. Its TSM did not send packets on the wire and it had no RSM functionality. So, these were merged into a single component called *Group Membership*. Another interesting feature about this component is that it is asymmetric in nature. The TSM and RSM functionality differs depending on where the component is deployed at the end-host or at the leaf multicast router. So, in order to make the state machines symmetric both the state machines contain exclusive transitions for end-hosts and routers. At the end-host: The TSM responds to *Control events EJoin* and *ELeave* (These events are generated by the application when the host wants to join or leave a particular multicast group). It also updates the local *group cache* when these events occur. The RSM responds to the Query packets from the leaf-router by sending back a *Report packet* containing the list of group addresses it belongs to. At the multicast-leaf router: The TSM periodically multicasts *Query packets* on the local network to the "all-hosts-group" and the RSM processes the Report packets received from its attached hosts and updates the local *group cache* and the global memory structure *Group Members Table*. It should be noted that the component at the end-host is initialized "actively" and that at the router "passively" through EActiveInit and EPassiveInit events respectively. This component thus creates and maintains the Group Members Table structure in global memory. Each multicast router contains in its Group Members Table the list of group addresses to which its attached hosts have joined.

3.5 Pruning

This component forms a part of the multicast routing stack deployed at multicast leaf and core routers. The primary purpose of this component is to create and maintain the global data structure *Prune Table* that stores the list of pruned downstream interfaces for each source/group pair. This along with the *Spanning Tree* component constructs per source-group multicast trees at each node. (Note: the *Spanning Tree* component by itself constructs a per-source broadcast tree at each node). The sender side of this component is responsible for sending prune packets for a particular source-group pair addressed to the corresponding upstream neighbor under the following conditions:

1. If all its downstream dependent neighbors have sent prunes and all its IGMP interfaces are also pruned.
2. If all its downstream dependent neighbors have sent prunes and there are no IGMP interfaces (at multicast core routers).
3. If there are no downstream dependent neighbors and all IGMP interfaces are pruned (at multicast leaf routers).

The receiver side of this component is responsible for updating the global memory *Prune Table* with entries containing source, group and incoming interface (interface to be pruned). Note that the TSM reads from the *Prune Table* and the RSM writes to the *Prune Table*. Components from other stacks also write to the Prune Table. The Multicast Forwarding component writes to this structure when there are no members for the source-group present in all attached host interfaces. The Join Leave component (router side) of the group membership stack also writes into this structure when a last member of a particular group leaves a multicast group. Thus this design of this component addresses some intra-stack communication issues. The global memory Prune Table is used here to communicate between the two stacks. These issues are discussed further in section 4.

3.6   Grafting

This component also forms a part of the multicast routing stack deployed at multicast core and leaf routers. This component is responsible for removing the appropriate pruned branches of the multicast tree when a host rejoins a multicast group. When a group join occurs for a group that the router has previously sent a prune, the global Prune Table is updated by the Join Leave component to un-prune the local IGMP interface for that particular group. The sender side of this component reads from the global Prune Table, and sends a separate graft packet to appropriate upstream routers for each source network under the following conditions:

1. On leaf-routers if the interface attached to all hosts is un-pruned.
2. On core routers if a graft packet is received on all previously pruned downstream interfaces.

The receiver side of this component on receiving a graft packet writes to the global Prune Table to update the list of grafted interfaces per source-group. Thus, this component along with the Pruning component maintains the global Prune Table by dynamically updating the list of pruned/grafted downstream interfaces for each source-group pair. This component assumes a Reliable component underneath it for reliability of its Graft packets. This obviates the need for this component to handle Graft ACK packets as in traditional DVMRP.

3.7   Multicast Forwarding Component

This is a part of the multicast data stack deployed at all nodes. This component is responsible for multicast of traffic on all the branches of the source-group multicast tree.

Initially when the branches of the tree are not pruned, packets follow the source broadcast tree. But when pruning comes into operation and builds the source-group multicast trees, packets are multicast on the un-pruned branches of the multicast tree. The TSM is operational only on nodes, which act as Multicast senders. On all other nodes, which either multicast the traffic (core and leaf routers) and end-hosts (multicast receivers) the TSM remains inactive and only the RSM is operational. The receiver first performs the RPF (Reverse Path Forwarding) check on the packet. This checks if the packet is received on the correct upstream interface, which is the one that is used to reach the source of the multicast packet. If the RPF check is successful, the RSM forwards the application data on (a) Each attached IGMP enabled interface if there are group members on that interface. If there are no group members then it writes to the global memory *Prune Table* to prune the interface and drops the packet. (b) On all un-pruned branches of the tree to its downstream dependent neighbors. On multicast receivers it delivers the data to the application.

3.8   Multicast Reliability and Security Components

These components can be optionally inserted to the multicast data stack if needed by the application. The multicast reliable component if inserted below the Multicast Forwarding component provides hop-to-hop reliability. Several protocols have been developed to address reliable multicast. This component can be either designed as a sender-initiated component based on ACKs or as receiver-initiated component based on NACKs. The flexibility of the composite protocol framework supports the easy addition and removal of different versions of these reliable multicast protocol components. The security components consist of the Authentication or the Encryption components, which provide hop-to-hop authentication and privacy of application data. Different versions of these security components like Encryption based on DES or IDEA and Authentication based on MD5 or SHA can be used.

4   Inter-stack Communication and Global Memory

One of the challenging problems in designing a network service is to identify and address the issue of how different protocols interact with each other. Network services require the cooperation of two or more network protocols; that is they need to share information. In this section, we will describe our solution to this challenging problem.

Our services use a active node based global memory object (GMO) shared between the protocols. This GMO is independent of any protocol that uses it. The scope and extent of the GMOmust be greater than that of any single protocol, which accesses the information, stored in the global memory object. Access to read / write the contents of the shared information is provided through a functional interface. A protocol component expresses its requirements for access to global memory object(s) by listing the external functions it uses in its implementation. For example, the RouteExchange component uses a function to write new routes into the Routing Table. It would use *addNewRouteEntry (rt-entry)* to add a new route entry to the routing table. The IP forwarding function needs to know the nexthop address for each destination. It would use an external function *ipaddr getNextHopForDest (dest-addr)* to get the nexthop address. These functions *addNewRouteEntry()* and *getNextHopForDest()* are provided through the functional interface of the global Routing Table object.

Generally, the GMOcan be regarded as a server, providing access to shared information to protocols reading or writing shared information. For example, in the TCP/IP world the IP Routing Table is created and maintained by protocols like RIP or OSPF and is accessed by IP while forwarding data packets. In our framework, the routing table is maintained as a GMO that is external to both protocols IP and RIP.

4.1 Global Memory Attributes

Functional interface: In our framework, global memory is abstracted through a functional interface for both reading and writing data. The functional interface model helps in encapsulating the data and hides the internal representation of the object.

Synchronization: Protocols access the GMO only through the functional interface, so the use of semaphores and/or any other control mechanisms to provide necessary synchronization are embedded in these functions in a uniform and robust manner. Synchronization is not delegated to the users of the shared object(s). Furthermore, since the interface is truly functional, no pointers are shared, which eliminates any possibility of conflicts from implicit sharing through multiple references to the same object. In a similar manner, implementation of the functional interfaces can apply access-rights controls to limit access to sensitive data. This approach makes protocol interfaces to the global memory are very simple. Complex issues of synchronization and access control are addressed just once in the design and implementation of the global memory object, instead of requiring each protocol which shares the information to incorporate these controls in its implementation. And the solution is much more robust, since the integrity of the shared data cannot be compromised by a single protocol, which does not correctly implement synchronization algorithm.

Extensibility: The GMO definition can be extended by adding new functions to its functional interface, to provide services for new protocols developed which use/access information in an existing global memory object. This provides a powerful mechanism for developing new protocols and/or improving existing implementations, while maintaining backward compatibility for previous clients (protocols) that use the global memory object. Previous clients continue to use the existing interfaces while the new protocols use the new extended version.

4.2 Implementing Global Memory

We consider three approaches to implementing a global memory object: a process model, a shared memory model, and a kernel based (NodeOS) based model.

In the process model, each GMO is implemented as a separate process running as a server on each node. Typically, each global memory server is started during the node initialization sequence. This server process maintains a single internal representation for its global memory object. The server can choose any representation for the data, because this structure is entirely local to the server. The server implements an inter-process communication (IPC) interface according to the functional definition of global memory. Any protocol that accesses a global memory contacts the local server process as a client. Communication between the clients (protocols) and server is limited to the IPC interface advertised by the server process. This implementation strategy is a direct implementation of the abstract model we propose for a global memory object. Unfortunately, the overheads associated with inter-process communication, even within a single node, may limit performance of network protocol implementations.

In the shared memory model, the GMO is stored in shared memory. The functional interface containing the set of all functions provided by the GMO is packaged into a dynamic link library (DLL). The protocol stacks, which run as individual processes on a node, link to this library at run-time. Thus, each protocol stack imports a copy of the DLL code space.

The function implementation is visible only internally and is opaque to the protocols that use it. Each function internally invokes the shared memory functions for reading/writing into shared memory. The shared memory library routines handle synchronization.

The shared memory approach strongly preserves the abstract functional interface we want for global memory. Users of global memory have only an abstract view of it through the functional interface provided by the DLL. Thus, protocol components are not concerned with the details of the how the shared memory is accessed. Also, the semantics and syntax of shared memory access functions may differ depending on the operating system, but is has no effect on the protocol component. Shared memory function calls are generally faster than IPC function calls, thus providing faster global memory access.

A third alternative is to embed global memory objects directly in the operating system on which the protocols run. With this alternative, the operating system (kernel) interface must be expanded to incorporate the GMO functional interface. The operating system implicitly operates as the GMO server. This approach is worthy of consideration only for a few special and widely accessed global memory objects, such as the routing table. The solution is vendor/operating system specific. In addition, it requires extensions to the operating system interface. For example, the current TCP/IP implementations use a strategy similar to this (though not employing a pure functional interface) to provide shared access to the routing table.

4.3   Initialization

Each global memory is independent of any network protocol, which uses it. From the perspective of a protocol running on a node, the global memory is a "service" provided by the node. Therefore creation of, and initialization of the global memory is a responsibility of the active node environment. Dynamic deployment of network services must determine if the global memory object(s) used by the protocols, which form the service, are already available on the nodes.

The above figure illustrates different protocols of the multicast service cooperating by means of global memory objects. NeighborTable, RoutingTable, SpanningTree, PruneTable and GroupMemberTable are all global memory objects that provide a set of read/write functions through their respective functional interfaces. For example, the Route Exchange component of the multicast routing stack writes into global memory using the write interface of the global RoutingTable object and the Multicast Forwarding component of the multicast data stack reads using the read interface of the object. Each protocol component includes the list of

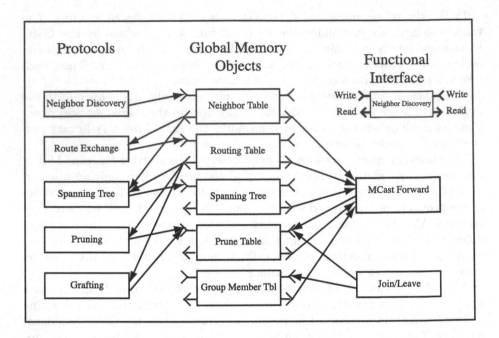

Fig. 3. The global memory of the multicast service and the protocols that access each memory section

external memory functions it accesses. getDownStreamNeighborsForSource(src-addr,group-addr), addNewRoute(route-entry) are typical examples of read and write external functions for the Route Exchange component.

4.4 Independence

The global memory objects are designed to be mutually independent of each other. A multicast service may need both the global memory objects Routing Table and Spanning Tree, but another network service might require only the Routing Table. Dependency of the Routing Table on the Spanning Tree is undesirable.

The global memory objects are designed so that it can be used across several services. For example, the Routing Table object can be used in unicast as well as multicast, with possible variations in its set of functional interfaces.

5 Conclusion

A multicast network service has served as a case study in understanding a composite protocol design framework. The basic functionality of traditional IP multicast protocols DVMRP and IGMP have been successfully expressed in the form of several protocol components and composite protocol stacks. Global memory has been proposed as a solution for inter-stack communication in our framework. Global memory design and features have been presented.

References

[1] D. Tennenhouse, J. Smith, W. Sincoskie, D. Weatherall, G. Minden, "A Survey of Active Network Research", IEEE Communications Magazine, Vol. 35, 1997.

[2] G. J. Minden, E. Komp et al, "Composite Protocols for Innovative Active Services", DARPA Active Networks Conference and Exposition (DANCE 2002), San Francisco, USA, May 2002.

[3] Pusateri, T. "Distance-Vector Multicast Routing Protocol Version 3."

[4] S. Deering "Host Extensions for IP Multicasting", RFC 1112, August 1989.

[5] W. Fenner, "Internet Group Management Protocol, Version 2", RFC 2236, Xerox PARC, November 1997.

[6] Yuri Gurevich, Sequential Abstract State Machines Capture Sequential Algorithms, ACM Transactions on Computational Logic, vol. 1, no. 1, July 2000, 77-111.

[7] M. Hayden, "The Ensemble system", Ph.D. dissertation, Cornell University Computer Science Department, January 1998.

[8] S. Subramaniam, E. Komp, G. J. Minden and J Evans, Building a Reliable Multicast Service Based on Composite Protocols, The University of Kansas, Information and Telecommunications Center, ITTC-F2004-TR-19740-11, Lawrence, Kansas, July 2003.

Network Programmability for VPN Overlay Construction and Bandwidth Management

Bushar Yousef[1], Doan B. Hoang[1], and Glynn Rogers[2]

[1] Advanced Research in Networking Laboratory, University of Technology Sydney,
Broadway NSW 2007 Australia
{byousef,dhoang}@it.uts.edu.au
[2] CSIRO ICT Centre, Epping NSW 1710 Australia
glynn.rogers@csiro.au

Abstract. Reliability and security concerns have increased demand for Virtual Private Networks (VPNs). Ideally, a VPN service should offer autonomous overlay networks with guaranteed bandwidth allocations over a shared network. Network providers seek an automated VPN creation and management process, while users of a VPN would greatly benefit from secure control over the handling of their traffic. Currently, network infrastructure does not support such partitioning services and, due to its static nature, it cannot be adapted to meet such new demands. Active and Programmable Network research has developed a number of adaptable architectures. However, its current focus is on theoretical service deployment rather than on applicability to large and shared networking environments. This paper presents the application of a new programmable architecture to enable on-demand VPN construction, bandwidth management, and secure autonomous VPN control onto shared commercial infrastructure.

1 Introduction

There is constant demand for new and sophisticated network services such as resource-assured networks for video conferencing. To support new services, network elements must perform new and unsupported tasks. As a result, many task-oriented devices have emerged such as web-switch, SSL, firewall modules, and new routers to support new QoS models. As these devices are 'closed', network providers are required to purchase new devices to support new services. However, an inspection of the underlying hardware of these devices reveals that they can be combined and reprogrammed to support new services.

Research in active and programmable networks has developed novel architectures that 'open up' network devices to support user-defined services [1, 2]. Such architectures enable users to modify network behaviour by placing software components in the forwarding plane or customising specialised forwarding plane hardware. These architectures are not designed to leverage current commercial platforms because of their inflexibility. Yet, commercial platforms are essential for the deployment of any service architecture into the real-life networking environments of the Internet.

G.J. Minden et al. (Eds.): IWAN 2004, LNCS 3912, pp. 114–125, 2007.

Recently, there have been increasing demands on ISPs to offer Virtual Private Network (VPN) services across the Internet. Conceptually, each VPN represents an autonomous, resource-assured, secure, and customisable network over shared infrastructure for each user (i.e. VPN owner). Such a VPN requires partitioning network bandwidth and providing users with the ability to secure and customise their VPNs. These are features beyond the support of current Internet infrastructure and, therefore, currently offered VPNs that fall short of expectation. A current VPN is either: a simple point-to-point encrypted tunnel with best-effort delivery; or a static overlay network of Service Level Agreements manually configured by ISP operators. The former type only addresses the security requirement of a VPN, while the later has a number of shortcomings. Firstly, an ISP cannot create or modify VPNs on-demand due to the long and manual setup procedure. Secondly, at the core of a network, bandwidth assurances can only be partially enforced for a large number of VPNs. Thirdly, users cannot customise or deploy services in their VPNs.

This paper presents a new model to support VPNs and their on-demand provisioning over shared commercial infrastructure. This model utilises a new programmable architecture called Secure, Extensible, and Deployable-Programmable Network Platform (SXD-PNP). SXD-PNP is used to deploy VPN support services onto current commercial modules, and to partition network nodes into customisable User Partitions for each VPN. VPN support services enable network providers to construct and manage customisable and resource-assured VPNs on-demand. Each VPN is allocated a series of SXD-PNP User Partitions, which enable VPN-owners safe autonomous control and secure path construction by deploying their own services within their partitions. To manage a number of VPNs across shared nodes, User Partitions separate internal resources and use traffic classification mechanisms to restrict their configurations to a permissible set of traffic. SXD-PNP employs a new differentiated allocation model called Control-plane Quality of Service (C-QoS) that manages internal node resources among competing partitions and among competing services within a partition.

This paper is structured as follows. Section 2 provides an outline of SXD-PNP and its implementation focusing on features that enable VPN provisioning. Section 3 presents the VPN support services. Section 4 describes an Edge-to-Edge QoS mechanism that provides VPN resource guarantees across the network core. It also discusses our experiences with its deployment onto current network devices. Section 5 gives a brief discussion of related works. The paper concludes in section 6.

2 SXD-PNP Overview

SXD-PNP is a flexible programmable router architecture that enables on-demand service deployment. SXD-PNP services modify the handling of traffic. This is achieved by configuring the forwarding hardware or by hosting the execution environments found in active networks. SXD-PNP is an ideal service architecture to deploy VPN support services and to facilitate VPN partition and customisation. This is due to its features of: QoS guarantees on internal node resources, isolation of users, traffic security enforcement, and commercial module utilisation.

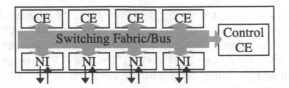

Fig. 1. Hardware Base Abstraction

SXD-PNP builds on an abstract node model called the Hardware Base Abstraction (HBA). The HBA, depicted in figure 1, represents a switching platform composed of a configurable realtime forwarding plane and separate extensible control plane. The forwarding plane is composed of Network Interfaces (NIs) represent the realtime hardware networking modules. These perform network traffic classification, forwarding, manipulation, and scheduling operations. The control plane is composed of Computational Elements (CEs) and a Control-CE. CEs accommodate User Services that construct Active Flow Manipulation [3] Paths (AFMP) among NIs to modify traffic handling behaviours. Operations beyond NIs capabilities are performed in the control plane by redirecting AFMPs to User Services that can use FPGA hardware to optimised packet processing. The Control-CE performs User Partition setup, security and C-QoS configurations, service deployments, load monitoring, and load balancing operations. All NI and CE components are interconnected by a high-speed communication bus. Both planes can be expanding by adding components to the bus.

Hosting a number of competing VPNs on shared network infrastructure requires all network resources to be partitioned amongst the VPNs. This involves partitioning network bandwidth and each customisable node along its control and forwarding planes. To partition link bandwidth, SXD-PNP deploys and configures bandwidth management services which enforce Edge-to-Edge Resource Discovery and Admission Control mechanisms [4]. At each customisable node (SXD-PNPs), the control plane is divided into separate, resource-assured, and secure User Partitions. These nodes allocate a User Partition to each VPN. The forwarding plane is partitioned among User Partition by restricting each partition from performing flow manipulations on traffic outside of its allocated VPN. The next subsection describes SXD-PNP control plane partitioning. Subsequent sections discuss the mechanisms that enforce this traffic access restriction (2.2) and the bandwidth partitioning mechanism (4).

2.1 User Partitions

A CE, depicted in figure 2, is composed of User Virtual Machines (UserVMs), a System Process, and a Bus Management Process. Each VPN is allocated a UserVM process with assured resources and access to AFM [3] on its traffic. This represents a User Partition. A UserVM manages a number of Runtime Environments (REs) that execute the User Services supplied by VPN owners. To ensure secure partitioning, UserVMs are restricted from hardware access and communications with the exception of through the System Process. The System Process guarantees to restrict UserVMs to their partitions. Details on service interaction and AFMP construction are in 2.2.

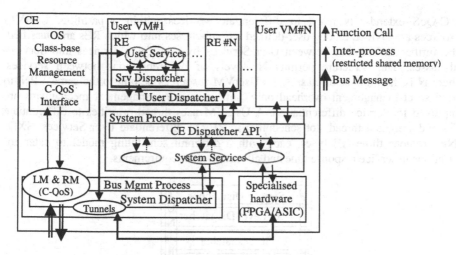

Fig. 2. Computational Element

The division and allocation of all internal node (control plane) resources among User Partitions are performed through C-QoS. User Partitions are classified into one of four C-QoS classes - Gold, Silver, Bronze, or Best Effort. C-QoS performs differentiated per-class allocation and fair allocation for partitions within each class. Due to the difficulty of determining user resource requirements or their availability in heterogenous infrastructure, C-QoS uses a dynamic allocation model - allocating resources from lower classes to an upper class as its load increase. Dynamic allocation is performed until a specified lower limit is reach. This limit is used to ensure a minimum level of resource availability to partitions. To allocate and reclaim resources, C-QoS utilises Resource Managers that interface with the Operation System (OS) resource management mechanisms. C-QoS Load Monitors track resource loads at CEs to balance UserVM load among CEs.

To maintain node integrity, a certain amount of resources is reserved before allocating resources among User Partitions. The aggregate capacity of links is reserved over the bus to ensure NI-to-NI (network) traffic is never delayed as a cause of service activity. All SXD-PNP management tasks and their messages are classified into a special *Realtime* class. *Realtime* resource requests are granted before the requests of other classes. This ensures that congestion will not affect the security or partitioning of a node.

C-QoS categorises resources as Computational or Internal Communication.

Computational resources are the traditional OS controlled resources of multi-user systems namely CPU scheduling, memory heap restrictions, I/O scheduling, and harddisk quotas. These resources are managed within each CE independently by its OS. The OS allocates resources to UserVMs in proportion to C-QoS classification and it restricts UserVMs to their allocation. The allocation details for each computational resource for each class are specified by the Control-CE and communicated via the C-QoS interface to the OS resource management mechanisms. The implementation, in section 2.3, interfaces to a modified Linux kernel.

C-QoS extends its reach to differentiate services within a partition. UserVM resources are divided among user-defined RE-subclasses into which REs are classified. REs further differentiate between User Services by classifying services into Service-subclasses. This structure permits N^3 levels of differentiations between services, where N is the number of classes. As UserVM resources belong to the same VPN, to avoid strict management overhead only 'soft' resource management mechanisms are employed for service differentiation. A UserVM uses thread priorities to differentiate REs and weighted thread slot scheduling in REs to differentiate User Services. SXD-PNP provides three RE types, each with a different scheduling model to cater for variations in service response time and allocation size requirements.

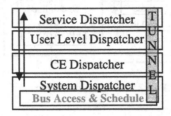

Fig. 3. Dispatcher Hierarchy

Internal communication resources are represented by a hierarchy of dispatchers, depicted in figure 3, which handle all internal communication. Scheduling mechanisms within dispatchers are used to divide and allocate internal communication resources among partitions. Computational and bus resources are allocated to dispatchers and dispatcher time is then divided into slots which are allocated to partitions or child dispatchers according to a dynamic class ratio. The bus is divided into channels or time slots, depending on the technology in use. For identification (used in traffic access restriction) and bus resource management, each partition is restricted by System Level Dispatchers to an allocated channel or timeslot(s).

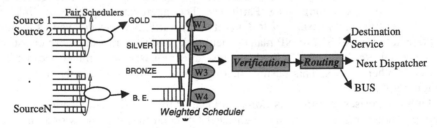

Fig. 4. Dispatcher Structure

Dispatchers share a common structure, depicted in figure 4. However, dispatchers differ in their verification scope and routing destinations depending on the hierarchy level. Each incoming message is placed in a limited queue allocated to its source. Source queues of the same class are serviced by the same fair scheduler that moves messages to the corresponding class queue. Messages in class queues are serviced by a scheduler weighted with the C-QoS class allocation parameters. Each serviced message is removed from the queue, verified as in figure 5, and routed to its next hop.

2.2 Network Abstraction and Traffic Partitioning

User Services construct AFMPs to configure new routing and manipulation operations on their traffic. An AFMP is composed of combination manipulation points, typically NPUs and CE specialised hardware modules, but may also include User Services for control flows. Each manipulation point along an AFMP is configured to filter ingress traffic into flows, perform specified manipulation operations on flows, and route flows to other manipulation points or onto the network.

User Services construct AFMPs by sending configuration messages to System Services. System Services are located at CEs to abstract the NPU configuration interfaces from User Services. System Services then send NI specific commands on the User Services behalf to each NI manipulation point. These commands are sent to the system dispatcher as message originating from the User Services partition.

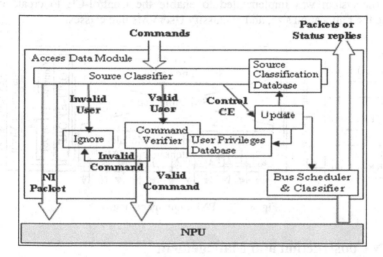

Fig. 5. NI Structure

An NI is divided into two logical components, depicted in figure 5, the Access Data Module (ADM) and the Network Processing Unit (NPU). NPUs represent the configurable traffic forwarding and manipulation hardware. These NPUs operate at wire-speed with no modification by SXD-PNP. ADMs ensure partitions only perform operations that affect their VPNs by verifying all user configuration commands to NPUs. This model partitions the forwarding plane without placing VPN classification or security checking in the path of network traffic.

At an ADM, each message arrives at the Source Classifier that identifies the type of each message by its source. This is established by the bus channel on which the message arrived. NI messages are traffic packets and are immediately passed to the NPU. Control-CE messages are configuration messages that update source classifications, User Partition-to-VPN associations, or the bus scheduling details. UserVM messages are verified by a Command Verifier before being forwarded to the NPU. The Command Verifier ensures that the flow filter of any forwarded configuration command falls within the Access Control List of its source partition's VPN.

2.3 Implementation

Figure 6 show the implementation of SXD-PNP a Passport 8600, an Alteon Web Switch Module, and a number of PCs. The Control-CE and ADM have been implemented in the Management Module's Java Virtual Machine. System Services have been implemented to interface with the manufacturer's Oplet Runtime Environment (ORE) [5] that configures AFM on its hardware modules. UserVMs are implemented as JavaVMs that initiate a specialised Java Security Manager and UserVM thread to manage control requests. UserVMs are hosted across a number of CEs that are implemented on PCs running a Linux kernel 2.6.7 patched with the Class-base Kernel Resource Management (CKRM) [6]. CKRM enables differentiated class-based resource management on CPU, memory pages, and I/O. A C-QoS interface to the CKRM file-system was implemented to enable the Control-CE to create classes, configure their allocation size, and to classify UserVMs into classes.

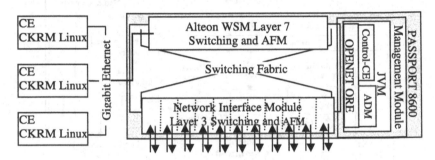

Fig. 6. SXD-PNP Implementation

3 VPN Construction and Management

This section presents the SXD-PNP VPN Construction and Management services depicted in figure 7. They consist are of sets of services. The first, VPN Activation &

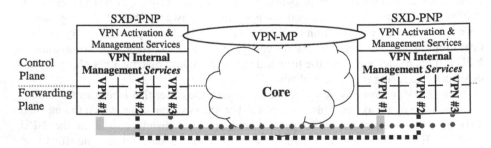

Fig. 7. SXD-PNP VPN Structure

Management Services, construct and manage VPNs. The second, VPN Internal Management Services, enable user autonomous control over their VPN.

3.1 VPN Activation and Management Services

VPN Activation & Management Services are SXD-PNP System Services that enable administrators to create, monitor, and modify VPNs across a network. These are composed of a distributed Network Division Service (NDS), and three local node services: a VPN Classification Service; a Bandwidth Management Service; and, a User Environment Service. These services are placed in Control-CEs and a NDS is placed at each node along VPN paths. NDSs collectively utilise the three local services to perform VPN activation and management.

Inter-NDS communication is achieved via an activated flow that spans all NDSs, called a VPN Management Protocol (VPN-MP) channel. A network administrator uses the VPN-MP channel to setup, monitor, and modify VPNs. VPN-MP employs security mechanisms to restrict NDS access to network administrators.

To perform VPN activation and management operations, network administrators construct a single VPN-MP *Request* and send it to the ingress edge SXD-PNP. This request is sent across the network and captured by NDSs along the *Paths* parameter. Each NDS fulfils the request, tightens the filters, and propagates it to nodes along the *Paths*. Filters are tightened using routing table information and subnet masks to eliminate filter ranges inapplicable to the current node or to nodes remaining in the propagation path. The VPN-MP Request structure is as follows:

1. *Paths* - Source and Destination network address combinations of all paths of the VPN.
2. *Instruction Type* – 0/setup 1/modify 3/remove 4/list details
3. *VPN Number* – 0 for new VPNs or operation on all VPNs
4. *Credentials* - User ID and Encrypted Password
5. *VPN ACL* (Access Control List) - List of Traffic Filters
6. *Network QoS class*
7. *C-QoS class*
8. *Signature* – MD5 hash encrypted using admin private key

To fulfil a VPN-MP Request each NDS uses the three localised services. The *User Environment Service* sets up a SXD-PNP User Partition according to *C-QoS class*. The *VPN Classification Service* configures the appropriate NIs to classify traffic into a VPN and configures their ADMs to restrict configuration access to the associated User Partition. The *Bandwidth Management Service* configures the link bandwidth for the VPN according to *Network QoS class*.

The *User Environment Service* uses C-QoS Load Monitors to locate the least loaded CE for new UserVM deployment. This service then sends a Control-CE request to Management Processes of the least load CE. This request creates a new UserVM with the *C-QoS class* specified. Once the UserVM is started, it is instructed to deploy the *VPN Internal Management Services*. These services are configured to restrict access according to the *Credentials* specified in the request.

The *VPN Classification Service* utilises ORE System Services to configure appropriate ingress NPUs to classify traffic according to the *VPN ACL* and mark its traffic with the *VPN number*. It also configures ADMs to allow the newly created UserVM to configure operations on traffic marked with *VPN number*.

The *Bandwidth Management Service* partitions network link resource among VPNs by configuring the *Edge-to-Edge QoS Services*, which are presented in section 4.

3.2 VPN Internal Management Services

VPN Internal Management Services are User Service running within each User Partition to provide users with a configuration interface to the routing and manipulation operations on their VPN traffic. They are composed of a *VPN Command Interface Service*, an *AFMP Construction and Management Service* that is used by two specialised services providing VPN specific features: a *VPN Overlay Management Service* and a *Secure Path Construction and Management Service*.

The *VPN Command Interface Service* provides a remote interface for users to interact with their User Services. It provides a command-line interface with username and password authentication (the *Credential* in VPN-MP request). It parses user instructions and parameters, calls the appropriate service, and displays the results. We plan to develop this service to be accessible via an active path similar to VPN-MP, enabling users to configure all nodes in a VPN with one request.

The *AFMP Construction and Management Service* provides the user and other VPN Internal Management Services with the capability to construct, monitor, modify, and remove AFMPs. It allows users to specify an AFMP Number, flow classification filters, and a sequence of actions to be performed on the flow. To construct a AFMP, this service uses the ORE System Service. Firstly, it locates a NI that is capable of performing the specified action and configures it. It then configures redirection and classification operations, to direct the path from the ingress NI, to the action NI, and finally to the egress NI. It also maintains a database to track AFMPs and their associated filters and actions, facilitating quick removable or modification of paths.

The *VPN Overlay Management Service* enables users to modify routes within their VPN by adding or removing route entries. For a new entry, it constructs an AFMP to redirect VPN flows to new destinations. It maintains a viewable table of routes, and their AFMPs. To remove a route, this service removes its table entry and AFMP.

The *Secure Path Construction and Management Service* enables users to secure sensitive flows in their VPN. As selective encryption at user hosts leads to security holes, this service allows VPN users to guarantee security encryption mechanisms on critical traffic at the network layer. It also allows the sharing of costly and specialised equipment that guarantees high-speed encryption and decryption. This service sets up AFMPs to redirect sensitive flows to encryption accelerators at ingress edge nodes, and to decryption accelerators at egress edge nodes.

4 Bandwidth Management

Networks must enforce bandwidth management mechanisms to partition link resources among VPNs. Current bandwidth management is performed by a DiffServ [ref] model that employs proprietary QoS mechanisms locally at each router. These mechanisms classify traffic at ingress into QoS classes by placing packets into a queue for each class. A Weighted Round-Robin algorithm services these queues, spending more link resources on higher-class queues than lower queues.

To provide bandwidth resource partitioning among VPNs, traffic of each VPN is classified into a single flow that is placed in a QoS class. However, this partitioning cannot be mapped to the DiffServ model for two reasons:

1. *Per-flow fairness* – In DiffServ, same class flows are placed in the same queue where packets are randomly dropped as the queue reaches its limit size. This model does not treat all flows within the same class fairly. Therefore, it cannot be applied to VPNs, as VPNs of the same class do not get equal treatment.
2. *Congestion Control* – DiffServ does not employ admission control mechanisms to prevent uncontrolled flows from causing congestion. Therefore, a VPN can affect the resources of others by causing congestion.

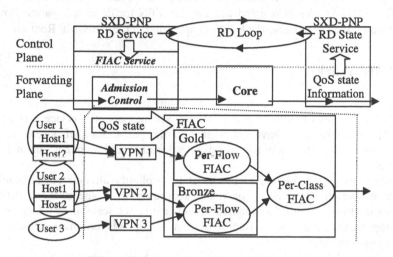

Fig. 8. Bandwidth Management Services

SXD-PNP uses Ed*ge-to-Edge QoS Services* to partition bandwidth fairly among VPNs and prevent congestion. These services configure existing QoS router mechanisms to enforce a Fair Intelligent Admission Control (FIAC) [4] scheme, as depicted in figure 8. It uses a Resource Discovery (RD) feedback loop to gather the congestion state information of the network. At each ingress node, an Admission Control Module (ACM) reconciles with available resources via the RD loop, and admits traffic intelligently according to the FIAC algorithm. The FIAC algorithm guarantees to admit traffic according to class weights while providing fairness among flows, and, based on the RD state report, prevent congestion by dropping packets at ingress intelligently.

Two services implement the RD feedback. At edge nodes, we implement an *RD Service*, which sends and receives "RD packets" along the feedback loop of VPN paths. These packets are captured by a *RD State Service* at each node in the path where the packets are updated with the congestion report. A demonstration of the RD loop implementation can be found in [7].

At edge nodes, the ACM is implemented through a *FIAC Service*. This service configures ingress NI to classify VPN traffic into flows and to classify the flows into its appropriate QoS class. It periodically uses state information supplied by *RD State Service* to configure NI queue lengths and drop rates to prevent congestion.

FIAC required per-flow fairness mechanisms at NIs. Unfortunately, most networking modules manufactured today are DiffServ compliant and do not provide a scalable per-flow management model. To achieve per-flow fairness in our implementation, presented in 2.3, we construct a static AFMP to redirect flows to the Web Switch Module where Load Balancing mechanisms perform flow management. However, this approach is still in initial design and testing stages.

The *Bandwidth Management Service* presented is section 3.1 uses the *Edge-to-Edge QoS Services* to partition the network link resources among VPNs. It instructs the *RD Service* to initiates feedback loops along VPN paths, if loops do not already exist. The *FIAC Service* is updated to treat the VPN traffic as a separate flow and classify the flow into the *network QoS class* specified in the VPN-MP Request.

5   Related Work

The extensive research in the field of Programmable and Active Networks has developed a number of flexible and relatively secure network service architectures [1, 2]. These architectures have not addressed the partitioning of access to traffic among users/VPNs, while few addressed the allocation and management of internal node resources.

Architectures [8-10] provide mechanisms to explicitly allocate each resource to services, collection of services, or paths according to a specified or estimated requirement. However, this fine-grained model is it is not scalable to a large number of heterogeneous users and is impractical as it depends on prior knowledge of resource requirements.

Due to these deficiencies, separate projects have been conducted to address active node resource management [11-13]. These projects throttle the input of packets to services to control their resource consumption. Their models hinge on the difficult task of pre-determining or estimating the resources consumed by each packet. Furthermore, these projects do not manage memory or internal communication resources. They also do not account for services resource consumption outside of packet input influence.

6   Conclusion

We have presented a new platform programmability architecture, SXD-PNP, that allows practical, secured, and true partitioning of network resources on commercial devices. We deployed this architecture to construct programmable VPNs, address difficult issues such as VPN traffic classification, bandwidth management, user service deployment, and secure path construction. We described a solution that enables a VPN on shared infrastructure as close as ever to a privately owned WAN.

Currently, VPN support service and bandwidth management services are partially implemented on our SXD-PNP testbed. Performance evaluation and VPN separation analysis on a complete implementation will be presented in future publications.

It is anticipated that the SXD-PNP will be deployed both in the network core and at the network edge. As a core router, it can be used to partition network resources into separate and secured user domains (such as VPNs), and allow operators to introduce services for the timely resolution of various traffic-engineering problems.

SXD-PNP is most useful when used in an edge device where all designed features can be deployed. A service provider can rapidly introduce new services to address the mismatches between domains in terms of network boundary, technology, and administration. Our next step is to deploy the platform for constructing overlay networks where network resources can be safely partitioned and shared in Grid service environments.

References

1. Campbell, A., H. De Meer, M. Kounavis, K. Miki, J. Vicente, D. Villela, *A Survey of Programmable Networks*. ACM SIGCOMM Computer Communications Review, 1999. **29**(2): p. 7-23.
2. Gottlieb, Y., L. Peterson, *A Comparative Study of Extensible Routers*. IEEE Open Architectures and Network Programming Proceedings (OPENARCH), 2002.
3. Lavian, T., P. Wang, F. Travostino, S. Subramanian, D. Hoang, V. Sethaput, D. Culler, *Enabling Active Flow Manipulation in Silicon-based Network Forwarding Engines*. IEEE Journal of Communications and Networks, March 2001
4. Li, M., D. B. Hoang, A. J. Simmonds, *Fair Intelligent Admission Control over Differentiated Service Network*. The Computer Communication Journal: the Special Issue on Quality of Service, 2004.
5. Nortel Network's Openet Lab, http://www.openetlab.org/.
6. Class-based Kernel Resource Management (CKRM), http://ckrm.sourceforge.net/.
7. Hoang, D., T. Lavian, I. Zhao, C. Nguyen, *Implementation of a Quality of Service Feedback Control Loop on Programmable Routers*. Submitted to IEEE International Conference On Networks (ICON'04), 2004.
8. Shalaby, N., L. Peterson, A. Bavier, G. Gottlieb, S. Karlin, A. Nakao, X. Qie, T. Spalink, and M. Wawrzoniak, *Extensible Router for Active Networks*. Proceedings of DARPA Active Networks Conference and Exposition, 2002: p. 92-116.
9. Tullmann, P., M. Hibler, J. Lepreau, *Janos: A Java-Oriented OS for Active Network Nodes*. Proceedings of DARPA Active Networks Conference and Exposition, 2002: p. 117-129.
10. Braden, R., B. Lindell, S. Berson, T. Faber, *The ASP EE: An Active Network Execution Environment*. Proceedings of DARPA Active Networks Conference and Exposition, 2002: p. 238-254.
11. Qie, X., A. Bavier, L. Peterson, S. Karlin. *Scheduling Computations on a Software-Based Router*. in *Proceedings of the ACM SIGMETRICS 2001*. 2001.
12. Ramachandran, V., R. Pandey, S-H. G. Chan. *Fair Resource Allocation in Active Networks*. in *Proceedings of the IEEE International Conference on Computer Communications and Networks (ICCCN)*. 2000. Las Vegas, Nevada.
13. Pappu, P., T. Wolf. *Scheduling Processing Resources in Programmable Routers*. in *Proc. of the Twenty-First IEEE Conference on Computer Communications (INFOCOM)*. 2002. New York, NY.

A Framework for Developing Mobile Network Services*

M. Sifalakis[1], S. Schmid[2], T. Chart[1], and A.C. Scott[1]

[1] Computing Department, Lancaster University,
Lancaster, LA1 4YR, U.K.
{mjs,chart,acs}@comp.lancs.ac.uk
[2] NEC Europe Ltd, Network Laboratories,
69115 Heidelberg, Germany
schmid@netlab.netlab.nec.de

Abstract. Service mobility is a highly desirable feature of future networks and will be a key factor in supporting mobile users and meeting the increasing demand for service resiliency and efficient resource management. Currently the main approaches for developing mobile services are active capsules and mobile agents but these are limited by design and fail to deliver sufficiently generic and broadly scoped solutions. In this paper we propose a framework for developing mobile (active) network services that aim to provide a more generic functionality over that offered by current approaches, promoting a more flexible and intuitive way of developing mobile applications.

1 Introduction

Despite these manifold developments of active and programmable network research, little attention has been paid to improving aspects of service mobility. So far, the main model considered for migration of code and state of a running service from one active node to another is that of active capsules [1, 2, 3], whilst most programmable network solutions [4, 11, 20] account only for out-of-band loading of code rather than migration of executing 'active services'. However, active capsule based approaches are quite restrictive in terms of code and state mobility as they operate in-band only and at a packet level granularity (i.e. carrying code and state in a single data packet). This tends to restrict the implementations to very simple and short-lived services, as both state and code for the service have to fit in a single data packet and code only executes while the packet is forwarded through a node along the data path. Furthermore, service mobility is restricted to the routing path of the packet hosting the service.

Service mobility is expected to play an important role in future network environments for various reasons. Mobile services can improve the user experience as he/she roams between heterogeneous and diverse network environments. Another key aspect of service mobility is its application for efficient resource management usually by means of load sharing, or by protecting network resources from being exhausted. Last but not least service mobility can facilitate service resiliency as it enables service-and-state migration to network locations where resources and network availability are plentiful.

---

* This work is part of the research funded by the EPSRC grand GR/R31461/01 in Lancaster University.

In developing generic and flexible solutions to tackle these classes of problem one needs to address a multiplicity of issues such as the handover of network flows, the composition of autonomic services through cooperating control components, the management of active services outside the data path, and so forth. Technologies such as mobile agents and active capsules provide ways of tackling only a subset of the problem. Yet, as both of these technologies were introduced with a specific application domain in mind, they are either not scalable or lack the features and capabilities that would make them more generic and applicable to a wider range of applications.

In this paper we propose a framework for developing active services that can be mobile and migrate to different programmable nodes at run time. The novelty lies on the fact that it enables code and state migration in an application independent way by mitigating the functionality at the execution environment (EE). This type of functionality was not previously considered in programmable network based solutions and was therefore expected to be internal in the applications that need it. To provide a generic model that is flexible, as well as effective, we tried to incorporate the benefits of active capsule solutions and out-of-band mobile agent based technologies.

The remainder of this paper is organised as follows: In the next section, we discuss the motivation for the work by considering a scenario that aims to illustrate the limitations of existing technologies, namely mobile agent and active capsule based solutions. In section 2, we investigate the requirements of a framework supporting the development of mobile services. Then, in section 3, founded on the requirements of section 2 we present the proposed architecture. In section 4 we exemplify the intended use of the framework with an example responding to distributed denial of service attacks. In section 5 we consider related work in the area of service mobility and the tools to facilitate it. Finally in section 6 we conclude this paper summarising our work.

1.1 Motivation

Before we examine the requirements of a framework for mobile active services, we consider a scenario (Figure 1) that exemplifies the problem domain at hand. Through this example we try to expose the limitations and inefficiencies of other approaches such as mobile agents or active capsules to facilitate generic service mobility. Scenarios such as the one described here motivated the development of the proposed framework.

In figure 1 nodes B, C and D are active routers, node A is an end node featuring active network support and node E is a commodity network node. Node A wants to exchange traffic with node E using a service deployed on the active routing infrastructure provided by the other three nodes (B,C,D). Initially A sends an active service request to B, which is the first active node on its data path towards E. Node B, intercepts the request and installs the requested active service. At the same time node B forces the installation of a flow monitoring and management active service component on node A and node D. Finally the service provisioning is activated and data is routed from A through B and D to E. At a later time due to some external factor (for example, congestion, resource utilisation, etc) node B cannot continue providing the active service for node A. Instead of shutting down the service, node B may force the migration of the active service to another active router (node C); subject to resource availability. Using the flow management components previously loaded onto nodes A and D the data flow can be redirected through node C so as to continue providing an uninterrupted service. Alternatively in an even more "extreme" case where node B dies suddenly, the management components on nodes A and D could detect the "malfunction" and correct the problem by re-installing the service on node C and recover if possible the flow state.

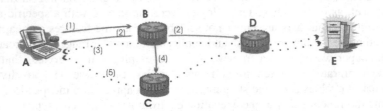

Fig. 1. Service Mobility

Despite the seemingly specialised setup of this example, it is by no means restrictive and rather broadly scoped. We have tried to include in it all the characteristics that need addressing when targeting the generic provisioning of mobile services: the support for in-band and out-of-band programmability, the support for service mobility in the data, management and control planes, the support for service composition and integration, and the need to support user space services as well as low-level network services (deployable in the forwarding path).

Using active capsules for the aforementioned scenario could address some of the issues but not all (at least not without highly specialised design or extensions to the basic concept). For example, it would be easy for an active capsule based solution to trigger the installation of the active service on node B in the first place, since it resides on the data path. However, using capsules to control the redirection of data flows is counterintuitive. For this, the active node needs information about alternative nodes that are ready and able to take over, necessitating long-lived state to be gathered and managed by the service (especially for the situation where node B and C are more than 2 hops apart). Unfortunately, active capsule based services are typically limited as the service state migrates with the capsule packet – few systems allow inter-capsule state to be stored at intermediate nodes and this is always restricted by the transmission path.

Also, as active capsules target in-band programmability, and only along the data path, another limitation is the lack of support for the out-of-band transfer of service state required for migrating the service from node B to C. Finally, as active capsules advocate a per-packet processing approach, they do not scale and introduce unnecessary overhead when coarser grained processing is preferable (e.g. per flow).

In addition to providing support for processing active services, there is also need for a management framework that can control service components running on active nodes with regard to node local state (for example, during the migration or "cloning" of a service in response to resource extinction). Although the use of mobile agent technologies may seem like a solution, their use would only introduce additional problems as they are typically implemented as high-level user-space solutions and are unsuitable for low-level data processing on the forwarding path. Aside from the obvious performance implications, this severely limits the range of applications that can be deployed using mobile agents. Returning to the example scenario in figure 1, if the active service provided by node B was a media caching or a NAT component, it would be impractical to implement it using conventional mobile agent systems.

As a result, to overcome the aforementioned shortcomings of one or the other technology, we anticipate the need for a framework for developing mobile network services that, in addition to being flexible, scalable, extensible and generic, combines the strengths of existing mobile agent and active capsule technologies. The framework proposed in this paper is based on the LARA++ [4] component-based active router architecture. The extremely flexible design of LARA++ enables functionality in the data path as well as the control path, allows deployment of mobile services vertically in the network stack and accounts for micro- as well as macro- composition[1] (see section 2.1 for details).

The benefits of introducing a framework for the development of mobile active services as opposed to promoting the direct top-down design of active applications as mobile services are twofold since it entails advantages both for the active node administrators and for the service developer:

- It promotes a single point of trust for the active node administrator. If the framework is trusted by the active node policies, then so are the applications running within it.
- If the framework provides a reasonable level of security, it removes the need for the developer to build application specific protection mechanisms.
- It simplifies the development of mobile active service components through design reuse.
- It introduces a level of abstraction that reduces apparent complexity and improves the manageability of the system.

2 Framework Requirements Specification

In developing a framework to support mobile active services, one must consider the range of supported functionalities. The overall design is dictated by a set of fundamental principles that advocate its viability in a real world environment and its usability by future applications. Before we describe our framework, we discuss the fundamental requirements and basic design principles that have guided our design:

- *Portability* over any existing or emerging active node platform. This will be typically guaranteed by means of the execution environment (EE) that hosts the framework.
- *Extensibility* without re-engineering the system or violating the specification.
- *Isolation* of individual active services in order to prevent unwanted interaction between services executing in the same EE.
- *Modularity* to facilitate dynamic binding to the framework at run-time. Individual components of the service components at run time.
- *NodeOS and EE compatibility*.

---

[1] We define Micro-composition as being within the framework and Macro-composition as being outside the framework on the active node or network.

2.1 Framework Functionalities

The main functionality of the framework should be based on a mechanism that enables code migration in a (semi-) transparent way to the mobile services. Although the framework services should be ubiquitously provided to the mobile service, yet it must also be possible to control/customize them whenever needed.

An important requirement is the support of an open and flexible mobility model facilitating both, *forced mobility* as well as *intended mobility*. The former refers to the case where the mobile active service is 'forced' to move by the framework as a direct result of some external. Forced mobility will typically be as a result of decisions intended to ensure service resilience and will account for node-related problems such as resource exhaustion and network related issues such as routing problems. In the case of 'intended mobility', the active application itself decides to move in response to application specific conditions.

So far we have argued that the most important reasons for enabling service mobility are the support of mobile users and the provision of service resiliency. These two reasons are motivated from two different application domains. Derived from this distinction also comes the need distinguish between the active nodes that can host the service in case of forced migration (*alternative active nodes*), and those that can be chosen by the application as candidates to host the mobile service in case of intended migration (*next active nodes*).

Once an event necessitating service migration occurs, different way of migrating services can be chosen depending on the situation. For example, if the service code is not broadly available on the new active node as might be the case with a personalised user service, it might be necessary to move both the code of the active service and its state. In other cases, where the service component is already cached or already running on the new active node, it would be more economical to simply transfer the state. The different types of transporting the services have been extensively considered by both the active network as well as the mobile agent communities. The framework should support all migration approaches and allow the mobile service to select the preferred one.

The migration of the mobile service state (and potentially code) between different active node platforms and diverse network environments is an interesting as well as challenging problem. As new code loading mechanisms emerge, the complexity of the problem increases. Therefore, the framework needs to provide a mechanism/protocol that allows negotiation and deployment of an available code loading method among the active nodes (work in this area has been considered in [9, 19]).

A critical factor determining the viability of any mechanism aiming to support the migration of services from one network node to another is security. This accounts both for the protection of the confidentiality of the information carried as part of the service state, as well as the authenticity of the nodes and also that of the information (both code and state) exchanged between the active nodes. It is unlikely that one active node will "accept" and execute code with predefined state unless it can trust the sending node and can check the authenticity of the transferred data. Therefore, the framework needs to provide appropriate mechanisms that allow active nodes to establish and verify trust relationships between mobile service components.

To avoid the limitations often seen in today's mobile agent systems, the framework must account for *micro-* as well as *macro-composition* of services. Very often the design of composite active services (such as the one described in section 1.1) follows the model of a loosely coupled distributed system. Other times a high level service is decomposed into code components interoperating through a node local composition model such as the one proposed as part of the LARA++ [4] active component framework. Both these cases illustrate what we refer to as macro-composition. The framework must be able to provide basic mechanisms or services through which the different service components can interact when required – typically in the control path. On the other hand, when the developer of a mobile service favours a modular design of tightly coupled components that implicitly trust each other, it should be possible to facilitate composition within an instance of the framework therefore favouring micro-composition.

Lastly, the framework requires appropriate authentication and access control mechanisms to regulate access to individual functions of the framework API. Depending on the author and user of the mobile service, access to individual API calls must be controlled (for example, only authorised services should be able to update the *alternative active nodes* table). Ideally, these security mechanisms will be closely integrated with the node local access scheme to NodeOS services.

In order to develop a functional and extensible framework the design of the APIs and the exported functionality needs to be considered carefully. The goal must be a level of granularity that permits the active service developer to use the framework services at their full potential, while at the same time hiding the internal implementation details of each service. Wherever possible, a set of primitives must be used in order to abstract the underlying structure of one mechanism over another. To exemplify this requirement, consider the need for providing different ways of transferring state (and code), over the network, between instances of the framework. In most cases, the mobile active service developer should be able to call *"send (state_object, destination, my_credentials)"* without caring if ftp, http, or some other proprietary data transfer mechanism is used. In this way, as new data transfer mechanisms emerge, they can be integrated in the framework without breaking existing applications. On the other hand, for reasons of speed, efficiency, etc., a specific data transfer method may be preferred. Therefore, the API should provide ways of querying at runtime the existence of a specific method and select its deployment.

3 Design and Implementation

Founded on the requirements analysis presented in section 3, we developed a framework for mobile active service components as part of the research carried out for the ProgNet [5] project in Lancaster University. The current prototype is implemented as an extension to a .NET [6] based execution environment (EE) running on the LARA++ active node [4] while ports of Java [7] and OpenCOM [8] are also under consideration as LARA ++ EEs.

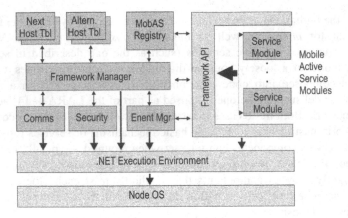

Fig. 2. Framework Architecture

LARA++ [4] is component-based active router architecture based on the program-mable switch paradigm. It uses a filter-based composition model particularly suited to supporting this framework and allows mobile components to be "hooked" directly into the forwarding path. The generic programming model provided by LARA++ enables our framework to support both in-band as well as out-band network pro-grammability. This makes our framework suitable for control and management appli-cations as well as services on the data path. Finally, LARA++ provides a filter-based pattern matching mechanism, enabling the flexible selection of packets subject to active processing. In this way it provides a generic solution of overcoming the effi-ciency and scalability problems of per-packet processing of active capsules.

3.1 Overview of Operation

A framework instance can host one or more closely coupled components that com-pose a *Mobile Active Service (MobAS)* at a micro-composition level. We herein refer to them as *MobAS modules* or simply *service modules*. If no MobAS modules are executing within the framework, then the framework operates in so-called *passive mode,* waiting for a MobAS from the network.

When an active application is implemented as a MobAS it initialises and executes within an instance of the framework. During the initialisation process (or at any time during normal execution) the MobAS may register with the framework a set of mobil-ity events. These are typically application specific events or external triggers that depict certain system and/or network conditions.

Parallel procedures related to the MobAS (for example, population of the *next ac-tive node table,* callbacks for the registered events, etc.) can be either handled inter-nally by the module that provides the actual service, or by separate module executing concurrently to the one providing the service – thus promoting a more scalable design based on separation of roles. Furthermore, the various service modules can interact either directly or through the framework provided inter-module communication (IMC) mechanisms.

When a registered event, representing either an application specific condition, for example, a serviced user has moved, or an external condition such as resource exhaustion is triggered, its callback signals the *framework manager* to initiate the MobAS migration.

The implemented mobilisation mechanism uniformly supports intended and forced mobility. Since the service should be suspended while in consistent state, the framework always tries to allow the MobAS time to continue until it reaches a point where execution can be safely suspended. The MobAS developer can select and indicate such points in the program by using appropriate annotations. Then, control is passed back to the framework that takes action to package and send the MobAS.

Depending on the event source (application specific versus system/network related events) the framework must choose, either from the *alternative active nodes table* or the *next active nodes table,* a prospective host for the MobAS. Once a suitable active node has been selected, the framework installs, configures, and activates a new copy of itself on the chosen node using the ASDP [9] based service deployment interface.

Finally, when everything is ready the framework packages (serialises) the MobAS with its current state, adds a digital signature and if required encrypts it; the packages are then sent to the remote active node using a commonly available, and previously agreed, transmission mechanism. The framework instance at the remote end, will receive, the MobAS, (decrypt it, if required), verify its authenticity using the local node's public key, and resume execution where it was previously stopped.

Depending on the migration model the above process may vary slightly: i.e. only the service state may be serialised and sent to the remote active node where it is used with a freshly activated installation of the MobAS.

3.2 Architecture

As illustrated in figure 2, the framework consists of several building blocks each facilitating a distinct functionality. The proposed architecture augments the functionality provided by the EE, while regulating the access to the EE API. Figure 2 also shows the interactions among the distinct parts of the framework as well as between the framework and the EE/NodeOS.

- The *framework manager* is the "heart" of the framework. It is responsible for the coordination and the interfacing between the framework components, thus promoting a modular design whereby any component can be replaced (or upgraded) independently without impacting the integrity of the rest of the framework.

- The *MobAS registry* is the component responsible for the registration of the MobAS components with the framework. It holds the configuration of the MobAS regarding its operation (for example, service module scheduling priorities), and the MobAS user/author credentials that determine the API access privileges.

- The *event manager* is the component that handles the mobilisation events. Both application specific as well as external system and/or network events that can trigger the migration of the MobAS are registered with this component along with any callbacks (that will be called upon firing an event).

- The *communication/control broker* component is responsible for the communication with instances of the framework installed on remote active nodes. Furthermore, this component handles the transmission of the MobAS from one active node to another, by negotiating a suitable data transfer method that is available on both active nodes. This is facilitated by means of a service deployment interface based on ASDP protocol [9].
- The *security broker* is responsible for providing the mechanisms to secure the code/state transmission between two active nodes. It holds a copy of the local node's private key and maintains a cache with the public keys of the active nodes that have been contacted in the past. It provides digital signing and encryption services for the framework.
- The *alternative hosts table* and *next hosts table* data structures maintain lists of potential future hosts for the MobAS. The *next host table* is maintained by the MobAS and holds a list of active nodes that may host the MobAS when an application specific event is triggered. The *alternative host table* on the other hand, is maintained by the framework (currently populated from the contents of a configuration file), and holds a list of alternative neighbour active nodes willing to host the MobAS.
- Finally the *framework API* controls access to the framework and the EE services.

4   A Case Scenario

To demonstrate the intended functionality of the framework, in this section we describe an example scenario whereby a server in the internet is assumed to be a victim of a DDoS SYN flooding attack [10]. It should be noted that with this example we do not aim to propose a comprehensive solution for the specific problem, but rather to exemplify the functionality of our framework.

Under this attack strategy, one or more malicious machines in the Internet send TCP SYN packets with various spoofed source IP addresses, at a very high rate to a victim server. The server replies with a TCP SYN/ACK packet to the spoofed IP addresses and waits for the ACK response to establish the TCP connection. Since the IP addresses are spoofed, and since the receivers of the SYN/ACK packets have not initiated the connections, the packets are dropped, leaving the victim node with a set of dangling TCP connection requests waiting to time out. The effect of this condition when it takes place at high frequency is the backlog queue exhaustion that leaves the server unusable as there are so many TCP connections waiting to be established.

Fighting against such types of DoS attacks is particularly tedious as it is impossible to filter the spoofed packets based on their source IP address. The most common countermeasure is to perform "traffic shaping" at the nearest to the victim router. Although this salvages the victim server resources, it usually cannot prevent the disruption of the service as new incoming connections are difficult to establish.

To counteract this attack we propose the use of a mobile active component that ultimately aims to track the source of the attack by following the spoofed traffic flow from the victim to its source, based on the exhibited traffic pattern (of the attack) [12]. Then, "move" as close as possible towards the attacking host and install a firewall to block the malicious traffic.

The overall functionality would be provided by three cooperating mobile service components: (i) one that performs in-line network measurements to detect congestion patterns in the network (herein called measurements component), (ii) another one that samples the network traffic and performs SYN flooding detection (herein called flooding detection component), based on techniques proposed in the literature (such as SYN-FIN differentiation [13]), and (iii) one that processes the measurements of the other two components, classifies them, identifies the traffic pattern of the attack, and migrates to the next active node closer to the source of the malicious traffic (herein called DoS tracker component).

Initially, the DoS tracker component is installed in an active node close to the victim server. It then instruments the installation of several flooding detection components in neighbour active nodes and receives periodically the feedback from them. Once a DoS SYN flooding attack has been detected by the flooding detection component, the DoS tracker deploys within a range around the "abused" network interface, several measurement components and tries to identify the traffic pattern of the attack and find the originating point in the immediate network neighbourhood. If such a point is located then the DoS tracker "clones" itself on an active node closer to that network location. The same process is repeated again and again and the DoS tracker component "crawls" through the network closer to the source of the attack; for as long as there are available active nodes. When it cannot progress anymore or it has reached the network of the attacker, it can install a filter to block the malicious traffic as close as possible to the attacker's machine.

This scenario advocates the usefulness of the active service mobility to address problems that are otherwise difficult to tackle with conventional approaches, and demonstrates the functionality of our framework.

5 Related Work

Traditionally, service mobility has been facilitated by means of (mobile) agents. Their applications cover a wide range of distributed services ranging from processing of scientific data [13], evaluation of security algorithms [14], scalable network management [15], and so forth.

The development of distributed services is often supported by middleware solutions such as .NET [6], Java [7] and OpenCOM [8] that provide abstraction of system and network services (reflective middleware), portability, type safety, and other high level facilities that ease the development of distributed applications. As these platforms often don't provide complete support for developing mobile agent applications, a few frameworks have been proposed [16], [17] that extend or enrich the functionality of the aforementioned middleware platforms accordingly. The approach presented in [17] is perhaps the closest related to our work in this paper; yet like all mobile agent solutions, it accounts for user space applications, and cannot support the development of network services that can be deployed on the forwarding path.

On the other hand, the emergence of active networks research has enabled alternative ways of developing (low level – even within the forwarding path) mobile services. Certain classes of network applications such as traffic flow management in ad-hoc networks [18] can be efficiently developed by means of active capsule based solutions [1, 2, 3]. However, as we have argued in this paper capsule based solutions exhibit limitations with regard to their flexibility, applicability and the scalability outside the scope of their original application domain. On the other hand, programmable network approaches, like [4, 11, 20], have not considered the issue of generic run-time service mobility, apart from the simple case of remote loading/installing of code out-of-band.

6 Conclusion

In this paper we have presented the requirements analysis and the implementation of a framework for the development and management of mobile active services.

Initially, we outlined the need for service mobility in order to support mobile users and facilitate resilient and resource efficient servicing, in unreliable network environments. We then, examined the functional requirements of a generic framework that would enable the development of mobile services vertically across the network stack, in-band as well as out-of-band in the data path.

Finally, based on these requirements we presented an implementation that takes advantage of the flexibility and efficiency offered by the LARA++ programmable node platform, in combination with the portability and modularity provided by middleware platforms such as.NET, to deliver a generic, extensible and flexible development platform. The proposed framework overcomes the limitations encountered in mobile agent and active capsule technologies and provides a more viable, practical and complete solution (combining the best of the two worlds), which can be used to develop user space applications as well as low level network services targeting the data, control or management planes.

References

[1] D.J. Wetherall, J. Guttag, and T.L.Tennenhouse, "ANTS: A toolkit for building and dynamically deploying network protocols", Proceedings of IEEE Openarch, April 1998.
[2] M.W. Hicks, P. Kaddar, J.T. Moore, C.A Gunter and S. Nettles, "PLAN: A Packet Language for Active Networks", In Proceedings of 3rd ACM SIGPLAN International Conference on Functional Programming, pages 86-93, 1998.
[3] B. Schwartz, et al. Smart packets: applying active networks to network management. ACM Transactions on Computer Systems, 2000.
[4] S. Schmid, J. Finney, A. Scott and D. Shepherd, "Component-based Active Network Architecture", in Proceedings of 6th IEEE Symposium on Computers and Communications (ISCC), Tunisia, July 2001.
[5] "Programmable Network Support for Mobile Services", Research Project funded by EPSRC Programmable Networks initiative, Lancaster University, 2001.
[6] "Microsoft.NET Overview White paper" http://www.microsoft.com/technet/itsolutions/msit/dotnet.mspx, January 1, 2002
[7] J. Gosling and H. McGilton. The Java language environment. White paper, May 1995. Sun Microsystems, 2550 Garcia Avenue, Mountain View, CA 94043, USA.

[8] Coulson G., Blair G.S., Clarke M., Parlavantzas N., "The Design of a Highly Configurable and Reconfigurable Middleware Platform", ACM/ Springer Distributed Computing Journal, Vol. 15, April 2002.

[9] M. Sifalakis, S. Schmid, T. Chart, D. Hutchison. "A Generic Active Service Deployment Protocol". In Proceddings of 2nd International Workshop on Active Network Technologies and Applications (IECE ANTA), p. 100-111, Osaka, Japan, May 2003.

[10] CERT advisory ca-1996-21. "TCP SYN flooding and IP spoofing attacks". http://www.cert.org/advisories/CA-1996-21.html, Sep 1996.

[11] A. Galis et al. "A Flexible IP Active Networks Architecture". Proceedings of 2nd International Working Conference on Active Networks (IWAN), Tokyo, Japan, October2003.

[12] H. Wang, D. Zhang, and K. G. Shin. "Detecting SYN flooding attacks" in Proceedings of IEEE Infocom'2002, June 2002.

[13] E. Korpela et al. "SETI@home: Massively Distributed Computing for SETI". IEEE magazine "Computing in Science and Engineering". January 2001.

[14] http://www.distributed.net/projects.php

[15] A. Bieszczad, B. Pagurek, and T. White. "Mobile agents for network management". IEEE Communications Surveys, September 1998.

[16] J. E. White. "Telescript technology: Mobile agents". General Magic white paper, 2465 Latham Street, Mountain View, CA 94040, 1996.

[17] N. Suri et al. "An overview of the NOMADS mobile agent system". Proceedings of 6th ECOOP Workshop on Mobile Object Systems, Sophia Antipolis, France, June 2000.

[18] S.-B. Lee, G.-S. Ahn, X. Zhang, and A.T. Campbell, "INSIGNIA: An IP-Based Quality of Service Framework for Mobile Ad Hoc Networks," J. Parallel and Distributed Computing, special issue on wireless and mobile computing and communications, vol. 60, no. 4, pp. 374-406, April 2000.

[19] Prince D., Scott A., Shepherd W.D. "On Demand Network Level Service Deployment in Ad-Hoc Networks". Proceedings of 8th Conference on Personal Wireless Communications, Italy, September 2003

[20] R. Keller et al. "PromethOS: A Dynamically Extensible Router Architecture Supporting Explicit Routing". Proceedings of the 4th Annual International Working Conference on Active Networks (IWAN), Zurich, Switzerland, December 2002.

Using Active Networking's Adaptability in Ad Hoc Routing

Seong-Kyu Song and Scott M. Nettles

Electrical and Computer Engineering Department
The University of Texas at Austin
{sksong,nettles}@ece.utexas.edu

Abstract. The early goals of Active Networking (AN) were to increase the pace of network evolution and to facilitate application specific protocols. Our aim is to demonstrate that for a specific application domain, Ad Hoc network routing, these goals have been substantially met. We argue that Ad Hoc networking is a domain that is well suited for this demonstration, due to its needs for both evolution and adaptation.

We support our claim by building a series of Ad Hoc routing protocols, based on both DSR and AODV, that demonstrate heavyweight evolution, lightweight evolution, and routing adaptation. We based our design and implementation on our Mobile Active Networking Environment (MANE). MANE is a direct descendant of PLAN/PLANet and, as such, supports both Active Packets and Active Extensions as programmability mechanisms, thus giving us maximum flexibility in our demonstrations.

Keywords: MANET, Ad hoc Routing, Active Networking, Adaptation.

1 Introduction

The original goals of Active Networking (AN) were clear: First, to make it easier to deploy new protocols or alter existing protocols to allow the network to evolve more readily; and, Second, to allow protocols to be customized to specific application needs. AN attempts to meet these goals by adding programmability to the network infrastructure. Although there have been a significant number of AN systems proposed and implemented [1,2,3,4,5], there has been less work done to show that these systems meet AN's original goals. The purpose of this paper is to show that, for a specific application domain, a mature, well-understood AN system can meet these original goals.

For the AN system, our Mobile Active Network Environment (MANE) [6] was the obvious choice. MANE is the most recent embodiment of our work on PLAN [1,7] and is a direct descendent of PLANet [8]. Like our earlier work, MANE combines programmable Active Packets (APs) with downloadable node resident Active Extensions (AEs), thus allowing us to explore both of the two principle AN programmability approaches in the same context. In MANE, APs carry PLAN programs that execute as the packet moves through the network.

G.J. Minden et al. (Eds.): IWAN 2004, LNCS 3912, pp. 138–155, 2007.

APs provide the programmable "glue" that binds the network together. AEs form the basis of the node-resident programmable infrastructure by allowing new functionality to be downloaded into the nodes, either to modify node behavior or to provide new services callable by APs. MANE goes further than any of our PLANet implementations in its support for AEs since it provides not just *plug-in extensions*, but also *dynamic-update extensions* [9,6]. When used in conjunction with plug-in extensions, APs can use new node-resident services specialized to their needs if the standard services are not sufficient. Further, dynamic-update extensions can update a system's functionality while the node remains operational and can affect the operation of existing functionality, even if there has been no pre-planning to provide a plug-in interface. The distinction between plug-in and update extensions is discussed in more detail in [9,6].

As an application domain, we chose routing for mobile ad hoc networks (MANETs) [10]. There are a number of reasons for this choice [11]. First, MANET routing is a very active area of research and the potential protocols of interest are still changing. Thus, if AN does facilitate evolution, it would be possible to deploy existing routing algorithms with the expectation that they could be easily replaced by better algorithms as they are developed. Second, MANET environments can vary greatly and the preferred routing algorithm can be different for different environments. Thus, if AN does facilitate application specific protocols, it should be possible to choose and dynamically deploy the best algorithm for the environment at hand. Third, the conditions present in a MANET may change so that the algorithm currently in use is no longer optimal. The ideal routing protocol may need to change dynamically. AN offers the possibility of adapting the algorithm dynamically as conditions change. Finally, because MANETs are not widely deployed or standardized, it is quite possible that a node will not have the desired algorithm present. It is even possible that a node will have no available MANET routing algorithm. AN can provide us with the ability to deploy the desired algorithm on-the-fly.

In this paper, we focus on two well-known MANET routing protocols, Dynamic Source Routing (DSR) and Ad-hoc On-demand Distance Vector routing (AODV). We chose these protocols because they are perhaps the most widely accepted and studied of the myriad of possible choices. Using these protocols, we demonstrate implementations that realize the possibilities discussed above. First, we show how a simple version of DSR could be deployed on a network where it was not currently deployed and where perhaps no ad hoc routing protocol was available. Second, we show how that simple version can be evolved dynamically into a superior version even without changing the code resident on the nodes. Third, we show how AN enables us to create a hybrid of DSR and AODV that allows us to adapt to changing conditions in the network dynamically.

The remainder of this paper is organized as follows. Section 2 is an overview of the two ad hoc routing protocols, DSR and AODV. In Section 3, we discuss AN technologies and our AN platform. Section 4 presents our implementation of a simple version of the DSR protocol. Section 5 demonstrates how we can deploy a new ad hoc routing protocol on a network where no ad hoc routing protocol is available. In Section 6, we describe how to use active packet evolution to evolve our simple version of DSR into a more efficient one without modifying node-resident code. Section 7 presents a protocol that is a hybrid of DSR and AODV that can adapt to changing network conditions. Finally, Section 8 concludes the paper.

2   Ad Hoc Routing Background

Understanding the examples we present requires some basic knowledge of how the routing protocols we have chosen work. The two protocols, DSR and AODV, are both reactive (or *on-demand*) protocols. This means that rather than always maintaining a route to all destinations (proactive routing) they find a route on-demand when it is actually needed. When a packet needs to be sent and a route is not already known, both protocols find routes by flooding the network with a route request packet. When the destination is found, a route reply packet is sent, which sets up the needed data structures for each protocol to actually send the packet. The protocols differ in the exact nature of this discovery process, in the nature of the routes, and in many details of the basic process.

2.1   Dynamic Source Routing

The DSR protocol [12] uses data packets that carry source routes that specify each next-hop node directly in the packet. It is composed of *Route Discovery* and *Route Maintenance* operations. In the Route Discovery phase, when a route is needed, a source node (S) attempts to obtain a source route (the sequence of nodes that the packet should visit) to a destination node (D) by flooding ROUTE REQUEST packets throughout the network. The request packets collect route information as they are propagated through the network. The first route request packet to reach the destination returns a ROUTE REPLY packet with the sequence of nodes it visited. When the route reply packet reaches the source, the source route it contains is used to send the data packet. In order to reduce routing overhead and make the best possible use of route information, each node maintains a *route cache* into which the new route is also entered. As described in Section 6, in more highly optimized versions of the protocol, this route cache can be used to short-cut route requests. In the Route Maintenance phase, S is notified of the link failures, if any, by nodes adjacent to the broken link. Then, S will initiate another route discovery operation by generating a new route request packet.

2.2   Ad-Hoc On-Demand Distance Vector

The AODV routing protocol [13] is the on-demand version of the Destination Sequenced Distance Vector routing protocol [14]. Unlike DSR, AODV data packets carry only a destination address; next-hop addresses are maintained in routing tables on the intermediate nodes. However, AODV still has the same basic Route

Discovery structure as DSR, the route reply packets simply must set up the intermediate nodes' routing table while returning to the source. AODV also uses sequence numbers to discern stale routes and maintain route freshness. AODV also has a Route Maintenance aspect, which is similar to DSR's. All of this means that the basic implementation structure of AODV is similar to DSR, but many of the key details are different.

In spite of their similarities, it has been shown that the two protocols perform differently under various network conditions, especially the degree of network mobility [15,16]. It appears that DSR may be more sensitive to mobility than AODV. Under lower mobility, since there are relatively few link changes, DSR's aggressive caching strategy is effective in achieving better performance than AODV. However, in high mobility cases, AODV seems to do better than DSR because of more conservative routing management [16].

3   Active Networking and MANE

AN provides adaptability to facilitate application-specific customization and speedy network service evolution [17]. In this section, we describe the programmability mechanisms of AN and the modifications we made to MANE to support ad hoc networking.

3.1   Programmability Mechanisms

There are two basic mechanisms for adaptability in AN: *Active Packets* and *Active Extensions* [17]. APs carry programs that execute as they pass through the nodes. Packet execution can perform management actions on the nodes, affect their own routing, or form the basic distributed computational framework of larger protocols. Since packet programs can accomplish protocol implementation on-the-fly, they are a quick and effective way of deploying new services in existing networks. Also, packet-by-packet adaptivity enables the network to adjust agilely to changing environments.

Complementary to APs are AEs, which form the basis of the node-resident programmable infrastructure by providing the services callable by APs. AE's can be dynamically downloaded to modify a nodes behavior [18,6]. When used in conjunction with *plug-in extensions*, packet programs can use new node-resident services specialized to their needs if standard services are not sufficient. Further, *update extensions* can update a system's functionality while the node remains operational. Update extensions can affect the operation of existing functionality, even if there has been no pre-planning to provide a plug-in interface.

The flexibility of these two mechanisms together makes AN a good choice for environments that require a high degree of adaptivity, such as MANETs. In MANETs, as the nodes move, link conditions may change frequently; thus the routing protocol needs to cope with those variations nimbly. Moreover, because ad hoc networks can occur without prior planning, it is entirely possible that the ideal routing algorithm may not be known in advance and may change as the network is in use. To overcome such *routing heterogeneity*, it is desirable to promptly conform to a unified protocol. AN's ability to implement a protocol on-the-fly makes it possible to agilely evolve and adapt routing protocols.

3.2 MANE

Our Mobile Active Network Environment (MANE) [6] implements the Switch-Ware architecture [1] and is the descendant of our previous AN testbed, PLANet [8]. Active packets are written in the Packet Language for Active Networks (PLAN) [7] and service functions are written in Popcorn [19], which is a C-like type-safe language based on TAL (Typed Assembly Language) [20]. Here we describe the modifications of MANE needed to support ad hoc networking in general and in particular to support on-demand routing protocols. Note that the first two modifications are really to our underlaying emulation, in a "real" network they would not be needed. The last two modifications would be needed in real networks and in Section 5 we discuss how they could be achieved dynamically using our AN mechanisms.

Addressing. Like an IP address, MANE addresses are globally unique and hierarchical. A node is identified by a network number and a host number. The hierarchy is based on sub-nets of nodes and each node on a sub-net can broadcast to all other nodes. Communication with nodes on other networks must be mediated by routers. Based on this hierarchy, MANE supports Mobile-IP-like mobility by utilizing AN's evolution techniques [6]. For ad hoc networks, where each node works as a router, we modified MANE to use a flat addressing scheme, where host numbers are used as a unique address.

Mobility Emulation. MANE emulates broadcast networks by keeping track of which nodes are on a particular sub-net and using UDP to communicate between neighbors. Broadcast is achieved by repeatedly unicasting to every neighbor.[1] This also supports emulation of physical node mobility, allowing a node to leave a sub-net and to join new sub-nets. Even though this emulation is transparent to higher-level protocols, MANE needed to inject special APs to disconnect and connect a node [6].

For ad hoc networks, we need a more scalable and distributed way of emulating physical mobility. Therefore, we adopted a method similar to that used by **ns-2** for wireless network simulations [21]. There is a pre-generated mobility file describing the physical movement. Also, there is a virtual master node with a global "bird's eye" view, whose role is to update neighbor information by sending neighbor information packets periodically to every node. The virtual master obtains neighbor information from the mobility file. Neighbor information is used only in emulating physical mobility and wireless link broadcasting, not in network-layer routing.

---

[1] It should be clear from this description that the goal of MANE is to allow flexible experimentation with models and functionality, not to provide a high performance AN implementation.

Routing Buffer in the Network Layer. Since we are experimenting with reactive ad hoc routing protocols, there needs to be a buffer – *the routing buffer* – to hold the packets during route discovery. When a route is discovered, the corresponding packets are released from the routing buffer and pushed into the lower layer queue for transmission. To support reactive routing protocols, MANE implements the routing buffer in the network layer. If there is no route information for a packet, a sender saves the packet in the routing buffer and initiates route discovery. Route reply packets cause the sender to free the packet from the routing buffer and resume the transmission of the packet.

Link Layer Acknowledgements. Any link can be broken due to either node movements or channel deterioration and ad hoc routing protocols need to be able to discover these failures. For route maintenance and detecting link breakage, we added link-layer acknowledgements to MANE. After transmitting a packet, the link layer saves the packet in the *interface queue* and waits for acknowledgement. If there is no acknowledgement during a timeout period or if a negative acknowledgement is received, the link layer retransmits the packet. When a certain number of trials fail, the node recognizes it as link breakage.

4   A Simple Version of DSR

We first present a simple version of the DSR protocol[2], which we will later show how to deploy and evolve. In our initial simple version, no use of the route cache is made at the intermediate nodes. All intermediate nodes simply re-broadcast the first instance of a route request received after appending their own address, and ROUTE REPLY packets are generated only by the destination.

In MANE, a protocol is implemented in two levels; active extensions and active packets. AE's are node-resident and implement the service functions needed for the protocol, while APs serve to glue together the AE functionality and actualize the protocol. We first present the services needed for DSR, followed by the AP's that are used by the protocol.

4.1   An Active Extension for DSR

Table 1 shows node resident services needed by DSR. Get_ID() generates a unique identification number for a new route request. There are two functions, LookUp_RouteCache() and SaveIn_RouteCache(), for managing the *Route Cache*. To filter out duplicate requests, Mark_Dup_Request() and Check_Dup_Request() are used to manage the *Duplicate Request Check List*.

4.2   Active Packets for Basic Route Discovery

Figure 1 shows the pseudocode for route discovery, while Figure 2 shows the PLAN implementation. The pseudocode shows that as the packet executes at

---

[2] In referring to the DSR protocol, we mean the basic idea of DSR, not literally the DSR standard.

Table 1. Service Functions for DSR

Functions	Types
Get_ID()	null $\Longrightarrow$ int
LookUp_RouteCache(dest)	host $\Longrightarrow$ host list
SaveIn_RouteCache(dest, srcRoute)	host*(host list) $\Longrightarrow$ null
Mark_Dup_Request(source, ID)	host*int $\Longrightarrow$ null
Check_Dup_Request(source, ID)	host*int $\Longrightarrow$ bool

each node duplicates are discarded. Then, if the packet is at the destination a route reply is sent and the route is saved, anticipating the possibility of data being sent back to the source. If the packet is not at the destination, the current address is simply added to the route and the packet is reflooded.

In addition to the service functions above, the PLAN code uses a number of PLAN core services and language constructs. thisHostIs() returns a boolean value indicating whether the given network address matches the address of the current node. getSrcDev() returns the interface on which the packet arrived, and thisHostOf() returns the network address corresponding to the given device. Using these functions and the list operator for concatenation, ::, the route request packet can obtain the source route as it is propagated through the network (Lines 9–13). OnNeighbor() is a network primitive that generates a child AP executing on a neighbor of the current node. getRB() returns the amount of resource bound available in the packet.

```
1: INPUT: destination address D, list of hosts R
2: if this is a duplicate request then
3:    discard this packet
4: else
5:    if arrived at D then
6:       send Route Reply with R
7:       save R in route cache
8:    else
9:       append my address to R
10:      flood this request to all neighbors
11:   end if
12: end if
```

Fig. 1. Pseudocode for Basic Route Discovery

The actual implementation corresponds closely to the pseudocode. In Line 2 route discovery starts by checking for duplicate requests. If the request has been already seen, this packet is discarded (Line 15). If not, it will save the tuple <source address, request id> in the Duplicate Request Check List (Line 3). If the request has arrived at the destination, D saves the source route to S and generates a route reply packet (Lines 4–7). Based on the assumption that links

```
1: fun routeDiscovery(src, dst, id, srtRecord) =
2: if(not Check_Dup_Request(src, id)) then (
3:   Mark_Dup_Request(src, id);
4:   if(thisHostIs(dst)) then (
5:     SaveIn_RouteCache(src, srtRecord);
6:     routeReply(src, dst, srtRecord, reverse(srtRecord))
7:   )
8:   else (  (* intermediate nodes *)
9:     let val myAddr = thisHostOf(getSrcDev())
10:    in
11:       OnNeighbor(|routeDiscovery|(src, dst, id, myAddr::srtRecord),
12:                  broadcast, getRB(), getSrcDev())
13:    end
14: )
15: else () (* dup req. discard *)
```

Fig. 2. PLAN for Basic DSR Route Discovery

```
1: INPUT: source address S, list of hosts R
2: if arrived at S then
3:    save R in cache
4:    exit route discovery
5:    send data using R
6: else
7:    forward this packet to S
8: end if
```

Fig. 3. Pseudocode for Basic DSR Route Reply

```
1: fun routeReply(src, dst, srcRoute, routing) =
2: if(thisHostIs(src)) then (
3:   SaveIn_RouteCache(dst, srcRoute);
4:   exitRouteDiscovery()
5: )
6: else (
7:   let val nexthop = hd(routing)
8:       val routing = tl(routing)
9:   in  OnNeighbor(|routeReply|(src, dst, srcRoute, routing),
10:                 nexthop, getRB(), getSrcDev())
11: end
12: )
```

Fig. 4. PLAN for Basic DSR Route Reply

are bi-directional, the source route is reversed to be used as a route for the route reply. If this is an intermediate node, the nodes address is prepended to the current source route and OnNeighbor is used to broadcast the request to all the 1-hop neighbors (Lines 8–14).

Figure 3 shows the pseudocode for route reply, while Figure 4 shows the PLAN implementation. The pseudocode shows that a packet is simply forwarded at intermediate nodes, while at the source the route is saved in the cache and then any data destined for the destination is sent.

Again, the PLAN code corresponds closely to the pseudocode. If the reply has arrived at the source, the route is saved and route discovery exits, triggering (implicitly) the data packets to be sent. Lines 7–11 show how the reverse source route is used at an intermediate node. In Line 7 the nextHop is read from the front of the list and in Line 8 it is removed from the list. In Line 9–10 OnNeighbor is used to send the reply to the next hop, along with the truncated route.

5   Deploying DSR

Given the varied environments faced by MANETs, it is quite possible that the most appropriate routing algorithm will not already be deployed on all the nodes. In fact, given that MANETs are a new technology, it is possible that no routing algorithm of any kind is deployed. This is exactly the sort of problem that AN was designed to solve. In particular, let us consider how we could deploy our simple version of DSR.

Our DSR implementation has two components, the AE making up the service routines and the APs that use these routines. Since the APs carry their own code with them, deploying them is trivial, we simply inject the required APs into the network. Deploying the AE is only slightly more complex.

In MANE, code for an AE can be dynamically linked into a running node [9]. During this linking process, the AE can define new services that can be called from PLAN. Once this has been done the APs that use those services will be able to function. Now the only question is how to discover which nodes need to have the AE installed and how to transport the code to those nodes. There are many possible approaches, for example, we could imagine an ANTS-like [2] system where APs implicitly discover whether the needed code is node-resident and then download it from predecessor nodes or perhaps from some global repository. Another possibility is that AEs could be downloaded from a central repository, perhaps on demand.

For illustrative purposes and implementation simplicity, our implementation uses a simpler approach. The route request packet carries the extension in the packet itself and tests to see if it needs to be loaded as it floods the network. Figure 5 shows the pseudocode for this simple solution. In Line 2, the packet checks if the extension it needs is present. If not, it will dynamically load and install the extension on the node before executing route discovery. This simple use of *plug-in evolution* [6] allows us to deploy the DSR protocol dynamically and in a timely manner. Although simple and elegant, it does seem likely that space and security considerations may make this approach less desirable in real systems.

We have swept one potentially important point under the rug. Most of the changes we made to MANE that were described in Section 3.2 were really concerned with improving our emulation of mobility and would not be needed for a

1: INPUT: destination address D, list of hosts R, Extension E
2: **if** DSR Service Not Present **then**
3:    Load DSR Extension From This Packet
4: **end if**
5: *DSR Route Discovery*

Fig. 5. Dynamic DSR Deployment

real network. However, some of the changes would actually need to be made to support DSR or AODV. In particular, the proactive routing algorithms typically used in wired networks have no need to potentially queue packets when a route does not exist, they simply drop those packets. Adding this queue is not simply a matter of plugging in a new PLAN callable service function, it requires more fundamental changes to the node implementation.

This is an excellent example of where MANE's support for "update extensions" comes into play. Using dynamic updating technology [9], we can load an extension that makes significant changes to the node implementation, including inserting the new queuing mechanism. Similarly, we could used update extensions to add the link-level acknowledgements needed to support route repair.

6 Evolving DSR

The ability to deploy a new protocol on-the-fly using AEs is a powerful mechanism for evolving the network. However, it is also a heavyweight mechanism, requiring that code be dynamically linked into a running node. Using update evolution is even heavier weight, since it enables almost arbitrary changes to be made to a node.

It seems likely that only a few network users will be trusted to make these kinds of heavyweight changes to running network nodes. Does this mean that only those privileged users will be able to evolve or customize the network?

In this section, we show that significant protocol evolution can be achieved without resorting to making permanent changes to the node. The key mechanism is, of course, packet programmability. If there is a need to evolve or customize a routing protocol, APs can implement the new one without modifying the services of the nodes in the network. This kind of *Active Packet evolution* [6] enables the network to promptly evolve with the help of common and reusable AE's. PLAN plays an important role here, because its strong safety and security guarantees allow unprivileged, third party user to safely program the network.

6.1 Active Packets for Optimized DSR

Our initial DSR implementation is quite simple and does not take advantage of many of the optimizations that are possible. In particular, intermediate nodes simply implement flooding, despite having route caches that might contain the route that we are searching for. To utilize route control packets efficiently and

```
1: INPUT: source address S, destination address D, list of hosts R
2: if this is a duplicate request then
3:     discard this packet
4: else
5:     save R in cache for S
6:     if arrived at D then
7:         send Route Reply with R
8:     else
9:         if route found in route cache then
10:            send Route Reply with R and found route
11:        else
12:            append my address to R
13:            flood this request to all neighbors
14:        end if
15:    end if
16: end if
```

Fig. 6. Pseudocode for Optimized Route Request

```
1: INPUT: source address S, destination address D, list of hosts R
2: save R in cache for D
3: if arrived at S then
4:     exit route discovery
5:     send data using R
6: else
7:     forward this packet to S
8: end if
```

Fig. 7. Pseudocode for Optimized Route Reply

to reduce routing overhead, the protocol needs to be optimized by allowing intermediate nodes to aggressively participate in routing. Specifically, request-broadcasting nodes can obtain a source route to S, and reply-forwarding nodes can acquire a source route to D. They keep those route information in their route caches for later use. Before re-broadcasting the request, intermediate nodes can search their route cache. If there is a valid entry, they can respond without re-broadcasting the request further. Most importantly, we can implement this optimized DSR by only re-programming APs, and we do not need to modify the DSR services in a node-resident AE.

Figure 6 and Figure 7 show the pseudocode for optimized DSR route discovery. The underlined portions indicate the parts that have been added to our initial simple implementation. We have not included our PLAN code, as with the simple DSR implementation, it mirrors the pseudocode closely.

At intermediate nodes, route discovery changes in two basic ways. First, in addition to flooding the route discovery packet, the packet also saves the partial route in its cache (Line 5), thus increasing its knowledge of possible routes at essentially no cost. Second, the packet looks in the intermediate node's cache for a route to the destination (Line 9). If the route exists, then the node returns the packet's route record concatenated with the cached route (Line 10), thus short-cutting the route discovery process. Route reply adds a single optimization, replies also add routes to the route caches on intermediate nodes (Line 2).

Although in this example, new APs are used to perform a general optimization, they can also be used to perform application-specific customizations as well. For example, in the current protocol, if no route reply short cutting occurs, the route that is chosen is the one taken by the first route request packet to arrive at the destination. An application might desire to use a different metric, say the route that has the largest bottleneck bandwidth. Assuming we had service routines that could tell us link bandwidths, then we could easily program a route request packet that would measure the bottleneck bandwidth and return a route reply for any route request that arrived at the destination with a better value than previous route requests.

7   A Hybrid Routing Protocol

We have seen how AN can be used to deploy new, improved, or customized protocols in a MANET environment. These examples show that AN's adaptability can help to accommodate the wide variety of environments MANETs face. Because of their dynamic nature, not only do we expect MANETs to be used with widely varying network conditions, but we also would expect that those conditions may well change while a network is operational, perhaps rapidly. In this section, we show that AN can be used to adapt to such changing conditions.

In Section 2, we presented some background information on both DSR and AODV. A key point is that AODV appears to work better when levels of mobility are high, while DSR appears to work best when mobility is low. Thus, even if the preferred protocol is in use, it is entirely possible that the level of mobility may shift, making it desirable to change protocols.

Our approach is to build a hybrid protocol that can easily switch between AODV and DSR as mobility levels change. The possible design space for such hybrid protocols is immense and it is important to keep in mind that our goal is to demonstrate that AN has achieved its goals with respect to adaptability, not to explore this design space or to propose the "best" protocol. By showing a fairly simple example, it should be clear that AN techniques will facilitate the implementation, development, and exploration of a wide variety of such adaptive protocols.

7.1   An Active Extension for the Hybrid Protocol

The key to creating a hybrid protocol that can switch rapidly between differing algorithms is to create a set of generic AE services that can be used by all algorithms. Once this is done, we can then accomplish the actual switching between protocols quite easily using APs. This general idea is an important aspect of AN, by providing generic, reusable, composable node resident components,

Table 2. Service Functions for Hybrid Protocol

Functions	Types

LookUp_RIB
(routing protocol, dest)
	`string*host`
	`⇒ host*int*int`
	or `⇒ host list`

SaveIn_RIB(dest, destSeq,
hopCount, nextHop)
or (dest, source_route)
	`host*int*int*host`
	or `host*(host list)`
	`⟹ null`

Get_RREQ_ID()	`null ⟹ int`
Mark_Dup_Request (source, RREQ_ID)	`host*int ⟹ null`
Check_Dup_Request (source, RREQ_ID)	`host*int ⟹ bool`
Get_SrcSeq()	`null ⟹ int`
Get_DestSeq(dest)	`host ⟹ int`

we can then use packet programs to create many different protocols and enable switching between protocols easily.

Here, we take this idea only so far by creating generic services common to both DSR and AODV as shown in Table 2. The most important of these, LookUp_RIB() and SaveIn_RIB(), manipulate a generic *Route Information Base (RIB)*, which is a combined form of DSR route cache and AODV route table. Notice that we have used parametric polymorphism so that these functions can take arguments and return values that are appropriate to either DSR or AODV. The next three services, Get_RREQ_ID(), Mark_Dup_Request(), and Check_Dup_Request(), are concerned with duplicate elimination during flooding. These are good examples of general services that we might expect to see reused by many different protocols and in fact, they have already appeared in our simple DSR implementation. The final two services, Get_SrcSeq() and Get_DestSeq(), are concerned with manipulating sequence numbers. Although here they are specific to the AODV aspect of our protocol, we can certainly imagine that with more experience, we could define a general set of sequence number manipulation services that would be reusable across a variety of protocols.

7.2   An Active Packet for the Hybrid Protocol

Using the services above, we can now program an AP that can adapt to changing conditions. If we actually wished to deploy an adaptable protocol, a key question would be *when* to adapt. However, our goals is to show that adaptation is feasible, not to research how best to do it. Thus we assume there exists some global policy module that monitors mobility and informs us as to when to adapt. That AN makes such a adaptive protocol feasible means that it would be interesting future work to explore how to build such a monitor.

```
 1: fun routeRequestAtSrc(src, dst) =
 2: if(mobility = 0) then
 3:  OnNeighbor(|dsrRREQ|(src, dst, Get_RREQ_ID(), [ ]),
 4:              broadcast, getRB(), getSrcDev())
 5: else
 6:  OnNeighbor(|aodvRREQ|(src, dst, Get_RREQ_ID(), Get_SrcSeq(),
 7:       Get_DestSeq(dst), 0), broadcast, getRB(), getSrcDev())
 8:
 9:  fun dsrRREQ(src, dst, id, srtRecord) =
10: if(not Check_Dup_Request(src, id)) then (
11:   Mark_Dup_Request(src, id);
12:   SaveIn_RIB(src, srtRecord);
13:   if(thisHostIs(dst)) then
14:     dsrRREP(src, dst, srtRecord, reverse(srtRecord))
15:   else ( (* intermediate nodes *)
16:    let val myAddr = thisHostOf(getSrcDev())
17:        val newSrtRecord = myAddr::srtRecord
18:    in ( try (
19:      let val srcRt:(host) list = LookUp_RIB("DSR", dst)
20:      in dsrRREP(src, dst, listcon(reverse(srcRt),
21:                 newSrtRecord), reverse(srtRecord))
22:      end )
23:     handle NotFound => (
24:         OnNeighbor(|dsrRREQ|(src, dst, id, newSrtRecord),
25:             broadcast, getRB(), getSrcDev())
26:     ) ) end ) )
27: else () (* dup req. discard *)
28:
29: fun aodvRREQ(src, dst, id, srcSeq, dstSeq, hopCount) =
30: if(not Check_Dup_Request(src, id)) then (
31:   Mark_Dup_Request(src, id);
32:   SaveIn_RouteCache(src, srcSeq, hopCount+1, getSrc());
33:   if(thisHostIs(dst)) then
34:      aodvRREP(src, dst, dstSeq, 0)
35:   else ( (* intermediate nodes *)
36:    try (
37:     let val rt_entry:(host*dev*int*int) = LookUp_RIB("AODV", dst)
38:     in (
39:       if(dstSeq > #3 rt_entry) then (
40:          OnNeighbor(|aodvRREQ|(src, dst, id, srcSeq, dstSeq,
41:            hopCount+1), broadcast, getRB(), getSrcDev()))
42:       else
43:          aodvRREP(src, dst, #3 rt_entry, #4 rt_entry)
44:     ) end )
45:    handle NotFound => (
46:      OnNeighbor(|aodvRREQ|(src, dst, id, srcSeq, dstSeq, hopCount+1),
47:                 broadcast, getRB(), getSrcDev()) ) ) )
48: else () (* dup req. discard *)
```

Fig. 8. PLAN for Hybrid Route Request

Figure 8 shows the PLAN program for hybrid routing request. The AP for the hybrid route request contains three functions: `routeRequestAtSrc()`, `dsrRREQ()`, and `aodvRREQ()`. The source, S, evaluates `routeRequestAtSrc()` and decides which protocol to use. At low mobility, S injects a DSR route request packet by calling an `OnNeighbor()` that evaluates `dsrRREQ()` on all the neighbor nodes (Lines 2–4). At high mobility, S spawns a child AP that executes `aodvRREQ()` with the appropriate sequence numbers and a hop counter (Lines 5–7). The two functions, `dsrRREQ()` and `aodvRREQ()`, contain the algorithm for the route request of the corresponding routing protocol.

In the interest of space, Figure 8 shows only our functions for the route request. The complete AP would include the route reply functions as well. When there is valid information for the request (on intermediate nodes or the destination node), a reply packet is generated by the function call, `dsrRREP()` (Lines 14 & 20) or `aodvRREP()` (Lines 34 & 43). The optimized DSR protocol allows intermediate nodes to reply to the request (Lines 19–22). In replying with cached information, the reply-generating node needs to concatenate the route record and cached information (Lines 20–21). In AODV, the destination sequence number is compared to validate freshness of the cached information (Line 39).[3]

7.3   Discussion

Our results show that it is not difficult to take two protocols that are similar in structure, but which differ in many key details and essentially combine them. But what if the protocols differ significantly in their basic structure? An obvious example would be our current reactive algorithms compared to proactive algorithms which always maintain routes to all destinations. Designing a system that adapted between reactive and proactive would be more challenging than our current approach. However, the key point is that if, such a hybrid was designed, AN would make it easier to deploy and evolve. However, it is important to be clear that AN is just an implementation and deployment approach, it offers no silver bullet for making hard design problems easier.

7.4   Simulation of the Hybrid Protocol

One significant limitation of our MANE based implementation is that it is difficult to generate meaningful performance results. This is because MANE nodes are virtualized and typically run many instances on each real node and because the physical network is emulated by using unicast UDP transmission. Thus it is impossible for us to usefully quantitate the overheads imposed by our approach. Despite this, and despite our goal not being primarily to explore the design of hybrid routing algorithms, we still wanted to see if we could show that such an algorithm could indeed result in improved performance when faced with changing mobility. To explore this question we simulated our algorithm as well as DSR and AODV.

---

[3] In PLAN, $\#n$ returns the n-th element of a tuple. In Figure 8, $\#3$ of `rt_entry` is a destination sequence number and $\#4$ is a hop count.

Experimental Setup. As a simulator, we used ns-2, which is a discrete event simulator widely used in networking research [21]. As a measure of performance, we used the Packet Delivery Ratio (PDR). PDR is the ratio of the number of packets received to the number of packets transmitted and larger numbers are better. For a direct comparison, we used CBR traffic rather than TCP traffic because congestion control and flow control offer different loads according to network conditions for TCP. Each node moves according to the "random waypoint" model [12], in which the nodes repeatedly move and then pause. In this model, the pause time and the movement speed characterize the mobility of the network. In each simulation, the same scenarios of movements and traffic are used for DSR, AODV, and the hybrid protocol. The reported values are averages taken from ten simulations under different movements and traffic scenarios.

The packet size is 512 bytes, and 4 packets are generated per second. The number of CBR sources is 25 out of 50 total nodes. For each simulation, 50 nodes move around in a 1000 m × 1000 m square space for 1500 seconds. To simulate changing mobility, we divided the simulation time into 3 parts of 500 seconds each. In the first part (0–500 seconds), there is no movement and the network is stationary. In the second part (500–1000 seconds), all the nodes move at a maximum speed of 10 m/s with a pause time randomly selected between 0 and 250 seconds. In the last 500 seconds, the maximum speed is 20 m/s and the pause time is 0 seconds. For the hybrid protocol, initially DSR is used and as the mobility increases the nodes switch to AODV. Specifically, during the first half of the simulation, route control packets follow DSR semantics and data packets are routed using DSR. After 750 sec., the interface for the routing protocol is changed to AODV and route control packets follow AODV semantics. For the simulation of DSR and AODV, we used the existing ns versions developed by the Monarch project [22].

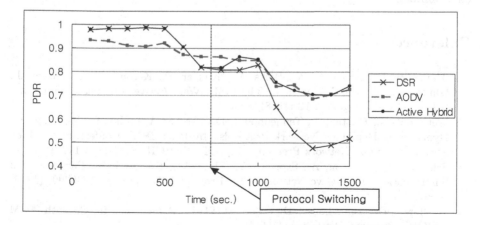

Fig. 9. PDR over time for DSR, AODV, and Hybrid

Results. The simulation results are shown in Figure 9. The x-axis is simulation time and the y-axis is the PDR. We observe that in general as mobility increases, the PDR decreases because of more frequent link failures or changes. However, DSR and AODV have different rates of decrease and there is a crossing point where which is superior changes. In particular, while DSR's is better than that of AODV under low mobility, DSR shows more degradation as mobility increases. On the other hand, AODV is relatively robust to changes in mobility.

Not surprisingly, since the hybrid protocol switches between DSR and AODV, its performance basically follows the better protocol in the whole range of mobility. At low mobility, the hybrid protocol adopts DSR's aggressive route discovery and caching scheme and it performs similarly to DSR. However, as mobility increases, it works like AODV and becomes robust to increased mobility. The region from 500 to 750 seconds is the only exception, because during that period, we have not switched away from DSR. From the simulation results, we see that the hybrid protocol is adaptive to network mobility and suitable for networks under varying mobility environments.

8   Conclusion

In this work, we have demonstrated how AN can be used to deploy, evolve, and adapt ad hoc routing protocols. In some cases, this has used both heavyweight AE programmability and lightweight AP programmability. However, we have also seen that if the right generic services can be provided, lightweight AP programmability can be a powerful tool by itself. These demonstrations argue that AN has achieved its initial goals of facilitating network evolution and customization, at least in this domain. Further we believe these demonstrations show than AN can play a significant role in building MANETs that are easy to deploy, experiment with, and which can respond to the challenges of the diverse MANET environment.

References

1. Alexander, D., Arbaugh, W., Hicks, M., Kakkar, P., Keromytis, A., Moore, J., Gunter, C., Nettles, S., Smith, J.: The SwitchWare Active Network Architecture. IEEE Network Magazine **12** (1998) 29–36
2. Wetherall, D., Guttag, J., Tennenhouse, D.: ANTS: A Toolkit for Building and Dynamically Deploying Network Protocols. In: Proc. IEEE Conference on Open Architectures and Network Programming (OPENARCH'98). (1998) 117–129
3. Schwartz, B., Jackson, A., Strayer, W., Zhou, W., Rockwell, R., Partridge, C.: Smart Packets for Active Networks. In: Proc. of IEEE OPENARCH'99. (1999) 90–97
4. Wetherall, D., Tennehouse, D.: The ACTIVE IP Option. In: Seventh ACM SIGOPS European Workshop. (1996)
5. Silva, S., Yemini, Y., Florissi, D.: The NetScript Active Network System. IEEE Journal on Selected Areas in Communications **19** (2001) 538–551

6. Song, S., Shannon, S., Hicks, M., Nettles, S.: Evolution in Action: Using Active Networking to Evolve Network Support for Mobility. In: Proceedings of the Fourth International Working Conference on Active Networks (IWAN'2002). (2002) 146–161
7. Hicks, M., Kakkar, P., Moore, J., Gunter, C., Nettles, S.: PLAN: A Packet Language for Active Networks. In: Proceedings of the Third ACM SIGPLAN International Conference on Functional Programming Languages, ACM (1998) 86–93
8. Hicks, M., Moore, J., Alexander, D., Gunter, C., Nettles, S.: PLANet: An Active Internetwork. In: Proceedings of the Eighteenth IEEE INFOCOM'99, IEEE (1999) 1124–1133
9. Hicks, M., Moore, J., Nettles, S.: Dynamic software updating. In: Proceedings of the ACM SIGPLAN Conference on Programming Language Design and Implementation, ACM (2001) 13–23
10. Perkins, C.E., ed.: Ad Hoc Networking. Addison-Wesley (2000)
11. Plattner, B., Sterbenz, J.P.: Mobile Wireless Active Networking: Issues and Research Agenda. In: Proceedings of the First IEICE International Workshop on Active Network Technologies and Applications (ANTA). (2002) 71–74
12. Johnson, D., Malz, D.: Dynamic Source Routing in Ad Hoc Wireless Networks. In: Mobile Computing. Kluwer Academic Publishers (1996) 153–181
13. Perkins, C., Royer, E.: Ad hoc On-Demand Distance Vector Routing. In: Proceedings of the 2nd IEEE Workshop on Mobile Computing Systems and Applications. (1999) 90–100
14. Perkins, C., Bhagwat, P.: Highly Dynamic Destination-Sequenced Distance-Vectore Routing (DSDV) for Mobile Computers. In: Proceedings of the conference on Communications architectures, Protocols, and Applications (SIGCOMM'94). (1994) 234–244
15. Broch, J., Maltz, D., Johnson, D., Hu, Y., Jetcheva, J.: A Performance Comparison of Multi-Hop Wireless Ad Hoc Network Routing Protocols. In: Proceedings of the Fourth Annual ACM/IEEE MobiCom'98. (Dallas, TX, Oct., 1998) 85–97
16. Perkins, C., Royer, E., Das, S., Marina, M.: Performance Comparison of Two On-Demand Routing Protocols for Ad Hoc Networks. IEEE Personal Communications 8 (2001) 16–28
17. Tennenhouse, D., Smith, J., Sincoskie, W., Wetherall, D., Minden, G.: A Survey of Active Network Research. IEEE Communications Magazine 35 (1997) 80–86
18. Hicks, M., Nettles, S.: Active Networking means Evolution (or Enhanced Extensibility Required). In: Proceedings of the Second International Working Conference on Active Networks. (2000)
19. (Typed Assembly Language) http://www.cs.cornell.edu/talc/releases.html.
20. Morrisett, G., Crary, K., Glew, N., Grossman, D., Samuels, R., Smith, F., Walker, D., Weirich, S., Zdancewic, S.: TALx86: A Realistic Typed Assembly Language. In: ACM SIGPLAN Workshop on Compiler Support for System Software. (1999) 25–35
21. (The Network Simulator - ns-2) http://www.isi.edu/nsnam/ns/.
22. (The Monarch Project) http://www.monarch.cs.rice.edu/.

Active Networking for TCP over Wireless

Seong-Kyu Song and Scott M. Nettles

Electrical and Computer Engineering Department
The University of Texas at Austin
{sksong,nettles}@ece.utexas.edu

Abstract. TCP assumes that packet losses are due to congestion. Unfortunately, for the increasingly common case of wireless last hops, this may not be the case. The result is poor TCP performance. There has been significant research into this problem, but the solutions either require widespread changes to the network, or are architecturally limited.

Network evolution of this sort is exactly the target of Active Networking (AN). We claim that if some network nodes were AN capable, the range of feasible and deployable solutions to this problem would be greatly increased. We support our claim by presenting a model and architecture of how AN might be deployed to address this problem. We then use this model and architecture to motivate a series of concrete implementations that address various aspects of the problem. These include an implementation of adaptive link control and of the Snoop protocol.

Keywords: TCP, wireless, Active Networking.

1 Introduction

The Transmission Control Protocol (TCP) is one of the central protocols of the Internet. Further, the widespread availability of IEEE 802.11 wireless LANs have made networks in which at least the last hop is wireless common. TCP's congestion control mechanisms assume that all packet losses are caused by congestion. Unfortunately, for wireless links, this is a poor assumption. The result is that over the many networks with wireless hops TCP performs poorly [1].

An obvious solution is simply to do the necessary research to understand how to mix TCP with wireless links and then deploy those solutions throughout the Internet. Not surprisingly, the first step, researching a solution has had significant progress [2,3,4,5,6]. The most general solutions require updating both the TCP implementations on the end hosts and at least some of the routers handling wireless traffic. Unfortunately, in today's Internet, such an update is very difficult to achieve. As a result, there has also been significant work on solutions that do not require updating the end hosts (or perhaps only the one connected wirelessly), essentially restricting the design space to transparent modifications of the basestation connecting the wired network to the wireless one [4,5]. Unfortunately, this architectural restriction can have adverse performance implications [7].

The goals of Active Networking (AN) are to facilitate network evolution and customization. Our claim is that if we had a network that incorporated AN in

G.J. Minden et al. (Eds.): IWAN 2004, LNCS 3912, pp. 156–168, 2007.
© IFIP International Federation for Information Processing 2007

at least some its nodes, the range of feasible and deployable solutions to the problem of TCP over wireless would be greatly increased. Of course, if AN in its most general form penetrated everywhere, it would clearly solve this problem, because it would be easy to simply deploy the best, most general solutions and as new solutions were developed to deploy them. Here we are interested in exploring the implications of more limited AN penetration on possible solutions.

In addition to presenting background material on TCP over wireless and our AN approach and platform, we make our case in two ways. First, to a large extent the issues at hand have to do with implementation architecture. Thus a key part of our argument is a presentation of a model of TCP over wireless systems that lays out the possible design space, followed by a consideration of the high-level architectural issues. Second, to make things concrete, we present implementations of some of the possible solutions.

To implement our demonstrations, we have chosen to use our Mobile Active Network Environment (MANE) [8]. MANE is the most recent embodiment of our work on PLAN [9,10] and is a direct decedent of PLANet [11]. Like our earlier work, MANE combines programmable Active Packets with downloadable node resident Active Extensions. MANE goes further than any of our PLANet implementations in its support for Active Extensions since it provides not just for "plug-in" extensions, but also for "dynamic-update" extensions [12,8].

The remainder of this paper is organized as follows. Section 2 presents background material on TCP over wireless. Section 3 presents our model and architectures and fundamentally addresses the question "How can AN Help?" Sections 4 and 5 present specific implementations and discusses alternative approaches. Section 6 presents performance evaluation and Section 7 concludes the paper.

2 TCP Background

TCP is a connection-oriented transport layer protocol responsible for end-to-end reliable data transmission. There are several problems with TCP's functionality and performance over wireless links. Over such links, there may be more fluctuation of bandwidth and delay than in typical wired networks, stressing TCP's ability to adapt. A key problem of TCP over wireless links arises because TCP's error recovery and congestion control are closely coupled due to the assumption that packet drops are only caused by congestion. Although this assumption is valid over wired links, wireless links are lossy and cannot be assumed to be reliable despite their link-level error recovery schemes [13]. These points are reinforced in the literature, where it has been shown that TCP's performance significantly degrades over wireless links [1]. A variety of solutions have been proposed for the problem of TCP over wireless links [2]. They can be classified into two main categories: *End-to-end* and *Transparent*.

End-to-end solutions require modifying TCP at both end points while maintaining end-to-end semantics [2,3,14,15,16]. These approaches are based on the distinction between congestion losses and corruption losses [14,17]. The drawback of these approaches is that they require fundamental changes to TCP on the hosts. The need to replace already deployed versions of TCP means that deployment of these approaches will be difficult and slow. Besides, this approach needs more care because it is unclear that the modified TCP will perform well both on wired and wireless links. From experience, we see that it may take time to find problems of newly deployed protocols that were thought to be well-designed.

In the transparent approach, link-level losses are hidden from the transport layer [4,5,6]. These approaches attempt to improve TCP performance either by using enhanced link control schemes [4] or by utilizing Performance Enhancing Proxies (PEP) [18,5,6]. Therefore, existing hosts operate normally without knowing whether the connection is over wireless or wired links. The main advantage of these approaches is that they can more practically be deployed incrementally. It is easier to modify link-layer protocols on the nodes with wireless links than the TCP protocol deployed on every end-host. However, as we will see from the TCP snoop protocol, link layers may be aware of the transport layers' semantics and session state information. In addition, this approach has the possibility of redundancy, inefficiency, or even ineffectiveness [7].

3   How Can Active Networking Help?

Our goal is not to devise fundamentally new schemes for solving the basic problem of TCP over wireless links, but rather to show how AN could be used to help to implement and deploy existing schemes. At a high-level, this is an architectural question, where and in what form can AN be useful? To answer this question, we begin by creating a model of the underlaying system. The section concludes by considering a variety of architectures that map AN capabilities on to this model. The rest of the paper is principally an exploration of some specific instances of these mappings.

3.1   Model

The model of a TCP session shown in Figure 1 captures many of the key architectural issues. Communication is between a Mobile Host (MH) and a Fixed Host (FH). A Base Station (BS) connects the wired network where the FH resides to the wireless one where the MH resides. Unlike most of the related work discussed above, we include the case where the MH may need multiple wireless hops to reach the BS. Also, the related work focuses on the case where the bulk of the data is being transmitted from the FH to the MH. In general, we are also concerned with the case where the MH is the primary source of data.

Figure 1 also illustrates some of our thinking about where and what kind of AN technology might be deployed. We subscribe to the SwitchWare [9] architecture of AN, in which there are both active packets (APs) containing executable code and active extensions (AEs) which are downloaded dynamically to modify or extend nodes. We assume that we have full control of the MH and thus can expect that both APs and AEs can be used there when needed. Similarly, we entertain the possibility that the wireless network is "all active" and thus that

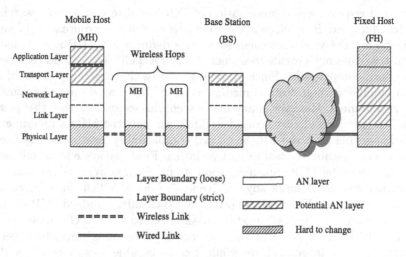

Fig. 1. AN model for TCP over wireless

we could potentially deploy both AEs and APs there. Three possibilities exist for the BS. First, if the BS can employ no activeness, then we are restricted to end-to-end solutions (and must have an active enabled FH). Second, perhaps for security reasons, the BS may allow AP processing, but not allow AEs to be downloaded. Finally, the BS may support both APs and AEs. The intermediate links between the BS and FH are not a source of the problems we are trying to address and so without loss of generality, we can assume they are not "active." However, in the case that the BS is not "active," some BS-centric approaches will work if deployed at an intermediate node. Finally, the FH has the same basic options as the BS. Of course, it is likely that a MH will have more control over the BS than the FH, so it is likely that in practice the FH will allow fewer "active" options than the BS.

Finally, Figure 1 also touches on the issue of layer-crossing. The problems we are addressing come fundamentally because TCP violates the basic layering principles of the network by making an incorrect assumption about the nature of the wireless physical layer. Thus it is not surprising that many of the approaches to solving these problems also violate layering. In fact, one of our premises is that since AN can support flexible controlled layer-crossing, it is well suited to these solutions. Thus the figure shows which layers we expect to be the most "permeable" as well as at which layers we most expect to deploy either APs or AEs. One case that is not illustrated is the use of "shim" layers. These are simply layers that are inserted between existing layers.

3.2 Requirements, Architecture, and Capabilities

Given the basic system model, we state two system requirements, consider the possible architecture of solutions and discuss several AN capabilities that potentially play an important role in the solution space.

The first requirement is preservation of TCP's end-to-end semantics: reliable, in-order, duplicate free delivery. We view this as a strict requirement of any solution; taking the view that these semantics define what TCP is and that any system that does not provide these features is not TCP. The second requirement is backward compatibility. Since in some scenarios the possibility exists of using AN to modify the end hosts implementation of TCP, we do not view this as a strict requirement. However, many other scenarios exist that deny this possibility and so it is important to consider. Since we view the MH as fundamentally more changeable than the FH, backward compatibility issues focus at the FH. Backward compatibility then takes two forms. First are systems where the FH is "active," but the TCP implementation is not. Such systems admit end-to-end approaches, but must mask any "activeness" from the TCP layer. Second are systems in which the FH is unchangeable and transmits standard TCP segments. In this case, any "activeness" must be masked before the FH. Given our assumption that the Internet is not active, this means "activeness" must be masked at or before the BS. In general, we would like to be able to support "islands" of AN functionality isolated by conventional networks. We will illustrate how this may be done in Subsection 4.3.

In our view, there are two basic architectural approaches: horizontal and vertical. The horizontal approach works between peer layers and does not cross layer boundaries. For example, link layer protocols over wireless hops can adaptively cope with fluctuating channel conditions and reduce link-level errors. An important special case is when the peer layers are dynamically inserted (and removed) shim layers. This is essentially the idea of Protocol Boosters [19]. In Section 4, we will discuss how our implementation system makes this idea especially useful. In contrast, the vertical approach allows layering violations and information sharing between layers. For example, the BS is allowed to cross layers in dealing with TCP-aware processing. To avoid congestion control on end hosts, the BS attempts to foil fast retransmit by adaptively manipulating duplicate ACKs.

One of the key AN capabilities that can be leveraged to assist us is the ability to adapt quickly, perhaps even on a packet-by-packet basis. This ability derives from the fact that the code (or data used by that code) contained in APs can change in each packet. We will show an example of this based on link error control in Subsection 4.3. A final AN capability of importance centers on AEs. AEs can be dynamically downloaded and can add to or modify the behavior of node resident code. The implication of this is that even protocols that need new or modified node resident functionality can be incrementally deployed on-the-fly. As an example, consider a MH that wishes to use an enhanced protocol that requires node-resident functionality at the BS. Assuming the BS supports AEs, then the MH can simply extend the BS. Essentially BS has been adapted to support the new protocol.

4   Horizontal Adaptive Link Error Control

One obvious approach is simply to improve the error characteristics of the wireless link. As our first example, we consider how to use the horizontal approach to

```
1: fun checkCRC(chk, crc) =
2:  let val crcCalcul = crc32(chk)
3:      val nexthop = defaultRoute(getSrc()) in
4:  ( if(crcCalcul = crc) then (
5:      eval(chk);
6:      OnNeighbor(|deQueue|(), #1 nexthop, getRB(), #2 nexthop)
7:  ) else ()
8:  ) end
9:
10: fun arq(dst, chk) =
11:  let val crc = crc32(chk)
12:      val nexthop = defaultRoute(dst) in
13:  ( enQueue(|checkCRC|(chk, crc), #1 nexthop);
14:    OnNeighbor(|checkCRC|(chk, crc), #1 nexthop, getRB(), #2 nexthop)
15:  ) end
```

Fig. 2. PLAN for basic ARQ

implement this idea. The tricky issue is that how best to do this is a function of the link error rate, which is changing dynamically. If the error rates are very low, it might make sense to have no link-level error correction. At higher, but still moderate error rates, a basic ARQ scheme is employed because of its simplicity and low overhead. However, as error rates increase, frequent retransmissions degrade performance. Thus at high rates, to control errors more efficiently, FEC is added into ARQ. By combining two coding procedures, hybrid ARQ/FEC can get the benefits of both [20,21]. In this section, we show how PLAN/MANE can be used to implement this adaptivity using a shim layer. For adaptive link error control, we place the shim layer between the link layer and network layer.

4.1 Basic ARQ

We begin with a simple ARQ scheme. For simplicity, we assume we have only one wireless hop. Thus we expect the round-trip times seen by the link-level ARQ to be small. Therefore, we adopt an idle RQ or *stop-and-wait ARQ* scheme rather than a *selective-repeat ARQ* or *go-back-N ARQ* scheme [22]; however it would be straightforward to include other ARQ schemes when desirable. In that case, we would not need to change the node-resident services, but would use a different PLAN program containing the required ARQ algorithm.

Figure 2 shows the PLAN code for our ARQ scheme. This code contains the ARQ scheme in chunks, such as CRC calculation, timeout and retransmission, and ACK reply. For error detection, the sender calculates a CRC-32 (Line 11) and sends a new chunk (checkCRC) containing the original chunk and the corresponding CRC (Line 14). It also stores the packet in the interface queue for retransmission (Line 13). The destination evaluates the chunk, thus evoking checkCRC, which executes to compute the CRC of the received chunk and comparing it with the original CRC (Lines 2,4). If the results are the same, the original chunk is evaluated on the destination (Line 5). The destination is also required to generate a chunk to invoke the deQueue() function on the sender. This chunk works like an acknowledgment and frees the packet in the interface queue (Line 6). Note in practice, this ACK chunk might also implement other functionality as well, such as updating an RTT estimate. This particular code is specialized for a single wireless hop because it always does the CRC check on its neighbor. However, it could be used from either the BS or the MH. Further, it would be easy to generalize this approach to support multiple wireless hops. In this case, if transmitted from the BS, it would simply defer execution of checkCRC until it reached its final destination and it would also need to carry with it the address of the BS to provide the "ack" with a destination.

4.2   ARQ/FEC

By utilizing ARQ/FEC at high error rates, we can maintain constant throughput at the expense of encoding/decoding overhead and complexity. The code for ARQ/FEC is similar to that for the basic ARQ. The key difference is that before the original chunk is transmitted it is encoded using Reed-Solomon coding and then when it is received, it is decoded. The code for this case can be found in Song [23]. By including the FEC strength in the chunks, we could control the level of error correction on a packet-by-packet basis.

4.3   Adaptive Link Control

Given basic ARQ and ARQ/FEC the question is how to combine them so that the appropriate one is used based on the quality of the channel. Figure 3 presents code which does this when sent from a FH. It depends on the BS to identify itself by returning true when isThisHostBS as well as to maintain a measure of channel quality, queried by isChanGood. The basic idea is that the packet single hops through the network (Lines 2,17) looking for the BS (Line 3). At the BS, it queries the channel state (Line 4) and if it is good, it uses no error control scheme (Line 5). If the channel is not as good, it uses either basic ARQ (Lines 9,10) or ARQ/FEC (Lines 13,14). Note checkCRC is the same as the previous code and decode is used for RS decoding. The fact that the algorithm is encoded in the packet means that we can apply this adaptation on a packet by packet basis. This is quite similar to protocol boosters, except that the packet itself decides whether "boosting" is needed or not.

4.4   AN for Channel Monitoring

For adaptive link control, we need to track the state of the channel. One approach is for the sender to use ACKs (or rather their lack) to tell when the channel is bad. With AN it is easy to do better. The key observation is that the receiver is in the best position to monitor the channel, while the sender is the one that needs this information. Assuming the receiver records channel information, we can use APs to query this state.

Figure 4 shows the code for an out-of-band channel monitor. The function getChanInfo() (Line 2) defines a standard interface to get information on channel characteristics. This function returns various channel information depending

```
1: fun adapLink(dst, chk) =
2:   let val nexthop = defaultRoute(dst) in
3:   (if(isThisHostBS()) then (
4:      if(isChanGood(#1 nexthop)) then
5:        OnNeighbor(|noControl|(chk), #1 nexthop, getRB(), #2 nexthop)
6:      else (
7:        enQueue(|adapLink|(dst, chk), #1 nexthop);
8:        if(isChanSoSo(#1 nexthop)) then (
9:          let val crc = crc32(chk) in
10:             OnNeighbor(|checkCRC|(chk, crc), #1 nexthop, getRB(),
11:                        #2 nexthop)  end )
12:       else ( (* if channel is worse, use RS coding *)
13:          let val codeword = fecEncoding(chk, "RS", 255, 223) in
14:            OnNeighbor(|decode|(codeword, "RS", 255, 223), #1 nexthop,
15:                       getRB(), #2 nexthop)  end ) ) )
16:   else
17:     OnNeighbor(|adapLink|(dst, chk), #1 nexthop, getRB(), #2 nexthop)
18:   ) end
```

Fig. 3. PLAN for Adaptive Link Control

```
1: fun report(indicator) =
2:   let val measure = getChanInfo(indicator)
3:       val src = defaultRoute(getSrc()) in
4:         OnNeighbor(|print|(measure), #1 src, getRB(), #2 src)
5:   end
6:
7: fun probe(dst) =
8:   let val nexthop = defaultRoute(dst) in
9:     OnNeighbor(|report|("RSS"), #1 nexthop, getRB(), #2 nexthop)
10:  end
```

Fig. 4. PLAN for Monitoring RSS

on the parameter, indicator, such as the Received Signal Strength or Signal-to-Noise Ratio. The code composes a query and sends it (Line 9). The query executes on the receiver and returns the result to the sender (Line 4). Note that this is much more flexible than the conventional approach, which would require specifying a special packet format and protocol for such queries.

An important variation would be to piggyback the query chunk on a data packet. This is easy to do because chunks are data and it is easy to compose various chunk oriented calculations. The result is that such queries can be done without sending additional packets and yet remain transparent to the data flow. This ability to piggyback control on data transparently, solves a key problem with Protocol Boosters [19], controlling when to add or remove a booster.

Finally, consider a system like IEEE 802.11 which precedes each data transmission with a request-to-send (RTS)/clear-to-send exchange(CTS). Then the

RTS could act as a channel probe, while the CTS could return the channel state to the sender, which would then be able to choose a error correction scheme or FEC strength. In a conventional network, this would require changing the format and function of the RTS and CTS. In however, if the wireless link sent APs for its RTS and CTS, then adding to or modifying the function of these parts of the protocol would become just a matter of packet programming.

5   Vertical Snoop Protocol

Even with adaptive link error control, packet drops may be still possible and the resulting congestion control action can cause performance degradation. In vertical adaptivity, collaboration and information sharing across layers on the BS are allowed to adaptively control the TCP flow. We claim that AN is advantageous because AN facilitates cross-layering implementation by allowing layer-specific information to be included in active packets.

In this approach, the lower layer protocols on the BS are aware of TCP semantics and adjust TCP flow information to prevent congestion control from taking place due to packet drops over wireless links. Further, by following up the parts of the end hosts' TCP Control Block (TCB) [24], the BS can take actions on incorrect congestion control, such as adjusting RTT measures and screening three duplicate ACKs. Using packet programming, we can deploy the snoop protocol onto the BS, which can improve performance of TCP connections from fixed hosts (FH) to mobile hosts (MH).

We have implemented these ideas in the form of a PLAN/MANE implementation of the snoop protocol, but space does not permit us to exhibit the code. It can be found in Song [23]. Substantial parts of the snoop protocol are implemented in active packets and this example shows how to easily deploy a new protocol. There is no need to update protocol stacks on the BS. Service extensions on the BS mainly implement the cross-layering mechanisms. As an adaptation layer, the service extensions transform active packets to TCP segments or vice versa. Evaluation of the PLAN packet on the BS actualizes the snoop protocol and enhances TCP performance over wireless links. This is fundamentally different from the Proxy Transport Service [25] in that our approach is transparent and maintains TCP semantics.

6   Performance Evaluation

In this section, present our performance evaluation, starting with some details of our implementation and the network setup. We then present a comparison of our adaptive link protocol with the nonadaptive protocols it is composed of. We conclude with an evaluation of our snoop protocol.

6.1   Evaluation Setup

To support our current experiments required some additions to the version of MANE discussed in [8]. The most significant was an implementation of an active

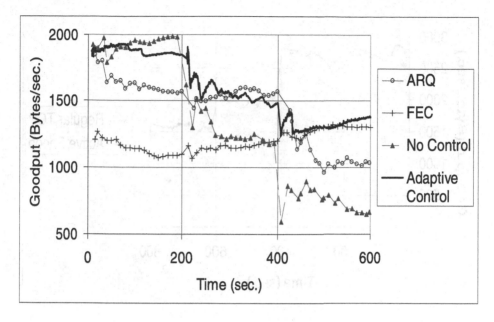

Fig. 5. Comparison of Link Error Control Techniques

version of TCP. To achieve this, we added a data structure called the Transmission Control Block (TCB) [24]. Each TCP host maintains information about TCP connections and TCB is used to store this information. Among the variables maintained in the TCB, we added the basic ones needed for the congestion control and the sliding window protocol, which included sequence numbers, round trip time (RTT) measures and variance, timeout values for retransmission, and the congestion window. In addition to TCP, we added the functions for calculating a 32-bit Cyclic Redundancy Check (CRC-32) to our frames as a Frame Check Sequence (FCS) and for Reed-Solomon encoding/decoding [26].

In all of our experiments, we used the same network topology. The MH and the FH are connected through the BS. The MH is one wireless hop away from the BS, and the BS is connected to the FH through one router using wired links. We emulated the lossy wireless channel by randomly changing bits in packets. The number of corrupted bits is determined by the channel's Bit Error Rate (BER); the channel's BER is changing on a scenario basis.

6.2 Active Link Error Control

In Figure 5, we present a performance comparison of four link error correction schemes: no error correction, ARQ, ARQ/FEC, and the adaptive hybrid protocol shown in Figure 3. Because we wanted to demonstrate adaptivity, rather than experiment with channel monitoring, we had our channel monitoring functions return the correct value, rather than trying to estimate it dynamically. In this case, the MH is the TCP sender.

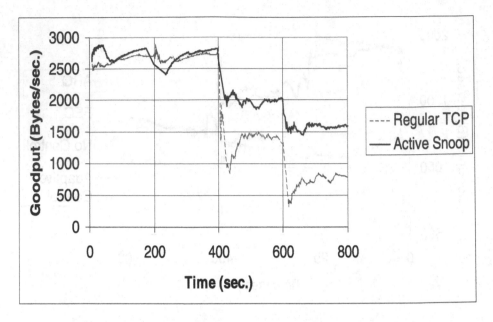

Fig. 6. Comparison of Regular TCP and Active snoop protocol

Figure 5 has time along the X-axis and goodput along the Y-axis. Initially, the channel is not lossy, but its error rate increases at time 200 and then worsens further at time 400. The individual protocols perform as we would expect, with the no error correction case showing the strongest dependence on the error rate and ARQ/FEC showing the least. The more interesting result is for the adaptive protocol. At low error rate it equals or sometimes betters the performance of ARQ. When it does better it is actually doing no error correction. When the error rate increases, it is able to detect this and adapt using ARQ or ARQ/FEC, respectively.

6.3   Active Snoop Protocol

Figure 6 shows a performance comparison of "regular" TCP when no snooping is done at the BS and with our snoop protocol. In this case, the FH is the sender. Again, time is along the X-axis and goodput is along the Y-axis. Initially, the channel is not lossy, but its error rate increases at time 200 and worsens further at time 400 and 600. As expected, when there are no or low errors, the performance of the two versions is similar. However, as error rates increase the snoop protocol outperforms the regular TCP by suppressing unnecessary congestion control.

7   Conclusion

TCP is not well suited to networks with wireless links. Conventional solutions to this problem are limited by the need to be transparent and backward compatible.

AN can ease these limitations by greatly increasing the possible implementation and deployment strategies. We demonstrated this by first modelling the TCP over wireless system and then showing how AN architectures and capabilities can apply to that model. We then showed a number of implementations that used these architectures and capabilities to help wireless TCP performance. We used MANE to evaluate the performance of these implementations, showing that they behave as expected.

We expect that future work will focus on further exploring our two architectural styles. For example, as one of the horizontal approaches, the network layers of the MH and the BSes could adaptively change paths between them so that link fluctuation do not affect the end-to-end flow. We could expand this approach into support for handoff. Another horizontal approach would be to adaptively change the Maximum Transmission Unit of the wireless link, so that smaller packets are sent when the link has a high bit error rate. On the other hand, if the FH is AN-capable, we can develop more efficient adaptive control over TCP flows. We expect to apply this advantage to handling handoff, during which harsh link deterioration and route changes happen at the same time.

References

1. Pentikousis, K.: TCP in Wired-cum-Wireless Environments. IEEE Communications Surveys (2000) 2–14
2. Balakrishnan, H., Padmanabhan, V.N., Seshan, S., Katz, R.H.: A Comparison of Mechanisms for Improving TCP Performance over Wireless Links. In: Proc. of ACM SIGCOMM'96. (1996) 256–269
3. Ramakrishnan, K., Floyd, S., Black, D.: The Addition of Explicit Congestion Notification (ECN) to IP. RFC 3168, IETF (2001) http://www.ietf.org/rfc/rfc3168.txt.
4. Ayanoglu, E., Paul, S., thomas F. LaPorta, Sabnani, K.K., Gitlin, R.D.: AIRMAIL: A Link-Layer Protocol for Wireless Networks. ACM Wireless Networks 1 (1995) 47–60
5. Balakrishnan, H., Seshan, S., Amir, E., Katz, R.H.: Improving TCI/IP Performance over Wireless Networks. In: Proc. of ACM MobiCom'95. (1995) 2–11
6. Bakre, A., Badrinath, B.: I-TCP: Indirect TCP for Mobile Hosts. In: Proc. of the 15th Int. Conf. on Distributed Systems. (1995) 136–143
7. DeSimone, A., Chuah, M.C., Yue, O.C.: Throughput Performance of Transport-Layer Protocols over Wireless LANs. In: Proc. of IEEE GLOBECOM'93. Volume 1. (1993) 542–549
8. Song, S.K., Shannon, S., Hicks, M., Nettles, S.: Evolution in Action: Using Active Networking to Evolve Network Support for Mobility. In: Proc. of IWAN 2002. (2002) 146–161
9. Alexander, D., Arbaugh, W., Hicks, M., Kakkar, P., Keromytis, A., Moore, J., Gunter, C., Nettles, S., Smith, J.: The SwitchWare Active Network Architecture. IEEE Network Magazine 12 (1998) 29–36
10. Hicks, M., Kakkar, P., Moore, J., Gunter, C., Nettles, S.: PLAN: A Packet Language for Active Networks. In: Proc. of ACM SIGPLAN International Conference on Functional Programming Languages, ACM (1998) 86–93
11. Hicks, M., Moore, J., Alexander, D., Gunter, C., Nettles, S.: PLANet: An Active Internetwork. In: Proc. of IEEE INFOCOM'99, IEEE (1999) 1124–1133

12. Hicks, M., Moore, J., Nettles, S.: Dynamic software updating. In: Proceedings of the ACM SIGPLAN Conference on Programming Language Design and Implementation, ACM (2001) 13–23
13. Chockalingam, A., Zorzi, M., Tralli, V.: Wireless TCP Performance with Link Layer FEC/ARQ. In: ICC'99 Proceedings. Volume 2., IEEE (1999) 1212–1216
14. Krishnan, R., Sterbenz, J.P., Eddy, W.M., Partridge, C., Allman, M.: Explicit transport error notification (ETEN) for error-prone wireless and satellite networks. Computer Networks **46** (2004) 343–362
15. Akyildiz, I.F., Morabito, G., Palazzo, S.: TCP-Peach: A New Congestion Control Scheme for Satellite IP Networks. IEEE/ACM Transactions on Networking **9** (2001) 307–321
16. Casetti, C., Gerla, M., Mascolo, S., Sansadidi, M., Wang, R.: TCP Westwood: End-to-End Congestion Control for Wired/Wireless Networks. Wireless Networks Journal **8** (2002) 467–479
17. Biaz, S., Vaidya, N.H.: Distinguishing Congestion Losses from Wireless Transmission Losses: A Negative Result. In: Proceedings of the Seventh International Conference on Computer Communications and Networks (IC3N). (1998)
18. Border, J., Kojo, M., Griner, J., Montenegro, G., Shelby, Z.: Performance Enhancing Proxies Intended to Mitigate Link-Related Degradations. RFC 3135, IETF (2001) http://www.ietf.org/rfc/rfc3135.txt.
19. Feldmeier, D.C., McAuley, A.J., Smith, J.M., Bakin, D.S., Marcus, W.S., Raleigh, T.M.: Protocol Boosters. IEEE Journal on Selected Areas in Communications **16** (1998) 437–444
20. Brayer, K.: Error Control Techniques Using Binary Symbol Burst Codes. IEEE Trans. on Communication Technology **16** (1968) 199–214
21. Burton, H.O., Sullivan, D.D.: Errors and Error Control. Proc. of IEEE **60** (1972) 1293–1310
22. Lin, S., Daniel J. Costello, Jr.: 15. In: Error Control Coding: Fundamentals and Applications. Prentice-Hall, Inc. (1983)
23. Song, S.K.: Applying Active Network Adaptability to Wireless Networks. PhD thesis, The University of Texas at Austin (2004)
24. Postel, J.: Transmission Control Protocol. RFC 793, IETF (1981) http://www.ietf.org/rfc/rfc793.txt.
25. Patil, S., Kumar, M.: TCP Enhancement Using Active Network Based Proxy Transport Service. In: Proc. of IWAN 2003. (2003) 103–114
26. Reed, I.S., Solomon, G.: Polynomial Codes Over Certain Finite Fields. Journal of the Society for Industrial and Applied Mathematics **8** (1960) 300–304

A Detection and Filter System for Use Against Large-Scale DDoS Attacks in the Internet Backbone*

Lukas Ruf, Arno Wagner, Károly Farkas, and Bernhard Plattner

Computer Engineering and Networks Laboratory (TIK)
Swiss Federal Institute of Technology (ETH) Zurich
CH-8092 Zurich/Switzerland
{ruf,wagner,farkas,plattner}@tik.ee.ethz.ch

Abstract. Distributed denial of service (DDoS) attacks in the Internet pose huge problems on nowadays communication infrastructure. Attacks either destroy information or impede access to a service. Since the significance of the Internet to business and economy is growing rapidly, efficient protection mechanisms are urgently required to protect hosts from being infected and, more important, sites from being attacked. Detection of DDoS attacks requires deep packet inspection at link speed, and context-dependent packet handling for countermeasures. This functionality is not achievable with nowadays commercial high-performance routers.

In this paper, we therefore present our problem space exploration of DDoS attacks and propose a flexible service architecture for detection and filter mechanisms to counteract DDoS attacks. To achieve the performance required for backbone routers together with the flexibility needed for services counteracting DDoS attacks, we base the proposal on our PromethOS NP router platform that manages and controls hierarchical network nodes built of network and host processors.

1 Introduction and Motivation

Present day communication infrastructure has been seriously threatened by large-scale distributed denial of service (DDoS) attacks in the Internet. These attacks destroy information or hinder customers from accessing specific services. Services provided in the Internet like on-line stock trading, virtual travel agencies or book-stores are very important to economy already today. The Economist reported in May 2004 [31]: "The 200m Americans who now have web access are

---

* This work is partially sponsored by the Swiss Federal Institute of Technology (ETH) Zurich, the Swiss Federal Office for Education and Science (BBW Grant 99.0533), the Swiss National Science Foundation under Grant 200021-102026/1 and Swiss Academic Research Network (SWITCH). PromethOS v1 has been developed by ETH as a partner in IST Project FAIN (IST-1999-10561). Moreover, we would like to acknowledge the great support received from the IBM Zurich Research Laboratory, and we acknowledge the valuable feedback and comments by the reviewers.

G.J. Minden et al. (Eds.): IWAN 2004, LNCS 3912, pp. 169–187, 2007.
© IFIP International Federation for Information Processing 2007

likely to spend more than US$120 billion online this year." But in eCommerce, brief inaccessibility of services results in loss of business [31]. Since the impact of eCommerce on economy is expected to grow further, the risk of economic damage resulting from a large-scale Internet attack increases [11]. The situation becomes more dramatic because the number of attacks increases at least at the same pace as the impact of eCommerce does. Of further threatening importance is the fact that newly discovered errors in soft- or hardware are exploited more rapidly for fresh attacks [32].

The effect of large-scale DDoS attacks in the Internet correlates with the number of infected hosts that launch attacks towards other sites. Hence the threat emerges as more and more private and insufficiently managed hosts are connected to the Internet by broadband lines. Home users are rarely aware of the problems and dangers in the Internet nor are they able to manage and protect their hosts effectively. But eCommerce flourishes not at least thanks to the widespread use of the Internet by home users [31]. Companies afford security and system administration teams quite often, but they suffer from similar problems.

To effectively protect the Internet, hosts need to be protected from becoming an attacker as well as from being attacked at any site. It is hard if not unfeasible to install protection mechanisms at this level of granularity without blocking daily business. Hence, detection and countermeasures are required that approach this problem at the level of border routers or gateways to protect larger areas in the Internet.

Fighting DDoS attacks requires in-depth packet inspection to identify malicious streams in the flood of traffic. With today's commercial high-performance routers, however, payload analysis is not possible, usually. Or if it is, the functionality is coded either in firmware or hard-wired in the box. Attack schemes vary a lot over time. In addition, the period becomes shorter between the first detection of an exploit and the widespread launch of the attack. So, it is crucial that large-scale DDoS attacks are defeated on routers as close to the core of the Internet as possible. Specific Anti-DDoS components must be installed, configured and removed on request. For obvious reasons, the deployment of the specific detection and countermeasure components must not interfere with other services. Further, they must be able to tackle the problem of known as well as unknown attacks semi-automatically according to predefined policies.

Active Networking (AN) [30] has proposed the concept of execution environments (EEs) to address the challenges of exchanging and extending service functionality on the routers at run-time. So far, EEs have been instantiated only on a single general purpose processor (GPP) as found in legacy personal computers. But single GPP configurations are not able to cope with the demands of nowadays border or backbone traffic in the Internet. To increase the degree of programmability and simultaneously of flexibility at interface level, processor manufacturers have proposed the architecture of Network Processors (NPs) [14, 15, 22] to be embedded in network interface cards (so-called NP-blades).

Built of control and packet processors[1], they provide additional processing capabilities and capacity in addition to the host processors. A hierarchical network node provides, thus, a perfect hardware platform for the envisioned Anti-DDoS service since packet processors are able to process packets at line rate, and processors on upper tiers provide the management and control functionality besides room for further packet processing. However, it is extremely difficult to provide a dynamically extensible router platform that provides the required abstractions and is able to manage a hierarchical network node if component based services must be able to span all tiers of the processor hierarchy. We propose PromethOS NP [24,25] as the dynamically code-extensible router platform for the envisioned Anti-DDoS service. It provides the abstractions required for node-internal communication among service components by which services are allowed to span arbitrary processors. Further, it provides the mechanisms to install, configure, instantiate and remove service components on any code-extensible processor of the processor hierarchy. Hence, the goal in this paper is to propose an architecture of an Internet backbone Anti-DDoS service for our powerful PromethOS NP router architecture.

Therefore, we structure the remainder of this paper as follows: in section 2, we present a problem-space exploration of detection mechanisms and countermeasures against large-scale DDoS attacks in the Internet to extract commonalities required for our service architecture. We briefly present the concepts and architecture of PromethOS NP in section 3. In section 4, we propose our Anti-DDoS service architecture for PromethOS NP, and present related work in section 5. Our paper is concluded by section 6, in which we give a summary and an outlook to further work.

2 Large-Scale Internet Attacks

The main type of large-scale Internet attacks we focus on here is an initial worm-driven [29] compromise of a large number of hosts, followed by an optional Distributed Denial-of-Service (DDoS) attack that uses the freshly compromised hosts as attack platform. We identify three main activities [32] during this type of attack: target identification, target infection and DDoS attack. The first two activities together are also called *worm propagation*. Worm propagation can sometimes also be done in a single step, e.g. when host probing and compromise can be done with a single data packet.

The attack activity can be started by a trigger, for example a time, reception of a message from an attack control network (see e.g. [33]) or completion of a specific number of infection attempts. It can be done in parallel to worm

---

[1] NP vendors do not use a consistent naming scheme to refer to the code-extensible processors: the Intel IXP-architecture refers to the first-level processors as *micro-engines* while the IBM PowerNP identifies them as *picoprocessors* or *core language processors*. Second-level processors are named differently, as well. For this reason, we refer to the first level of processing engines as *packet processors* and to those of the second level as *control processors*.

propagation, however this usually impacts worm propagation speed negatively and is generally not done.

We now describe the basics of the attack model in more detail and identify common characteristics.

2.1 Activity 1: Target Identification

A vulnerable host offers network functionality that can be compromised. The vulnerability can be located in an application, for example a P2P filesharing client or web server, or in the operating system itself, e.g. in the network stack. It is also possible to use several different vulnerabilities in worm propagation. In order to recognize that a host is vulnerable, a vulnerable network functionality has to be found on it. This is done by sending a specific probe over the network. Probes consist of one or several specifically constructed packets that are sent to a host. A probe can consist of several sub-probes.

2.2 Activity 2: Target Infection

After a vulnerable host has been identified, it still needs to be compromised. This is done by using the vulnerability to transport to and start exploit code on the target. This may involve a multi-stage process where several steps are needed, each involving specific network activity. The end result is that the work code runs on the target host and is able to propagate further from it. Note that no complete host compromise is needed. Compromising a network application, e.g. an email client, or part of an operating system may already be enough. As an extreme case worms that use vulnerabilities in other worms (that have previously infected the target) exist. The new host is now called *infected*.

A border case is single packet propagation, were target identification and compromise are done with a single network packet, e.g. the Sapphire worm [5] needs only a single UDP packet of 404 Bytes for a successful propagation step. Single packet infection requires the use of a protocol that can transport data in the first packet, like UDP. Many vulnerabilities also do not allow single packet propagation, e.g. because several data transfers are needed. Code Red [9, 3] is an example of a worm that uses TCP with its three-way handshake [23]. As an example of a multiple protocol infection, the Blaster worm [6], uses TFTP [28] to retrieve code in a second step of the infection, after an initial exploit was used to initiate the second step.

2.3 Activity 3: Attack

The third step is to execute one or several attacks. Sets of compromised hosts have also been used for other purposes, e.g. as relay for unsolicited commercial email (SPAM), which is of interest to organized crime. This worm creation purpose has been predicted by Schechter and Smith in [26] and recently been confirmed to exist in practice by the German computer magazine c't [8]. In this paper we only deal with the use of compromised hosts as attack platform for DDoS attacks.[2]

2.4 Detection and Possible Countermeasures

We differentiate between the terms *byte-pattern*, *flow-pattern* and *traffic-pattern*. A *byte-pattern* is a sequence of bytes within a packet. A *flow-pattern* is a sequence of packets that together forms a specific attack. A *traffic-pattern* is an aggregation of multiple flow-patterns that target the same site. We do attack detection by trying to observe traffic anomalies. We argue that traffic-pattern need to be analyzed for this. For the identification of packets belonging to a specific attack, attack signatures need to be determined. Attack signatures can be detected either by byte-patterns or flow-patterns. Once this has been done for a specific attack, a countermeasure can be selected and activated. We base our detection and countermeasure service on four fundamental functional elements named *Capture, Identification, Filter* and *Slowdown*.

Data Capturing: In order to detect a worm during its propagation phase in a high-speed network, access to more than abstracted traffic data (e.g. NetFlow [7]) is desirable. One promising possibility is to obtain information about specific suspicious traffic from abstract data without payload information and then capture concrete packets to gain more insights. As an example, transferred worm code looks the same in most observed worms. If, e.g., a lot of TFTP transfers are observed, it would be desirable to find out whether most carry the same payload. Furthermore, it is desirable to capture complete instances of the transferred code. The same is true for the exploits used and for the packets sent in a DDoS attack. This information can then not only be used to better understand the worm, but is also essential in generating specific filters or slowdown mechanisms and in identification of infected hosts.

Identification of Compromised Hosts: One countermeasure desirable is the filtering of all traffic from infected hosts. This serves to block further infections as well as attacks or other misuse of compromised hosts. It also serves to force host operators to repair the compromised host software. In order to allow host filters, infected hosts have to be reliably identified. Generally, this needs payload information. The reason is that worms and DDoS attacks frequently use protocols that are also used for other purposes. Without payload based detection of infected and attacking hosts, the number of wrongly identified and blocked hosts could be large and this type of countermeasure can do more damage than good.

Filters: Besides host blocking, it is desirable to filter attack traffic out based on protocol and payload information. One reason is that the set of compromised

---

[2] Since worm spreading and host infection might be the attack itself, we refer to the combination of all three activities by the term *attack* if we do not state the different activities explicitly.

hosts may not always be identified fully, for example if some infected hosts do not propagate the worm but wait silently after infection until they start to participate in a DDoS attack. In a filter, it may, e.g., be desirable not to block all HTTP traffic to a site under attack, but just a specific query or query type as emitted by some known infected hosts. In order for this to work, byte-patterns have to be identified and then a filter for these patterns has to be constructed and installed on the fly.

Slowdown: A variant of a filter is a slowdown filter. Instead of dropping all packets, it limits the bandwidth for packets or connections matching a signature. The advantage is that legitimate use of the target over the network is still possible, but slower. This is especially useful when attack traffic cannot be reliably identified. Filtering infection traffic to implement slowdown is hard. Fast worms as have been observed in the recent past compromise most vulnerable hosts in a matter of minutes. Still filtering infection traffic is worthwhile, since worms have a tendency to stay active for months or longer and cause both network load and new infections of the occasional newly installed and unpatched hosts. While filters have a very high disruptive potential if used incorrectly or triggered by an attacker as a type of indirect attack, slowdown is far more benign. Slowdown filters may even be safe enough to be employed in an automatic fashion, at least initially. Countermeasures will still require some human input at some time for near future. However, they can buy humans time to think and to understand what is happening.

3   PromethOS NP Router Platform

We propose the PromethOS NP [24, 25] router platform to introduce, map and accommodate services, such as our Anti-DDoS service, on a hierarchy extended active network node. Services as built of service components may span all processing elements if required. To pave the way for the Anti-DDoS service architecture, we briefly present the component based service model used on PromethOS NP and the architecture of PromethOS NP with emphasizing specific components that are required to control and manage this platform.

3.1   Component Based Service Model

Fig. 1 visualizes the service model of PromethOS NP by a configuration that illustrates the capabilities of the model. Services for PromethOS NP are described as a graph of edges and vertices. Edges represent service components (emphasized with named boxes in Fig. 1) and vertices denote interconnection points. Service components provide data path functionalities. Classical data path functionality, for example, is payload dependent packet filtering, counting or even payload transcoding. Service components are configured and controlled by control components. A control component, as exemplified by F4 in Fig. 1, may control one or more service components. In addition, the control component itself may provide data path service functionality. Functionalities provided by the

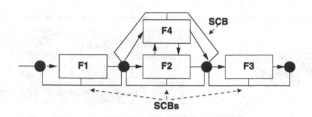

Fig. 1. Service Model

components depend on their implementation. While service components register for data communication only, a control component may register for timed events, too. At vertices, a service graph may be split into several subgraphs and combined by fork and join operations, respectively. Service components register with one data input and one data output port and bidirectional control communication is provided between the service and the relevant control components (symbolized by the connections between F4 and F2).

We refer to service components with the adjacent vertices by the term *service chain*. A *Service Control Bus* (SCB) accompanies a service chain. It propagates signals like packet discard notifications as well as the state of the service chain, i.e. whether the service chain is currently processing a packet or whether it is idle.

3.2 Architecture of PromethOS NP

Fig. 2 depicts the architecture of a PromethOS NP node using a three-tier processor hierarchy[3] and a node control layer.

On all tiers, PromethOS NP provides dynamically code-extensible processing environments (PEs). PromethOS NP creates a hierarchical EE by that an interface to the hierarchical EE is provided only via the control layer. Internally, PromethOS NP manages two different types of code-extensible PEs, in which service components can be installed and instantiated. On the GPP cores, the PE is implemented as an extended PromethOS EE [19] (cf. Host Processor Processing Environment in Fig. 2). This PE provides a binary compatible interface to the PromethOS EE. In contrast to the PromethOS EE, that runs on a single processor node only, the other PE (cf. Network Processor Processing Environments in Fig. 2) is embedded in the hierarchical router platform and provides the abstractions to build a service of distributed service components residing in other PEs. On the PPs, a PE is instantiated that provides the mechanisms to install and execute service components without stopping the PP.

The control layer contains components which are responsible for the whole node. The *Node Manager* provides the interface to create a service at node run-time and instructs the other components on the node to act according to its

---

[3] The current implementation creates a three-tier hierarchical router platform for nodes that are built of host processor and NP-blades. NP-blades consist of a control processor with a set of packet processors (Appl. Ref. Board [27] for the IBM PowerNP 4GS3 [14]).

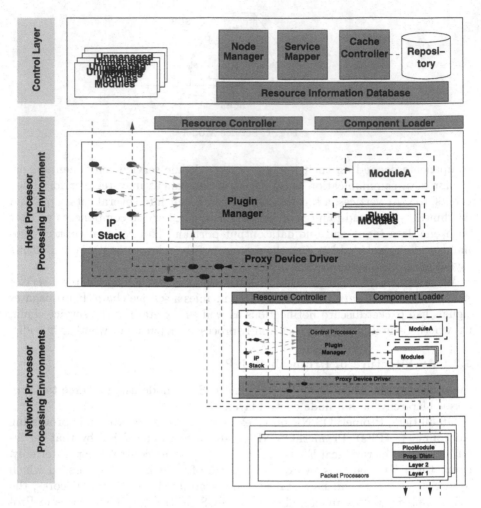

Fig. 2. PromethOS NP Node Architecture

decision. The *Service Mapper* creates the required map specification that provides the information to install and instantiate service components on specific processors such that, first, a service can be created and, second, the resources available are not overbooked. It instructs the PE specific *Component Loaders* to load, instantiate, configure and unload service components. To better differentiate between instantiated and uninstantiated service components, we refer to the latter by the term module. Every module is identified by a module identifier (ModID) that is unique for the whole hierarchical network node. The ModID is used to query and re-configure the module at run-time. Service components to be instantiated are retrieved by help of the *Cache Controller*. It is responsible to manage the node-local repository which contains service components for PromethOS NP nodes. Upon reception of a request, it either compiles service components from source or retrieves a service component in binary format if available. It does not deal with network-wide service component retrieval but assumes the availability of these components in the node-local repository.[4] The *Resource Information Database* is required to keep track of resources available and consumed. Therefore it interfaces with the *Resource Controllers* residing on the different GPPs. Each PE is controlled by its Resource Controller. The Resource Controller configures and controls the *Programmable Distributors* (PDs) according to instructions received from the Node Manager.

PDs implement the vertices of our service model on and between any processors. Hence, they provide the mechanisms to bind a service chain to specific flows. They are PE specific and provide the mechanisms required to forward packets between service components. Two types of PDs are implemented. One that interconnects service components on the same processor, and the second one that interconnects service components residing on different processors.

In Fig. 3, we illustrate the architecture of a PD. PDs consist of a receiving, classifying and forwarding element [24]. While the receiving and forwarding element eliminate the need of a service programmer to deal with the underlying hardware platform, the classifier element is replaceable. It provides the interfaces like common service components but is required to communicate with the receiving and forwarding elements along the SCB by a particular protocol.

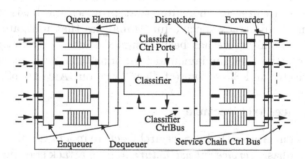

Fig. 3. Programmable Distributor

Packet classification is time-consuming. Therefore, we define cut-through PDs to avoid unnecessary classification overhead if two adjacent components are only linked directly. We extend the basic concept of service chains that consists of a edge between two adjacent vertices to a set of edges for which no classification and no inter-processor communication is required in between. On a PromethOS NP node, service chains are identified by the first ModID that starts the chain. A service chain is hooked to multiple outbound ports of a PD as well as multiple different service chains are attached to a PD if required. Dynamic replacement

---

[4] For proof-of-concept purposes, we have implemented a straightforward service component fetcher that is able to retrieve service components from a remote repository over a secured TCP channel if the service components are not locally available.

of service chains is based on a selector logic per outbound port. This logic provides the required semantic to install, replace and remove service chains at node run-time without disrupting other services. PDs on PPs are bound to the capabilities offered.

Our *Proxy Device Driver* provides the mechanisms to communicate between all processors of the processor hierarchy.[5] This Proxy Device Driver supports two types of communication channels between different processors. A fast path provides the mechanisms to interconnect service components without additional legacy classification overhead of the Linux Netfilter network stack architecture, while a slow path along the Linux network stack provides the full flexibility of iptables as described for PromethOS [19]. The *Plugin Manager* interfaces with the Linux *IP Stack*, as well as with the fast path. Based on its ability, service components may be executed on nodes with and without NP tiers. Moreover, PDs are implemented as part of the Plugin Manager on GPPs regarding the receiving and forwarding elements.

4   Anti-DDoS Service

Counteracting DDoS attacks requires continuous traffic observation and, if necessary, the installation of countermeasures. Traffic observation and the insertion of countermeasures, however, should not affect regular services. Therefore, we propose a service architecture hereafter that provides the basis infrastructure for the deployment of attack specific functionalities that mitigate the effect of the attacks. The architecture has been designed such a way to make it possible to instantiate the four fundamental functional elements, namely Capture, Identification, Filter and Slowdown (cf. Sec. 2), of our Anti-DDoS service.

4.1   The Service Architecture

Fig. 4 visualizes our Anti-DDoS service architecture in a particular configuration that consists of a basis *service infrastructure* and an attack specific *Service Handler*. While the Service Handler must make the required functionalities available to detect and counteract DDoS attacks, the other components are generic in the sense that they provide the fundamental service architecture. Since the path via the Service Handler creates the needed countermeasure functionality, we refer to this path as the *service path*. Irrespective of the functionality provided, for the PromethOS NP router platform service components are black boxes. As such not only the service path but also the service infrastructure are built of service components that provide the appropriate functionalities. The service specification is used by the Node Manager that triggers the installation and instantiation of the service as mentioned above. The service logic, however, is service specific.

---

[5] Our Proxy Device Driver is based on the code delivered with the IBM Advanced Software Offering Toolkit. It extends the original code base by a generalized, more abstracted communication infrastructure with resource control mechanisms for a hierarchical router architecture built of a multitude of NPs.

As such, the service logic may contain mechanisms to request the installation or removal of service components depending on service-internal policies. Due to this autonomous, policy based service-internal management, our service architecture provides the basis of a node-local *autonomous service*.

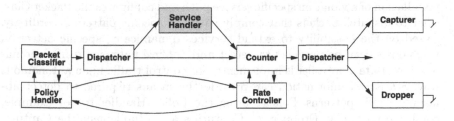

Fig. 4. Anti-DDoS Service Architecture

We argue that this autonomous service provides a suitable basis for detection mechanisms and countermeasures against well-known and unknown attacks. We exemplify three different, particular service configurations to illustrate the applicability of our service architecture for the mechanisms and measures introduced in Section 2:

- Without detection mechanisms or countermeasures installed, the *Packet Classifier* assigns a tag to the incoming packets and sends the packet to the first *Dispatcher*. Since no particular service path is specified by the tag, the Dispatcher forwards the packet to the *Counter*. The Counter increments tag-dependent counters and sends the packet to the next Dispatcher. This Dispatcher then re-inserts the packet into the common routing/forwarding path of the router.
- In case of a well-known attack, whose packets are classified according to specified criteria, our Anti-DDoS service with the detection and countermeasure mechanisms are implemented in the following way. An appropriate policy is given to the *Policy Handler* that creates the service path and configures the Packet Classifier implementing the Capture service function. Policies are specified beforehand and sent to the Policy Handler by service-external entities. Packets matching the criteria are sent to the respective service path (Identification). Service Handlers provide the mechanisms required to detect packets that belong to an attack. Their mechanisms give the specific operations necessary for in-depth payload inspection or multi-protocol attack handling to detect, for example, the W32/Blaster worm [6]. Service Handlers are installed on request to carry out the Filter or Slowdown service functionalities, as well. Multiple Service Handlers may exist simultaneously. A Service Handler signals the detection of a particular pattern to the subsequent Dispatcher. Depending on the service configuration, packets are sent to the *Capturer* or to the *Dropper*.
- In case of unknown attacks, our Anti-DDoS service follows a different configuration. These attacks, i.e. traffic anomalies, are detected by that the

Rate Controller queries the counters periodically and compares the values retrieved with specified thresholds. If the counters exceed these thresholds, the Rate Controller informs the Policy Handler of the violating tag and provides the violated condition. This message initiates a service extension or re-configuration process by the Policy Handler. The Policy Handler triggers the installation of a violation specific service path and configures the Packet Classifier to dispatch packets that comply with the specific pattern accordingly. Based on the possibility to extend services dynamically, specific detection mechanisms can be provided to detect and analyze unknown traffic anomalies. The Rate Controller is implemented to control traffic in an autonomous way. Statistical information can provide the means required to detect abnormal traffic patterns. Policies bring the Policy Handler to, for example, configure particular Droppers or Capturers as to implement the Capture, Identification, Filter or Slowdown service mechanisms, respectively.

Packets can be sent to the Service Handler by mistake if, for example, a packet matches a particular byte-pattern at the first classifier but the in-depth packet inspection carried out by the Service Handler reveals that the packet is not part of an attack. Were such packets simply discarded, denial of service results although not all flows are malicious. To avoid such malfunctioning, false positives must be re-inserted.

Attacks vary and provide attack-specific characteristics. These characteristics are yet unknown and may require specific countermeasures that are neither configurable with today's routers nor implementable within today's firmware. Large hierarchical routers located in or close to the core, however, need to be prepared to effectively mitigate future attacks without interruption of other services as it would be required if firmware would need to be upgraded.

4.2 Hardware Constraints

PDs enable service designers to focus on the specific functionality to be implemented according to a unified component model among all types of processors. Thus the challenge remains to decide where to place which service component. For the exploration of this problem space, we need to take hardware constraints into account before we can propose an appropriate classification scheme.

Today's packet processors provide very limited but highly specialized processing capabilities. The programming flexibility known from general purpose processors is not available there. For example, the number of timer events is small. Since PPs are focused on squeezing out the most of possible performance for packet processing, they are not well-suited for dynamic code updates. Memory is direct mapped; no address virtualization is available. This imposes hard constraints on the code layout of service components for packet processors, and makes the installation of code components at run-time extremely difficult. Fast memory on the NPs is an extremely scarce resource. Different types of memory exist therefore on an NP-blade. Packet processors differentiate between instruction memory and data memory. Often, the former provides room for a total of

32 kilo-instructions [14] only. Thus, the number of code components that can be installed is very limited if we assume that additional functionality, like routing, must be provided by the NP besides our services. While PPs provide fast, co-processor supported packet processing capabilities, control processors on the NPs increase flexibility by general purpose processor architectures. In addition, CPs are able to manage up to 2 GBytes of DRAM [16].

Packet processors are able to forward packets at line speed. But communication paths between service components on the PPs and those on the CPs are not able to cope with the aggregated throughput of all PPs. Neither are today's CPs able to process so high packet rates fully themselves. For example, our prototype implementation with the IBM PowerNP 4GS3, we have been able to receive packets at approx. 100 Mbit/s on the embedded PowerPC. while bi-directional communication resulted in a maximal transmission rate of 42.7 Mbit/s [25].[6] If we assume a hierarchical network node with multiple NP-blades, router-internal communication between NP-blades and the host processor is not able to cope with the data rate either. Actual NPs, like the Intel IXP28xx family, are able to forward packets lossless at rates of up to 20 Gbit/s [17] on the packet processors. Thus, forwarding all packets to host processors would overcharge any of them.

Hence, we argue that scalability of our node is achieved by that programmable network interfaces will be equipped with NPs in the near future. Thus they provide a fully programmable GPP together with a potentially large set of optimized and specialized PPs. Currently, control processors do not provide the processing capacity to run data path service components with the required performance [25]. However, as processor technology advances, performance of control processors will not be of a major concern. We can imagine that multi-core CPs are feasible soon as separated memory channels for CPs and PPs are. Separated channels are required such that the processing elements do not interfere with each other[7] when processing packets each. But challenge remains in deciding where to place service components most effectively.

4.3 Service Components on Our Hierarchy-Extended Router

Communication between different processor tiers is time consuming, imposes additional limits on packet throughput and comes at the cost of overhead that needs to be avoided by design if possible. To explore this problem space, we propose a classification scheme that is based on the complexity of the operation, the rate and the type of service functionality. This classification scheme is used hereafter to support the mapping strategy of an Anti-DDoS service onto our router platform.

We differentiate between three dimensions as illustrated in Fig. 5. The first dimension is the complexity of the function provided by the component. The complexity depends on the type of procedures to be applied. For example, if byte-patterns can be identified in a single packet only, the complexity of the

---

[6] The chip itself is able to handle nearly four times 1 Gbit/s.
[7] Some NP manufacturers provide this capability already today.

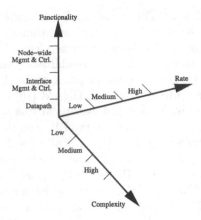

Fig. 5. Classification Dimensions

appropriate function is lower than if a series of packets needs to be kept in memory before the function can return its decision. The second dimension is the rate a service component must be able to receive packets or control messages. And the third dimension is the type of service functionality provided, i.e. data path, control or management functionality. For the PromethOS NP platform, it is important to know if a service component is triggered by a timer event or upon arrival of a packet at its data input port, and if a service component manages and controls rather a full node than a NP-blade only. We name the first dimension processing *complexity*, to the second we refer by the term *rate*, and the third is referred to as *functionality*.

For the classification of the service components of our service architecture, we decide on the complexity, rate and the functionality. The complexity of a function provided by a component is determined at specification time while the initial location of components in the second dimension is based on rough estimations of expected packet rates for data path service components. The location of control and management components in the second dimension depends on the frequency of triggers or queries the component is expected to handle. Placement of components in the third dimension is based on the type of service functionality a component is expected to provide. It is important to distinguish from service components that provide functionality on data packets and from those that are able to control manage other service components. Hence, the functionality differentiates between service components residing solely in the data path or providing functionality in the control and management plane as well.

In table 1, we present the classification of the service components of our service architecture according to the scheme introduced above. We exemplify the classification by explaining its application to the Packet Classifier, the Service Handler and the Policy Handler. The Packet Classifier needs to process all arriving packets. Hence, the rate is high. However, the complexity is low since packets can be classified based on data available in a single packet only. Remember that this Classifier decides if a packet needs further in-depth analysis. In addition,

Table 1. Classification

Component	Complexity	Rate	Functionality
Classifier	Low	High	Data path
Counter	Low	High	Data path
Capturer	High	Low	Data path
Dispatcher	Low	High	Data path
Dropper	Low	High	Data path
Rate Controller	Low	Middle	Interface Control
Service Handler	Low → High	Low → High	Data path/Interface Control
Policy Handler	High	Low	Node-wide Management & Control

the functionality provided is one clear representative of the data path. Classifier are therefore instantiated on PPs of all NP-blades most preferably. Functionality provided by the Service Handler is service specific. The operations to be applied can range from rather simple byte-pattern matching of payload in potentially fragmented IP packets up to complex multi-protocol attack detection, or the detection of commonalities found in traffic anomalies of which the reason is unknown. Thus, its complexity may range from low up to high. The same argumentation applies for the packet rate it must be able to process. Functionality provided by the Service Handler may reside in the data path and/or in the control plane. Since the Service Handler itself can be composed of various components, full flexibility is required of PromethOS NP to install the specific components on appropriate processors. It is important to notice that PromethOS NP distributes internal control messages between different processors on the same mechanisms as used for data communication, and imposes therefore no limitations. Depending on their complexity, service handlers are therefore instantiated either on CPs or PPs of the required NP-blades. The Policy Handler provides management and control functionality that supervises potentially all NP-blades. As an aggregating function with an expected low-bandwidth communication interface but high service complexity, it is predestined to be instantiated in the PE on the host GPP. Following this classification of the components, we specify the following mapping of components on the hierarchy-extended platform:

- Components with a low complexity and a high packet rate are placed on packet processors most preferably. Thus, promising candidates are the Packet Classifier, the Counter, Dispatchers as well as the Dropper. Depending on the complexity of the Service Handler, parts of it like byte-pattern matching are candidates as well.
- Components with a high complexity and a low rate are installed either on the control or on the host processor. The exact placement depends on the kind of interaction among components. Thus, candidates to be installed on these GPPs are the Rate Controller, the Policy Handler and the Capturer. For obvious reasons, particular components of the Service Handler may or must reside on GPPs, as well.

– The functionality dimension determines if a component can be installed on packet processors or must be placed on GPPs. Data path components can be installed anywhere. Although theoretically feasible on PPs, control and management components that are triggered by timer events are installed on GPPs. Thus we decide to place the Rate Controller on the respective CP of the PPs, and place the Policy Handler on the host processor.

PDs provide resource accounting and enforcement mechanisms. By the means of the Resource Controller, service re-configuration can be implemented to allow for the relocation of service components at service run-time. Thus, service components could be relocated if their location in the classification scheme changes. However, our platform provides no explicit support for state preserving or service component migration. Based on the measurements of the Rate Controller, the Policy Handler could provide the required functionalities to trigger a re-deployment of the service with different attributes.

5   Related Work

Various active router platforms following the component model have been proposed for single processor systems [1, 10, 20]. However, only a few addressed the problem of managing hierarchical active network nodes with integrated support of NPs.

VERA [18] introduced the hierarchy of classifiers as a chain of classifiers which is mapped on a model of a hierarchical router. It defines extensibility as the ability to provide resources for additional services. However, the core components of VERA do not provide at run-time extensibility, and VERA does not deal with the complexity of instantiating services that span all tiers arbitrarily. Compared with PromethOS NP, VERA takes programmability of packet processors into account, but packets are forwarded to a statically linked operating system running on the host GPP.

NetBind [4] proposes an approach to construct data paths dynamically on a network processor based router. Low latency on dynamic binding is achieved due to post-processing of intermediary object files before linking the components. For this reason, no overhead takes place at the execution time, except for the machine code changes. In comparison to PromethOS NP, NetBind is not a generic framework for adding new services on network processor based routers, i.e., NetBind does not deploy services on all tiers of the processor hierarchy in an integrated way.

SPLITS [12] creates a router architecture built of attached network processors line cards and host processors. While SPLITS provides the same functionality as VERA and NetBind for network processors, functionality is extended by stream handlers that allow for flexible interception of packet flows to attach arbitrary applications. Like VERA and NetBind, SPLITS does not address the potential of CPs for the execution of services. However, we are convinced CPs are and will be an important processing element on large hierarchical routers for router scalability reason. Therefore, we provide the concepts and mechanisms required for services of which service components reside on one, several or all processor tiers including CPs.

The potential of active countermeasures against large-scale distributed denial of service attacks in the Internet has been recognized before. FIDRAN [13] proposes a service framework similar to ours. However, the service architecture focuses on a single host GPP node only, and hence, is not able to benefit from additional processing capabilities offered by a hierarchy extended active network node. FLAME [2] built and evaluated a monitoring system that can be used to detect distributed denial of service attacks. Similar to FIDRAN, the system is designed for single host GPPs only. In [21], the application of re-configurable hardware to detect signatures in payload of packets is proposed. While we are convinced that the FPX is able to scan packets for signatures much faster than our architecture, we argue that our architecture provides more flexibility as required for, e.g. selective packet capturers.

6   Conclusions and Outlook

In this paper, we have analyzed the problem space of detection mechanisms and countermeasures against large-scale distributed denial of service attacks in the Internet, and presented briefly the architecture of PromethOS NP. PromethOS NP provides a dynamically extensible router platform for hierarchical network nodes built of host and network processors for high-performance packet processing. Motivated by the continuously increasing significance of the Internet to business and commerce, and the always quicker spreading of newly created worms and viruses, we have proposed a service architecture that allows for the efficient deployment of new service functionalities to detect and counteract DDoS attacks effectively on high-performance routers for the Internet backbone. The classification scheme proposed in this paper alleviates the design and implementation of specific Anti-DDoS service components that benefit from our service architecture, as well as from the flexibility and the capabilities of our PromethOS NP router platform. Hence, we are convinced that our service architecture in conjunction with PromethOS NP provides the flexibility and performance required for detection mechanisms and countermeasures against DDoS attacks in the Internet. Moreover, it is flexible enough to provide the basis for services in completely different fields like charging and accounting of traffic. Currently, we are implementing the proposed service architecture on PromethOS NP. The evaluation of this implementation with appropriate Anti-DDoS service components will show whether our claims hold.

References

1. D.S. Alexander, W. A. Arbaugh, M. W. Hicks, P. Kakkar, A. D. Keromytis, J. T. Moore, C. A. Gunter, S. M. Nettles, and J. M. Smith. The SwitchWare active network architecture. *IEEE Network*, 12(3), May/Jun. 1998.

2. K.G. Anagnostakis, S. Ioannidis, S. Miltchev, J. Ioannidis, M.B. Greenwald, and J.M. Smith. Efficient packet monitoring for network management. In *Proc. of IFIP/IEEE Network Operations and Mgmt. Symp. (NOMS) 2002*, Apr. 2002.

3. CAIDA. CAIDA Analysis of Code-Red. http://www.caida.org/analysis/security/code-red, 2003.

4. A.T. Campbell, M.E. Kounavis, D.A. Villela, J. Vicente, H.G. de Meer, K. Miki, and K.S. Kalaichelvan. NetBind: A Binding Tool for Constructing Data Paths in Network Processor-based Routers. In *Proc. of the 5th Int. Conf. on Open Architectures and Network Programming (OPENARCH)*, Jun. 2002.

5. CERT. CERT Advisory CA-2003-04 MS-SQL Server Worm. http://www.cert.org/advisories/CA-2003-04.html, 2003.

6. CERT. CERT Advisory CA-2003-20 W32/Blaster Worm. http://www.cert.org/advisories/CA-2003-20.html, 2003.

7. Cisco. White Paper: NetFlow Services and Applications. http://www.cisco.com, 2002.

8. Ferngesteuerte Spam-Armeen. c't Magazine, Issue 5, 2004.

9. R. Danyliw and A. Householder. CERT Advisory CA-2001-19 "Code Red" Worm Exploiting Buffer Overflow in IIS Indexing Service DLL. http://www.cert.org/advisories/CA-2001-19.html, 2001.

10. D. Decasper, Z. Dittia, G. Parulkar, and B. Plattner. Router plugins: A software architecture for next-generation routers. *IEEETNWKG: IEEE/ACM Trans. on Networking. IEEE Comm. Society, IEEE Computer Society and the ACM with its Special Interest Group on Data Comm. (SIGCOMM), ACM Press*, 8, 2000.

11. T. Dübendorfer, A. Wagner, and B. Plattner. An Economic Damage Model for Large-Scale Internet Attacks. In *13th IEEE International Workshops on Enabling Technologies: Infrastructures for Collaborative Enterprises (WET ICE 2004); Workshop on Enterprise Security, Modena, Italy*, 2004.

12. A. Gavrilovska. SPLITS Stream Handlers: Deploying Application-level Services to Attached Network Processors. Ph.D. Thesis, Georgia Institute of Technology, Jul. 2004.

13. A. Hess, M. Jung, and G. Schäfer. FIDRAN: A Flexible Intrusion Detection and Repsonse Framework for Actie Networks. In *Proc. of the 8th IEEE Symp. on Computers and Communication (ISCC), Kemer, Antalya, Turkey*, Jul. 2003.

14. IBM Corp. IBM PowerNP NP4GS3 databook. http://www.ibm.com, 2002.

15. Intel Corp. Intel IXP1200 Network Processor – Datasheet. http://www.intel.com, 2000.

16. Intel Corp. Intel IXP2800 Network Processor Hardware Reference Manual. http://www.intel.com, Nov. 2002.

17. Intel Corp. IXP2800 Intel Network Processor IP Forwarding Benchmark Full Disclosure Report for OC192-POS. http://www.intel.com, Oct. 2003.

18. S. Karlin and L. Peterson. VERA: An extensible router architecture. In *Proc. of the 4th Int. Conf. on Open Architectures and Network Programming (OPENARCH)*, Apr. 2001.

19. R. Keller, L. Ruf, A. Guindehi, and B. Plattner. PromethOS: A Dynamically Extensible Router Architecture Supporting Explicit Routing. In *Proc. of the 4th Annual Int. Working Conf. on Active Networks IWAN, Zurich, Switzerland*, number 2546 in LNCS. Springer, Dec. 2002.

20. E. Kohler, R. Morris, B. Chen, J. Jannotti, M. Kaashoek, and C. Modular. The click modular router. *ACM Trans. on Computer Systems*, 18(3), Aug. 2000.

21. J. W. Lockwood, J. Moscola, D. Reddick, M. Kulig, and T. Brooks. Application of Hardware Accelerated Extensible Network Nodes for Internet Worm and Virus Protection. In *Proc. of the 5th Annual Int. Working Conf. on Active Networks IWAN, Kyoto, Japan*, number 2982 in LNCS. Springer, Dec. 2003.
22. Network Processing Forum. http://www.npforum.org, Jun. 2004.
23. J. Postel. Transmission control protocol. RFC 792, ISI, Sep. 1981.
24. L. Ruf, R. Keller, and B. Plattner. A Scalable High-performance Router Platform Supporting Dynamic Service Extensibility On Network and Host Processors. In *Proc. of 2004 ACS/IEEE Int. Conf. on Perv. Services (ICPS'2004)*. IEEE, Jul. 2004.
25. L. Ruf, R. Pletka, P. Erni, P. Droz, and B. Plattner. Towards High-performance Active Networking. In *Proc. of the 5th Annual Int. Working Conf. on Active Networks IWAN, Kyoto, Japan*, number 2982 in LNCS. Springer, Dec. 2003.
26. S.E. Schechter and D.S. Smith. Access For Sale. In *ACM Workshop on Rapid Malcode (WORM)*, 2003.
27. Silicon Software System. Application Reference Board for the IBM PowerNP NP4GS3 Network Processor User Manual. http://www.s3group.com, 2002.
28. K. Sollins. The TFTP Protocol (Revision 2). RFC 1350, MIT, Jul. 1992.
29. S. Staniford, V. Paxson, and N. Weaver. How to Own the Internet in Your Spare Time. In *Proc. of the 11th USENIX Security Symp.*, Aug. 2002.
30. D. Tennenhouse and D. Wetherall. Towards an Active Network Architecture. In *Multimedia Computing and Networking (MMCN 96)*, San Jose, 1996.
31. The Economist. E-commerce takes off. *The Economist*, 371(8375):9, May 2004.
32. A. Wagner, T. Dübendorfer, B. Plattner, and R. Hiestand. Experiences with Worm Propagation Simulations. In *ACM Workshop on Rapid Malcode (WORM)*, 2003.
33. A. Wagner and B. Plattner. Peer-to-peer systems as attack platform for distributed denial-of-service. In *ACM SACT Workshop, Washington, DC, USA*, 2002.

Dynamic Link Measurements Using Active Components

D.P. Pezaros[1], M. Sifalakis[1], S. Schmid[2], and D. Hutchison[1]

[1] Computing Department
InfoLab21, South Drive
Lancaster University,
LA1 4WA, U.K
{dp,mjs,dh}@comp.lancs.ac.uk
[2] NEC Europe Ltd.
Network Laboratories
Kurfürsten-Anlage 36
69115 Heidelberg, Germany
schmid@netlab.nec.de

Abstract. Active and programmable network technologies strive to support completely new forms of data-path processing capabilities inside the network. This in conjunction with the ability to dynamically deploy such active services at strategic locations inside the network enables totally new types of applications. In this paper we exploit these network-side programming capabilities to realise a new active network application that dynamically evaluates network link costs based on in-line traffic measurements. The performance experienced by the data packets (e.g. delays, jitter and packet loss) along network or virtual links is used to compute link costs based on multiple cost metrics. The results are published by means of a routing metric broker, which enables available routing protocols to calculate different sets of routes for different QoS metrics – as for example suggested for ToS-based routing (RFC 1583).

1 Introduction

Active networks research over the last decade has led to new developments in a number of areas ranging from secure programming languages [1,2], mobile code techniques [3], execution environments [3,4], active node platforms [5,6,7,8,9], service composition models [9,10,11], and so forth. Despite these valuable advances, the number of genuine applications where active network technologies are provably useful in real world networks is still limited.

A large number of applications proposed so far [12,13,14] aim to demonstrate the functionality of certain active platforms, while others try to address problems that are best solved with conventional techniques such as (mobile) agents. Active networks are often regarded as a neat technology in seek of genuine applications, which would persuade operators that the benefit of active networks exceeds the corresponding cost and risk involved in deploying and managing them.

We anticipate that active network services expose some properties that allow problems arising from e.g. network operation and management or service deployment,

G.J. Minden et al. (Eds.): IWAN 2004, LNCS 3912, pp. 188–204, 2007.

to be tackled in a more generic/elegant way. Being dynamically deployable on-demand, in a transparent and potentially automatic fashion at relevant points in the network, active services are suitable for a much wider range of applications/problems.

In this paper we focus on the use of the in-line traffic measurement framework [15] as an active service to facilitate dynamic routing link-cost updates that reflect fluctuations in traffic performance attributes. Routing adjustment in response to varying service quality characteristics can improve overall network stability and performance, and presents a challenging task that really benefits from active and programmable networks. In-line traffic measurements are used to assess the performance experienced by the flows along a transmission path, and measurement results are used to periodically adjust the network link costs in the routing protocol. As traffic measurements typically encompass a range of different characteristics (i.e. delay, jitter, packet loss, etc.), the calculation of link costs can be based on a multitude of different cost metrics. This allows for route optimisations tailored to specific applications or classes of applications with different QoS requirements (e.g. real-time synchronous applications vs. asynchronous applications).

The remainder of this paper is organised as follows: In section 2 there is a brief presentation of in-line IPv6-based measurements technique, and a discussion of why it is a particularly well-suited application of active networks technology. Furthermore, we describe the LARA++ active router framework, which has been used for the deployment and operation of the proposed service. In section 3, we present the design of the proposed active service, and we show how it can be implemented and deployed using LARA++. Section 4 presents some experimental results demonstrating the applicability of the in-line measurements and the proposed active service. In section 5, we examine the related work in the area of network measurements, and on dynamic metrics-based routing. Finally, in section 6, we conclude this paper by summarizing the proposed work and motivating some directions for future work.

2 Background

2.1 In-Line IPv6 Traffic Measurement

In-line measurements [15] is a technique to assess the QoS properties experienced by IPv6 flows accurately, independent of a particular network topology and transparent to the end-user applications. The in-line measurements are carried out between two (or more) points in the network by piggybacking the relevant measurement data onto the actual data packets that are observed.

IPv6 extension headers [16] allow Type-Length-Value (TLV)-encoded data to be inserted between the main IPv6 header and the upper (transport) layer header. Depending on which type of extension header is used for the traffic measurements (for example, destination options header or hop-by-hop options header [16]), one can control where and when to trigger the measurement activity. For example, in case the destination options header is used, traffic measurements will only be triggered end-to-end; whereas in the case of the hop-by-hop options header, any node along the transmission path could be involved. Moreover, the use of measurement information in the destination options header in conjunction with the routing header allows precise definition of where the traffic measurements in the network should take place.

The main benefit of this technique is that the traffic measurements are based on the actual user traffic rather than on general measurements based on other traffic flows. In addition to this property, by enforcing option processing only at identified nodes in the network and not hop-by-hop, in-line measurements eliminate the concern of instrumented packets being treated differently than the rest of the traffic in the network. Consequently, the measurements really reflect the performance experienced by the user data transmitted.

At the same time, the header extensions for the traffic measurements are defined by the network layer protocol itself, making the technique native, and equally applicable to any type of traffic (independent of the actual transport or user application).

Several measurement TLVs have been defined to be encoded within the IPv6 destination options header, which is examined by the final destination or optionally pre-defined intermediate nodes (based on the routing header) of a packet. Different TLVs implement a variety of performance metrics[1] by carrying packet departure/arrival timestamps, IP-based sequence numbers, trace information, etc. [17].

The clear separation of concerns between the measurement mechanism and particular analyses engines or post processing measurement applications, makes in-line measurements a promising candidate-application for active and programmable networks; measurement instrumentation is deployed only where and when required, and the results are used as input for a variety of network operations tasks.

Figure 1 show different points along an end-to-end transmission path, where in-line traffic measurements can be deployed. End-systems as well as selected intermediate network nodes can be equipped with in-line measurement functionality. The node that starts the traffic measurement process inserts the desired extension header into the relevant data packets. These packets are then processed by the instrumented nodes along the transmission path. The measurement information is recorded, amended and/or extracted accordingly.

In this paper, we focus on a particular application of in-line traffic measurements, whereby the measurements of up-to-date transmission characteristics (such as delay,

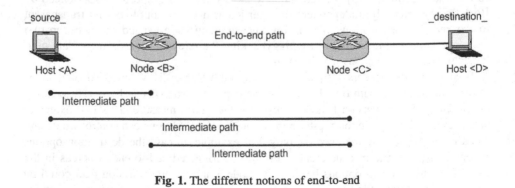

Fig. 1. The different notions of end-to-end

---

[1] A set of performance metrics are defined within the IETF's IPPM WG.

jitter, packet loss and so forth) are used to dynamically update network link costs, so that routing decisions can be made more accurately.

Suitably selected active routers are used to deploy the measurement modules as they are needed, in order to adjust network link costs according to the current transmission performance. In the context of figure 1, active routers can be nodes <B> and <C>, and the intermediate paths can be a point-to-point link or a virtual overlay link that spans across several hops in the underlying network.

The proposed traffic measurement application is particularly well-suited for active networks for a number of reasons:

- It is directly deployed on the data path
- It relies on direct access to data packets on the forwarding path (to support transparent measurements – independent from the applications)
- It needs to be deployed, activated, and configured dynamically whenever and wherever there is need for it

These characteristics advocate the realisation of the add-on service as an active service, offering the flexibility (and the ability) of on-demand deployment within the network.

2.2 The LARA++ Architecture

The LARA++ [9] active node framework is a software implementation of a programmable router that is designed for commodity operating systems. It augments the functionality of a conventional router/host by exposing a programmable interface which allows active programs, referred to as active components, to provide network level services on any packet-based network.

Since LARA++ "hooks" directly into the router's operating system, it enables the transparent interception of packets traversing the node. Intercepted packets can be processed by active components and then be re-injected back into the host OS for the default processing on the node. In this way, LARA++ can flexibly extend (as opposed to alter) the functionality of a router's conventional network services, enabling lightweight augmentation of existing network services and allowing for gradual replacement of conventional router functionality. We consider this feature especially useful for our in-line traffic measurements, since it facilitates transparent processing of the relevant data traffic within selected nodes.

LARA++ treats a router as a resource shared by all its users. The extent of programmability can be adjusted on a per-user or group-of-users basis, as well as based on resource availability. Active components of different LARA++ users are protected from each other by a safety model that gives each component a sandbox called a processing environment (PE). For performance reasons, however, LARA++ allows users that trust each other to execute their active code inside the same PE.

LARA++ uses a sophisticated model for service composition [18]. Each component that is to become part of the service composite on a running active router installs one or several packet filters into nodes of a directed graph, referred to as the classification graph. These packet filters specify rules that LARA++ uses to determine if traversing packets need to be processed locally. Once a packet is matched, LARA++ delivers the packet to the components that registered the filter for processing. The use of a configurable classification graph allows LARA++ to process packets of any type ranging from standard IP packets over active packets with ANEP-style [19] headers to completely bespoke packet formats. As a result, service composition on LARA++ active router is defined implicitly by the classification graph and the packet filters installed by the active components. This type of composition approach provides a means to control both co-operation and competition among active components [18]. Figure 2 illustrates this concept in more detail.

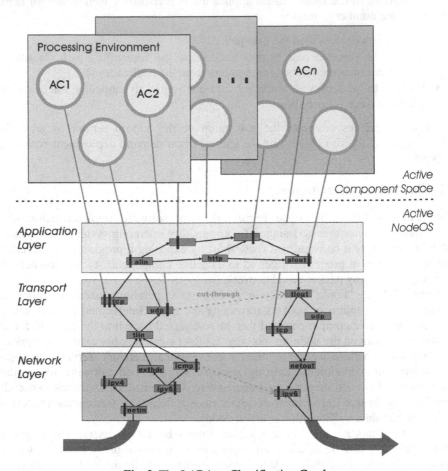

Fig. 2. The LARA++ Classification Graph

Packet filters are extremely flexible from the component developer point of view, because they enable the description of packets that are subject to active processing based on any bit or byte pattern. Yet, in most common cases it is sufficient to consider the flow information and/or the existence of specific header values in the packet. LARA++ filters are easily specified and installed by active components using an XML-based mark-up language.

The LARA++ active router framework also encompasses a generic service deployment protocol, called ASDP [20], that allows dynamic deployment and control of active services on remote active routers. We consider this particularly valuable in order to deploy traffic measurement support inside the network where desired.

3 Design and Implementation

The proposed mechanism consists of two main modules. The first module is responsible for carrying out the in-line measurements. It has been implemented as a standalone LARA++ active component that registers the relevant packet filters (depending on the flows of interest) at the IPv6 node of the classification graph [9]. It exposes an API that allows other components or user applications to use it. The second module is a user-space application that reads and processes the measurement data, and maintains a data structure with separate metrics for the different types of measured attributes in the network (e.g. delay, jitter, packet loss, and so on). In order for the two modules to interface effectively, the evaluation module registers a callback interface with the measurements module. Periodically, the measurements module contacts the broker through the callback interface to stream the raw measurement data. Figure 3 illustrates the design of the proposed mechanism and shows how the two modules interface with each other.

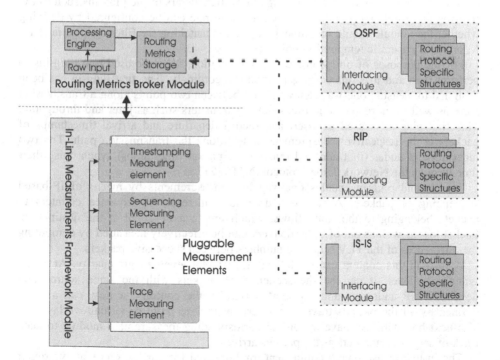

Fig. 3. Basic Design of the Active Service

The following sections describe in more detail the internal implementation and functionality of these two modules.

3.1 In-Line Measurements Active Components

The central functionality of this module is to perform the in-line measurements. As shown in figure 3, this module consists of two main parts: i) a plug-in framework and ii) a set of measurement plug-ins. The plug-in framework provides the functionality for creating the appropriate destination options extension headers and for inserting/extracting the measurement data of previous nodes (which are encoded as TLV options). It exposes the necessary API for other applications to access the measurement data, to manage (add/remove/configure) the plug-ins, and to configure the filtering parameters. Filtering can be based on the source and destination addresses and ports, on transport protocol, traffic class, and on flow label values.

The plug-ins are the code elements that carry out the actual measurements and generate the appropriate data that are inserted in the IPv6 packet header by the framework. Separate plug-ins are used for different types of measurements (e.g. transmission times and packet loss). The framework can accommodate several plug-ins simultaneously for performing different measurement (which results in more than one TLV options records in the IPv6 destination header), although this comes at the cost of reducing the data payload size. However, different plug-ins can create separate measurement TLVs for different data of interest.

The framework API provides an IOCTL-based interface for registering/attaching the plug-ins, and also adjusts the configuration parameters of the plug-ins such as the filtering and sampling granularity. The sampling rate can be configured by defining whether the module should instrument all packets matching the filtering criteria, 1-in-N, or act at a specific temporal sampling rate.

For the purposes of our prototype implementation, we have used two plug-ins to perform time and loss-related measurements accordingly. The first plug-in has been designed to measure one-way delay (OWD) between two points along a transmission path, as well as more synthetic time-related parameters such as jitter and throughput. This first plug-in is used to insert and record departure and arrival timestamps of packets at the respective measurement nodes along the transmission path. The two measurement nodes (that add and remove the packet timestamps) synchronise their time through the Network Time Protocol (NTP) [21].

The second plug-in enables one-way loss measurements by means of IP-based sequencing of packets. A source node inserts incremental sequence counters to packets belonging to the same flows, which are then observed at the destination. Packet loss as well as out of order delivery can be effectively measured by computing the differences of the TLV sequence numbers between successive packets.

A flow in this context can be defined at different levels of granularity. At a fine granularity level, it can be the sequence of packets with the same source and destination IP addresses and transport ports. On the contrary, a flow can also be defined by all the packets traversing a certain point-to-point or virtual/overlay link. The next hop will also have to run the corresponding measurement module to keep track of sequence numbers as the packets arrive.

The in-line measurement component implemented for our LARA++ active router architecture registers the following packet filters with the classification graph: one or more filters for the outgoing packets of interest (the number of filters here depends on the filtering parameters configured by the measurement application) and one filter for the incoming IPv6 packets that contain our measurement header. Once a packet of interest is filtered, it is pulled out of the forwarding path and handed to our in-line measurement component. Depending on which filter captured the packet, TLV-options are either inserted or extracted accordingly. The packets are then inserted back to the classification graph for further processing.

The information extracted from the incoming packets is delivered to the external broker module that has expressed interest in the respective measurement data. The role of the broker module is further described in the following section.

3.2 Routing Metrics Broker Module

This control module accesses the in-line measurement active component in order to configure the in-line traffic measurements and collect the results. It is responsible for extracting and processing the appropriate raw measurement data, and for updating the costs table according to the routing metrics of interest. Node-local running routing protocols can then access these up-to-date cost metrics and optimise their routing information. In this way, routing protocols can always decide optimal routing paths based on up-to-date link quality information (with regard to the chosen metrics).

The current prototype of the broker module is implemented as a user-space application. The traffic measurement process starts by initialising the broker module where the user specifies the (virtual) link and the packet flows that should be used for the in-line traffic measurements. The user also selects which measurement plug-in instruments which flows.

At start-up, the broker module instruments the installation and activation of the in-line measurement components on the respective active routers on both ends of the (virtual) link. Note that in the case of a virtual link (tunnel), the in-line measurements module will be installed several routing hops apart from each other, which enables the measurements for a whole routing path as opposed to a single physical link. This process takes place using the existing active network loading mechanism supported by LARA++.

The broker module then establishes the necessary communication channels with the in-line measurement components, to pass configuration parameters such as the packet filters and sampling rate, and to receive the measurement results. Based on this data, the broker computes the appropriate link cost metrics that have been registered by the routing protocol(s) or other applications.

Once the in-line measurement component starts performing the measurements and delivering the measurement results, the broker module processes the data and updates the cost metrics data structure. This data structure stores single-value link costs for each measured attribute. It is accessible by the routing protocols through a "well-known" API so that they can update their internal data structures periodically, in order to reflect the dynamic link cost changes.

Since our main goal is to demonstrate the proposed functionality, our current implementation simply sets the cost values by averaging the N most recent measurements. More sophisticated calculations could be based on averaging a set of past cost values combined with the N most recent results or any other algorithm that would deliver a less fluctuating set of cost values.

Furthermore, since existing routing protocols typically do not use generic data structures among them and neither share a common representation of link costs or routing metrics, those ones that want to benefit from the in-line traffic measurements have to be extended. As shown in figure 3, we propose that the routing protocol will interface with our broker module through its own proprietary interface adapter. For example, the interface adapter for OSPFv3 would calculate OSPF-specific link costs from the measurement results and update the internal data structures accordingly.

4 Evaluation of the In-Line IPv6 Measurements Mechanism

For the evaluation of our mechanism we used the IPv6 testbed infrastructure [22] at Lancaster University, where we have deployed two LARA++ active nodes (at points A and B) as illustrated in figure 4. We created an artificial, yet realistic, network condition, where we stressed the ADSL uplink (at the tunnel connection) by generating 512-byte TCP/UDP traffic at an exponentially increasing rate of up to 62 packets per second. The WaveLAN link on the other hand, being part of the campus WiFi network was subject to the usual (relatively congested) traffic encountered at midday hours.

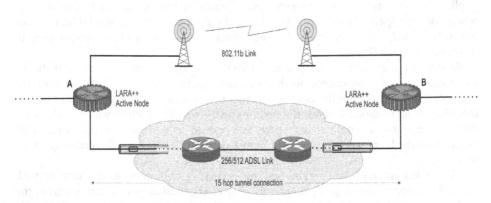

Fig. 4. Experimental Network topologies

We then triggered the installation of the proposed active service on node A and B according to the process described in section 3, and deployed the timestamping plug-in (for one-way delay and jitter) to instrument UDP traffic and the sequencing plug-in (for packet loss) for measurements on TCP traffic, respectively. These choices are justified by the fact that TCP performance is known to be vulnerable to packet loss (continuous back-off), whereas UDP performance is impacted by increasing delays and delay variations (buffer adjustment requirements).

After processing the measurements for appropriate time intervals using the broker module, we got the results illustrated in figures 5 (ADSL downlink), 6 (ADSL uplink) and 7 (802.11b), with regard to packet loss, delay and jitter. Table 1 summarises these results.

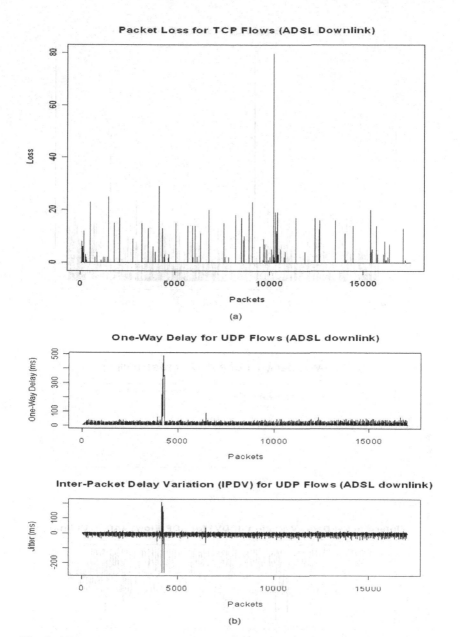

Fig. 5. ADSL Downlink Measurements - (a) TCP Packet Loss (b) UDP OWD and Jitter

Comparing figures 5 and 7, we observed that the packet loss on the tunnel link is approximately 5% versus 4.8% for the WaveLAN link, yet the wireless link exposes more bursty characteristics. The delay experienced by the UDP flows over the tunnel connection was slightly better than on the WaveLAN link: the mean delay was 15.4

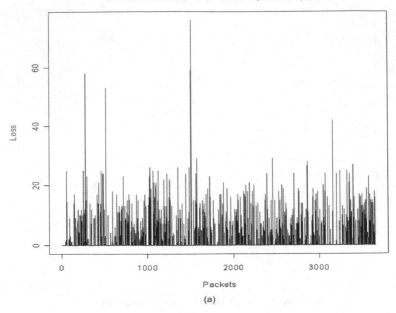

(a)

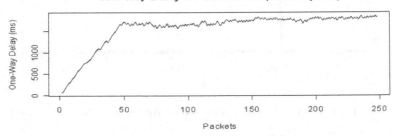

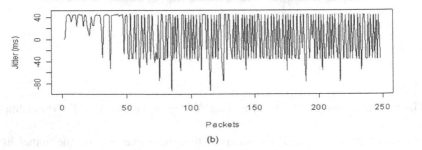

(b)

Fig. 6. ADSL Uplink Measurements - (a) TCP Packet Loss (b) UDP OWD and Jitter

Packet Loss for TCP Flows (IEEE 802.11b)

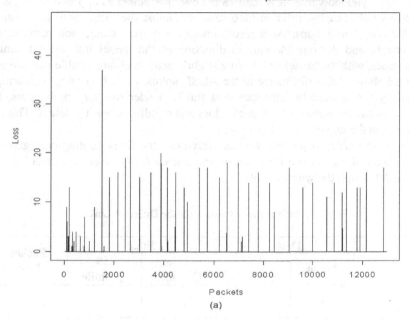

(a)

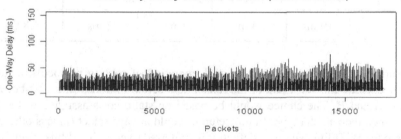

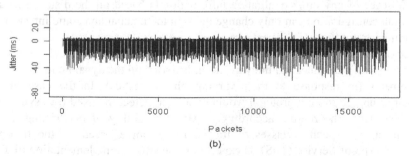

(b)

Fig. 7. IEEE 802.11b Measurements - (a) TCP Packet Loss (b) UDP OWD and Jitter

ms over the tunnel link versus 19 ms on the wireless link and 75% of the measurements yielded values less than 18 ms over the tunnel as opposed to 23 ms on the wireless link. Finally, jitter in both cases is almost the same, with most values laying between 1 and 2 ms. As a result, under the current congestion patterns, the WiFi network and the one (downlink) direction of the tunnel link exhibit similar characteristics, with the tunnel link having slightly better and more stable behaviour.

Figure 6 shows the performance of the ADSL uplink while becoming increasingly saturated by the artificially introduce data traffic. Under the very high stress, the tunnel link is hardly usable: 53.6% packet loss and rapidly increasing delays. This can be observed in the upper plot of figure 6(b).

Under these traffic conditions, we can derive that the fittest routing configuration in our testbed is the asymmetric routing of traffic from A to B over the tunnel link and from B to A through the wireless link.

Table 1. Performance Statistics for the Different Links

	Delay		Jitter		Packet Loss
	Mean	75% Quantile	25% Quantile	75% Quantile	
ADSL Uplink	1558 ms	1768	-35 ms	44 ms	53.6%
ADSL Downlink	15.4 ms	18 ms	1 ms	2 ms	5 %
IEEE 802.11b	19 ms	23 ms	1 ms	2 ms	4.8 %

Currently, according to the conventional operation of routing protocols, a router would select either the WiFi link or the tunnel connection to transport traffic between the points A and B. The choice would be based on static costs assigned to the two links based on their media type. In our setup it would always select (unless otherwise instructed) the WiFi link, since by default it is preferred over a virtual link, even if the latter had bigger capacity. This happens because the link cost assigned to the virtual link in absence of any other qualitative information is based on the distance metric. This default configuration can only change through the manual and static intervention of the administrator.

Based on our proposed mechanism, the routing protocol can dynamically adjust the link costs of both the tunnel and the wireless links based on the dynamic in-line traffic measurements (in response to their varying characteristics). In the case of our particular setup, the routing protocol would be able to detect the need for asymmetric routing and adapt the routing accordingly. Also, the ability of performing in-line measurements for specific classes of traffic, for example based on the transport protocol or Type-of-Service (ToS), is expected to benefit the implementation of ToS-based routing.

5 Related Work

Existing traffic measurement techniques and infrastructures fall into two main categories, namely active and passive techniques. Active measurement techniques inject additional traffic with known characteristics into the network to test particular attributes of a service [23, 24, 25, 26], and they have been focusing on characterising properties of end-to-end network paths between instrumented systems. Passive measurements give highly accurate results by observing and analysing real traffic on a link without disruption of the service. They mainly operate at a single observation point within an administrative domain and try to provide feedback for network operations tasks [27, 28, 29, 30].

Active and passive measurements rely either on the performance experienced by dedicated traffic or on the costly correlation of one-point observations to yield one-way performance results, and do not provide a framework for performing accurate and transparent service-quality measurements for different traffic flows that can be deployed on-demand in the network.

Work on QoS Routing research has considered adaptive routing based on dynamic cost metrics. Some early work focused on ToS routing [31], which is either based on using multiple instances of routing protocols or maintaining routing tables with multiple metrics for different network attributes (i.e. delay, throughput, etc). Nevertheless, the link costs considered were static according to the natural characteristics of the link as it is the case with most routing protocols today.

Other solutions that have been proposed in this area advocate the use of destination-driven/initiated routing path computations and updates towards them [32, 33]. Clearly, these solutions are neither scalable nor pervasive, since they typically involve flooding mechanisms that cause both significant traffic overhead and high complexity. As a result, they suggest viable solutions only for maintaining routing paths to a small number of frequently used destinations. And, although they are quite dynamic, they often don't account for multiple metrics needed for the different attributes.

A different approach for tackling congestion problems and therefore improving communication, has led to the idea of multipath routing. Work, such as the one presented in [34] and [35], propose probabilistic or other methods of load balancing the traffic across multiple routing paths. Although these solutions differ fundamentally from our approach, yet, we believe that our mechanism can complement these solutions to improve their performance through dynamic adaptation.

Finally, the deployment of reconfigurable middleboxes or active network-based solutions has been considered in [36] and [37] in order to adapt or change the network configuration to match current traffic requirements. However, most of these solutions are not embeddable in general routing fabrics, but rather focus on out-of-band allocation of QoS resources in order to improve communication for individual flows.

6 Conclusions and Future Work

In this paper we have presented a new service for active networks based on the concept of using in-line traffic measurements to improve intra-domain routing. The main idea and contribution of this work is to provide the necessary mechanisms to accurately measure dynamically changing link (or virtual link) properties including delay, jitter and packet loss. This measurement information is then fed to available routing protocols so that they exchange more accurate, performance information about the links, enabling more prudent routing decisions. We have focused on the functionality and the design of the proposed mechanism to advocate its feasibility and applicability in an active network environment.

Future work will investigate the impact of the proposed mechanism on the routing protocol behaviour, as well as on how the measurement results can be used to generate meaningful link cost values (for specific protocols). We aim to tackle the fine-tuning of the mechanism and its viability when used in conjunction with today's routing protocols, in wired, wireless, and overlay network environments. Steps in this direction include the investigation of optimal time and sampling intervals for the measurement processes, as well as of novel algorithms for the link cost calculations. Application-specific routing based on performance properties of interest to different flows can also be facilitated.

We expect the proposed traffic measurement solution to be particularly applicable to overlay networks and mobile ad-hoc networks, since it enables the deployment of an always-on active service at strategic locations, where network characteristics change rapidly. In overlay networks these rapid changes result from the combination of a (often varying) number of underlying physical links that form the virtual network links, whereas in the case of mobile ad-hoc networks it is a result of the often changing mobility patterns and the environment affecting the wireless interfaces. We anticipate the proposed solution to be particularly valuable in both these cases.

Acknowledgements

We are grateful to Agilent Technologies for the support of Dimitrios Pezaros' work through an industrial fellowship. We would also like to acknowledge the support of the EPSRC under grant number GR/R31461/01.

References

[1] Wakeman, I., Jeffrey, A., Owen, T., Pepper, D., SafetyNet: A Language-Based Approach to Programmable Networks, in Computer Networks and ISDN Systems, 36 (1). 2001.
[2] The Caml Language. Online Reference, INRIA, http://caml.inria.fr/.
[3] Wetherall, D., J., Guttag, J., Tennenhouse, T., L., ANTS: A toolkit for building and dynamically deploying network protocols, in Proc. of IEEE Openarch, April 1998.
[4] Hicks, M., W., Kaddar, P., Moore, J., T., Gunter, C., A., Nettles, S., PLAN: A Packet Language for Active Networks, In Proceedings of the 3rd ACM SIGPLAN International Conference on Functional Programming, pages 86-93, 1998.
[5] Paterson, L., Gottlieb, Y., Hibler, M., Tullmann, P., Lepreau, J., Schwab, S., Dandelkar, H., Purtell, A., Hartman, J., An OS Interface for Active Routers, IEEE Journal on Selected Areas in Communications, Volume 19, Issue 3, March 2001, pp. 473-487.
[6] Merugu, S., Bhattacharjee, S., Zegura, E., Calvert, K., Bowman: A Node OS for Active Networks, in Proceedings of IEEE INFOCOMM'00, Tel Aviv, Israel, March 26-30, 2000.

[7]   Keller, R., Choi, S., Decasper, D., Dasen, M., Fankhauser, G., Plattner, B., An Active Router Architecture for Multicast Video Distribution. In Proc. of IEEE INFOCOM (3), pp 1137-1146, 2000.

[8]   Keller, R., Ruf, L., Guindehi, A., Plattner, B., PromethOS: A Dynamically Extensible Router Architecture Supporting Explicit Routing, in Proceedings of the 4th International Conference on Active Networks (IWAN), Zurich, Switzerland, December 4-6, 2002.

[9]   Schmid, S., Finney, J., Scott, A., C., Shepherd, W., D., Component-based Active Network Architecture, IEEE Symposium on Computers and Communications, July 2001.

[10] Merugu, S., Bhattacharjee, S., Chae, Y., Sanders, M., Calvert, K., Zegura, E. Bowman and CANEs: Implementation of an Active Network, In Proc. of 37th Conference on Communication, Control and Computing, September 1999.

[11] Bossardt, M., Antik, R., H., Moser, A., Plattner, B., Chameleon: Realising Automatic Service Composition for Extensible Active Routers, in Proceedings of the 5th International Conference on Active Networks (IWAN), Kyoto, Japan, December 10-12, 2003.

[12] Bassi, A., Gelas, J-P., Lefevre, L., A sustainable Framework for Multimedia Data Streaming, in Proceedings of the 5th International Conference on Active Networks (IWAN), Kyoto, Japan, December 10-12, 2003.

[13] Lefevre, L., Pierson, J-M., Guebli, S., Collaborative Web-Caching with Active Networks, in Proceedings of the 5th International Conference on Active Networks (IWAN), Kyoto, Japan, December 10-12, 2003.

[14] Hand, S., Harris, T., Kotsovinos, E., Pratt, I. Controlling the XenoServer Open Platform, in Proceedings of IEEE OpenArch'03, San Francisco, California, April 4-5, 2003.

[15] Pezaros, D., P., Hutchison, D., Garcia, F., J., Gardner, R., D., Sventek, J., S., In-line Service Measurements: An IPv6-based Framework for Traffic Evaluation and Network Operations, in Proceedings of IEEE/IFIP NOMS 2004, Seoul, Korea, April 19-23, 2004.

[16] Deering, S., Hinden, R., Internet Protocol Version 6 (IPv6) Specification, IETF, IPNG Working Group, RFC 2460, December 1998.

[17] Pezaros, D.,P., Hutchison, D., Garcia, F.,J., Gardner, R., Sventek, J.,S., Service Quality Measurements for IPv6 Inter-networks, to appear in International Workshop on Quality of Service (IWQoS), Montreal, Canada, June 7-9, 2004.

[18] Schmid, S., Chart, T., Sifalakis, M., Scott, A., C., "Flexible, Dynamic and Scalable Service Composition for Active Routers", In Proc. of IWAN 2002, pp 253-266, December 2002.

[19] Alexander, D., S., Braden, B., Gunter, C., A., Jackson, W., A., Keromytis, A., D., Minden, G., A., Wetherall, D., A., Active Network Encapsulation Protocol (ANEP), July 1997.

[20] Sifalakis, M., Schmid, S., Chart, T., Hutchison, D., "A Generic Active Service Deployment Protocol". In Proc. of ANTA 2003, pp 100-111, Osaka, May 2003.

[21] Mills, D., Internet time synchronisation: the Network Time Protocol, IEEE Transaction on Communications, Volume 39, Issue 1, October 1991, pp. 1482-1493.

[22] MSRL – Mobile-IPv6 Systems research Lab". Research Project funded by Cisco Systems, Microsoft Research (Cambridge), and Orange Ltd, Lancaster University, 2001.

[23] Matthews, W., Cottrell, L., The PingER project: Active Internet Performance Monitoring for the HENP Community, IEEE Communications Magazine, Vol. 38, Issue 5, May 2000, pp. 130-136.

[24] Kalidindi, S., Zekauskas, M., J., Surveyor: An Infrastructure for Internet Performance Measurements, in Proceedings of the ninth Annual Conference of the Internet Society (INET'99) INET'99, San Jose, California, June 22-25 1999.

[25] Georgatos, F., Gruber, F., Karrenberg, D., Santcroos, M., Susanj, A., Uijterwaal, H., Wilhelm, R., Providing Active Measurements as a Regular Service for ISP's, in Proceedings of Passive and Active Measurement Workshop (PAM2001), Amsterdam, NL, April 23-24 2001.

[26] NLANR Active Measurement Project (AMP) Homepage, http://watt.nlanr.net//active/intro.html.

[27] Apsidorf, J., Claffy, K., C., Thompson, K., Wilder, R., OC3MON: Flexible, Affordable, High Performance Statistics Collection, in Proceedings of the seventh Annual Conference of the Internet Society (INET'97), Kuala Lumpur, Malaysia, June 24-27 1997.

[28] Fraleigh, C., Diot, C., Lyles, B., Moon, S., Owezarski, P., Papagiannaki, D., Tobagi, F., Design and Deployment of a Passive Monitoring Infrastructure, in Proceedings of Passive and Active Measurement Workshop (PAM2001), Amsterdam, NL, April 23-24 2001.

[29] Feldmann, A., Greenberg, A., Lund, C., Reingold, N., Rexford, J., True, F., Deriving Traffic Demands For Operational IP Networks: Methodology And Experience, in Proceedings of ACM SIGCOMM'00, Stockholm, Sweden, August 28 – September 1 2000.

[30] Claffy, K., C., Miller, G., Thompson, K., The Nature Of The Beast: Recent Traffic Measurements From An Internet Backbone in Proceedings of the eighth Annual Conference of the Internet Society (INET'98), Geneva, Switzerland, July 21-24 1998.

[31] Matta, I., Shankar, U., A., Type-of-Service Routing in Dynamic Datagram Networks, in Proceedings of IEEE INFOCOMM'04, Toronto, Ontario, Canada, June 12-16, 1994.

[32] Chen, J., Druschel, P., Subramanian, D., A New Approach to Routing with Dynamic Metrics, in Proceeding of IEEE INFOSOMM'98, San Francisco, USA, 29 March- 2 April, 1998.

[33] Di Fatta, G., Gaglio, S., Lo Re, G., Ortolani, M., Adaptive Routing in Active Networks, Proceedings of IEEE OpenArch 2000, Tel Aviv, Israel, March 2000.

[34] Nelakuditi, S., Zhang, Z-L., Tsang, R., P., Du, D., H., C., Adaptive Proportional Routing and Localised QoS Routing Approach, in Proc. of IEEE INFOCOMM'00, Israel, March 26-30, 2000.

[35] Bohacek, S., Hespanha, J., P., Obraczka, K., Lee, J., Lim, C., Enhancing Security via Stochastic Routing, in Proceedings of the 11th International Conference on Computer Communications and Networks (ICCCN'02), Miami, Florida, October 14-16, 2002.

[36] Matta, I., Bestavros, A., QoS Controllers for the Internet, In Proceedings of the NSF Workshop on Information Technology, Cairo, Egypt, March 2000.

[37] Vrontis, S., Sygkouna, I., Chantzara, M., Sykas, E., Enabling Distributed QoS Management Utilising Active Network Technology, in Proc. of Net-Con'03, October 2003.

Simple Active Mechanisms for Measuring and Monitoring Service Level Topologies

Gísli Hjálmtýsson, Ólafur Ragnar Helgason, and Björn Brynjúlfsson[*]

Network Systems and Services Laboratory
Department of Computer Science
Reykjavik University, Reykjavik, Iceland
{gisli,bjorninn,olafurr}@ru.is
http://netlab.ru.is

Abstract. Whether driven by security concerns, need for flexibility, deployment of advanced services or as a simplified outsourcing model, overlaying a virtual service topology over the underlying network infrastructure is common. To ensure and enforce consistent service quality, fairness and protocol behavior it is necessary to measure and monitor these service level topologies. In this paper we present extensible general purpose mechanisms to monitor and measure characteristics of a service level topology at the nodes of the topology. The mechanisms provide means to dynamically deploy a distributed observation function at the nodes of the topology and to collate the observations into a result given to the requestor on a subscription channel. These are control plane mechanisms, outside of the router datapath, where we assume programmability and low cost memory. We give several examples of how to use these mechanisms to compute interesting properties of the topology.

Keywords: Service aware networking, measurement, service management, overlays, VPN.

1 Introduction

Whether driven by security concerns, need for flexibility, deployment of advanced services or as a simplified outsourcing model, overlaying a virtual service specific topology over the underlying network infrastructure is a common solution approach for all types of network technologies. Static service topologies include "private networks" built using leased telephony lines to ensure isolation, and Internet "bones" based on statically allocated IP-in-IP tunnels such as the MBONE, 6-BONE and the A-bone, to provide the illusion of universal deployment over a virtual topology. More dynamic approaches include Virtual Private Network (VPN) services in ATM [1] established from dynamically allocated collection of ATM circuits, and Service Level Routing (SLR) over the Internet providing non-local redundancy and load balancing across a network of service locations [2]. Similarly, application level services, such as application layer multicast, build a service specific topology. Many proposed

---

[*] This work (all authors) was supported in part by The Icelandic Centre for Research under grant number 020500002.

G.J. Minden et al. (Eds.): IWAN 2004, LNCS 3912, pp. 205–216, 2007.

active networking services explicitly or effectively build an overlay topology. Recent interest in overlay networks can be viewed as an attempt to abstract out both the underlying topology and specific network technology.

To ensure and enforce consistent service quality, fairness and protocol behavior it is necessary to measure and monitor these service level topologies. The detailed technologies used to realize the various virtual topologies differ. However, significant and important commonalities make it desirable to design and implement general purpose mechanisms to support the monitoring and measurements and algorithms to compute values of common interest, rather than have each technology, service or application implement a fraction of such mechanisms.

End-to-end measurements and edge based solutions [3,4,5,6], requiring no cooperation from the core network, have been proposed to infer the service topology for multicast and network characteristics from edge observations. A significant drawback of these methods is that they only compute long term averages are inherently error prone and do not adapt well to membership changes in the service topology. We believe that rather than employing service ignorant long term observations from the edges, effective management of service level virtual topologies requires service specific observations from inside the service network for timeliness and relevance.

Commonly, virtual topologies are built from nodes such as boundary nodes where functionality beyond basic forwarding is common. These nodes are prime candidates and targets of active networking technology. Moreover services based on P2P networks, application layer multicast and overlays that are implemented at the application layer can reasonably be assumed to have high level of activity and programmability. Adding mechanisms for observations at the nodes of the virtual topology is therefore achievable.

Such general mechanisms must provide a) the right abstractions for results of importance, b) extensibility to support service specific observations, and c) interface that makes it easy to employ with a variety of service level topology approaches, such as application level overlays, ATM style VPN's, IP-bones and network layer multicast.

In this paper we present extensible general purpose mechanisms to monitor and measure characteristics of a service level topology at the nodes of the topology. These are control plane mechanisms, outside of the router datapath, where we contend assumptions of high programmability and low cost memory are valid. Moreover, we present algorithms to collect and use these observations to compute interesting properties of the topology. The mechanisms provide means to dynamically deploy a distributed observation function at the nodes of the topology and to collate the observations into a result given to the requestor on a subscription channel. We give examples of our use of these mechanisms in managing multicast distribution, as well as in an control overlay for router selection in sparsely deployed services. We furthermore discuss the use of our mechanism to collect information for load distribution in network wide service level routing.

The rest of the paper is organized as follows. In Section 2 we discuss related work and further position our work. In Section 3 we describe the basic mechanisms, and show in Section 4 how we have used them to monitor and manage multicast service over a dynamically constructed virtual service topology. In Section 5 we discuss how the same mechanisms are used in general overlay/virtual topologies with two examples of control level overlays for service aware route selection. Section 6 contains additional discussion. In Section 7 we conclude.

2 Related Work

Network tomography from end-to-end measurements has been proposed to infer service level topology and network characteristics from edge observations [3,4,5,6]. An attractive attribute of these methods is that they don't require any cooperation from the core network and therefore work for large scale discovery across multiple administrative domains. However, a major drawback of these methods is that they only compute long term averages and are therefore inherently error prone and do not adapt well to membership changes. While valuable as a fallback, effective service management requires more detailed and timely observations that can only be obtained inside the service network.

Overlays have been used for monitoring the underlying physical network for path outages and periods of reduced performance. In [7], path restoration in the overlay network is done by finding a route for the backup path that minimize the probability that the primary and backup overlay paths share a link in the underlying network. In [8] aggressive probing between application layer overlay nodes is used to do fault detection of Internet paths and recovery is performed by routing by way of the overlay nodes instead of the IP routing. Although using overlays to monitor the underlying physical network can be a powerful approach, with our mechanisms we are primarily interested in monitoring the overlay and service level topologies themselves. We are not aware of any mechanisms for monitoring general overlay and service level topologies.

Related to the monitoring of general service level topologies is the monitoring of multicast. A number of mechanism and tools for monitoring multicast topologies have been enunciated [9] but most of these mechanisms are protocol dependent, inflexible and can not easily be generalized to other services or topologies. The mechanisms presented in this paper on the other hand can be used to monitor more general topologies and we give an example of how they have been used to monitor the SLIM network layer multicast protocol.

Our mechanisms inherently implement a control plane that supports many-to-one and one-to-many operations for the purposes of measuring and monitoring general topologies. Essentially our mechanism can be viewed as combining active multicast and active gather-cast [10] to realize the measurement functions.

Some of the ideas behind our work are similar to what is presented in [11]. However, even though all state maintained by our mechanisms is soft and possibly short-lived it is not self destroying in the same sense as defined in [11]. In contrast the state maintained by our mechanisms is explicitly introduced and assumed to exist for a substantial amount of time.

3 Description of the Mechanisms

The mechanisms perform three main functions: 1) local maintenance and information collection from the local service level module, 2) a distribution mechanism to propagate (new query) functions and information from a collection point to the active nodes of the topology, and 3) information gather implemented by a protocol that propagates information from leaves in the topology towards a designated root applying a (query specific) summation function at each intermediate node. Fig. 1 depicts the gather and distribution mechanisms.

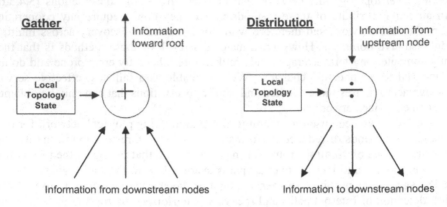

Fig. 1. The gather and distribution mechanisms

We refer to the single source tree rooted at the observer as the collection channel. Each node in the collection channel, apart from the root, has exactly one upstream neighbor and zero or more downstream neighbors. The local state at a measurement node consists of the topology identifier of the channel source, the source specific channel identifier (a single source can have multiple collection channels), a downstream state per each downstream neighbor and the local topology state from the service level module.

The mechanisms implement the collection and computation of three general base attributes that we believe are of sufficient value to most service level topologies, namely the number of leaves of a collection channel, the total number of nodes in a collection channel and the height (or max depth) of the collection channel. The mechanisms define local collection, sum and distribution operations that can be dynamically instantiated on a per service basis or service defined per flow basis. The mechanisms are designed for the control plane and outside of the data forwarding path.

3.1 Local Collection Mechanism

The information collection mechanism is a module that contains the service specific objects for each service level topology the node may be operating. Each object collects the service specific local state from the topology manager running on the node. We define an abstract interface that each service level topology manager implements, enabling it to export its local state to the object performing the local information collection.

```
Interface local_state;
local_state* getLocalState(void);
```

The `local_state` object and the `getLocalState` function must be implemented as part of an adaptation of our mechanisms for a given topology management system. The content of the `local_state` may vary between topology mechanisms, and may for example be different for a network layer multicast topology management, than for an application level overlay.

Our mechanisms support dynamic installation of local information collection modules on runtime, thus adapting and enhancing the local collection abilities of the node. This allows for dynamic installation of objects for new services.

3.2 Distribution Mechanism

The distribution mechanism propagates a query object from the root of the collection channel towards the leaves. The root creates a distribution message and sends a copy on each interface of the virtual topology where the destination address of the message is a collection channel specific identifier C. The format of the distribution message, shown in Fig. 2 lower half, consists of some (topology specific) *base* values, a *type identifier*, type specific *data* and the sum and distribution operations for the service type. If a new type identifier is provided the node installs the code for the summation and distribution methods.

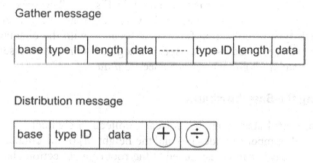

Fig. 2. The gather and distribute messages respectively

A node receiving a query object records the source address of the message as the root of the collection channel and the destination address as the channel identifier. The distribution method specified by the type identifier in the message is then applied to the message. The distribution method may retrieve the *local state* from the topology manager, before producing a new message to be forwarded to each downstream neighbor in the virtual topology. In the simplest case the new message forwarded downstream is the same as the arriving one. In other cases a different message may be forwarded to each neighbor.

From a functional point of view the primary use of the distribution mechanism is to allow the collection point to subscribe to the continually updated computation of results specified by the query object. Since the query object is an arbitrary code (supported by the execution environment of the topology) the range of queries that can be computed is substantial. A query subscription results in the gather process being activated to periodically to compute a distributed time dependent global state estimation at the collection channel root. A distribution message with a null value for the summation operation will cancel the subscription.

An important use of the distribution mechanism is to distribute information from the root of the collection channel to the nodes of the topology.

3.3 Gather Mechanism

The gather mechanism propagates information from the leaves of the collection channel towards the root by periodically sending updates upstream. At each node the gather involves two functions: a) Receiving and processing gather messages from downstream, and b) preparing the sending a gather result upstream. The two functions are performed asynchronously on each channel.

A gather message received from downstream on a given channel is simply stored as part of the channel gather state, and overrides any previous state on that channel from the same downstream node.

To compute the new gather result, for a given channel, the summation function of each message type associated with a given channel is invoked, each function producing a type specific result, that is appended to the message being prepared. The summation function uses the downstream gather state for each downstream neighbor and the local state from the topology manager.

The format of the gather message is shown in Fig. 2. The message consists of some topology specific set of *base* values (leaves, weight and height) at a node and a segment for each type of collection function associated with the channel (by a previous distribute message). Each service specific segment consists of a service *type ID*, service specific header *length* and service specific *data*.

3.4 Computing the Base Attributes

The general base attributes computed for each collection channel are the number of leaves (l), the total number of nodes (w) and the height (h) of the collection channel.

The number of leaves can be estimated at the root of a collection channel using the gather mechanism. The base field of the gather message contains a leafcount field used by the nodes in the collection channel for this computation. A leaf node sets the value of the leafcount field in the gather message to 1 and sends the gather message towards the source as usual. An upstream node n computes the number of its downstream leaves according as the sum of the leafcounts from all its neighboring downstream nodes. More generally the leafcount at a node n is computed according to

$$l_n = \begin{cases} 1 & \text{if } n \text{ is a leaf} \\ \sum_{j \in down(n)} l_j & \text{otherwise} \end{cases}$$

where *down(n)* is the set of neighboring downstream nodes of n. This way the leafcount at the root, l_{root}, is simply the current estimate[1] of the number of participants in

---

[1] Note that due to packet losses, delays in delivery and asynchrony across the topology the result may not be accurate, but is instead a (very good) estimate.

the collection channel. More generally the leafcount at any intermediate node is the number of participants in the subtree rooted at that particular node.

In a similar manner to the estimating of the number of participants the gather mechanism is used to estimate the number of internal nodes in a service level topology. We define the weight of a collection channel as the number of all nodes in the channel, both leaves and internal nodes. The weight at a node n is then given by

$$w_n = \begin{cases} 1 & \textit{if } n \textit{ is a leaf} \\ 1 + \sum_{j \in down(n)} w_j & \textit{otherwise} \end{cases}$$

The height of the collection channel can be computed by finding the subtree with the maximum height and adding one to that value. More generally the height h of any node n in the collection channel can be computed according to

$$h_n = \begin{cases} 0 & \textit{if } n \textit{ is a leaf} \\ 1 + \max_{j \in down(n)} \{h_j\} & \textit{otherwise} \end{cases}$$

To reflect the latest changes in the topology, each node periodically sends a gather message towards the root of the collection channel containing the latest values for l, w and h. The distribution mechanism can be used to propagate the number of participants estimate from the root to all nodes in the collection channel.

3.5 Characteristics and Implementation Assumptions

An important tradeoff in the realization of the gather mechanism is the length of the update period. A short update period gives better state estimates at the increased cost of bandwidth and processing at the nodes. In general the update period should depend on the packet volume of the service being monitored to ensure that the overhead of maintaining the gather state is a some small fraction of the volume of the service flow (say less than 1%) or overall resources. The mechanisms support the dynamic adaptation of the refresh period.

We do not assume reliable delivery of the distribute or the gather messages. Consequently, message loss may affect the effectiveness of the mechanisms. As queries are effectively subscriptions, repeated transmissions of distribution messages can be employed to ensure completeness, potentially resulting in some but inconsequential delay in query distribution.

A more persistent impact is caused by losses of gather messages, resulting in the current estimate at the collection point being a random number continually affected by losses. Our approach described above is designed to minimize the impact of a single packet loss, as the downstream state remains valid (for some significant time) until updated from below. Thus if an update is not received from a particular subtree in round T the update value for that subtree received in round T-1 remains in use.

4 Monitoring and Managing SLIM Multicast

We have used our mechanisms for monitoring and managing SLIM multicast sessions. The local collection mechanism communicates with the topology management module of SLIM. We use the mechanisms to compute estimates of a number of key properties of the multicast topology and monitor changes in these from our service management center. In addition to trigger queries, we utilize the distribution mechanism to trigger the proccess of updating running code in our implementation to enhance and update the monitoring abilities of the active nodes.

4.1 Self Configuring Lightweight Multicast – SLIM

SLIM [12] is a single source multicast paradigm for the Internet that self-configures over the unicast infrastructure by dynamically building network layer IP-in-IP tunnels as required. The SLIM signaling protocol thus constructs and maintains a dynamic service level topology for multicast. A multicast channel in SLIM is identified by the pair $<S, C>$ where S is the channel's source and C is the source specific channel identifier. To create the single source distribution tree a SLIM client sends a JOIN control message towards the source S. SLIM enabled routers intercept the messages and create the appropriate forwarding state in their flow based classifier and construct dynamic tunnels if the JOIN message has been forwarded through routers not supporting the SLIM protocol. When the JOIN message reaches the first router that is already a node in the distribution tree of $<S, C>$ the new branch is added to the distribution tree and the JOIN message suppressed. The only multicast specific functions of SLIM are the control plane topology management, which operates out of data-path and manipulates router classifiers (forwarding table) and tunnel facilities.

4.2 Implementation

We have implemented a monitoring system for SLIM based services using our mechanisms on the Pronto [13] programmable router using packet processors [14]. For the purposes of our implementation the Pronto router provides strong separation between services and protocols implemented in a user space execution environment and the data-path router facilities realized at kernel level. Data-path packet processors furthermore support the composition of paths through the router. In particular, a path can have multiple branches, each branch composed of one or more packet processors. Thus branches may differ in functionality. For our mechanisms this allows us to monitor the information volume sent on individual multicast branches by creating packet/byte count packet processors for each branch.

The monitoring mechanisms are implemented as a user-space daemon. The local collection object communicates with the Topology Management (TMP) daemon of SLIM to collect the local state information. We have implemented this through the use of shared memory. The TMP daemon maintains a table in shared memory that contains the local state for each active multicast flow. The local collection object creates a read-only instance of the class interfacing the shared memory upon which it can invoke a `getLocalState` method as described in Section 3.1.

Each SLIM channel corresponds to a collection channel where the root of the collection channel is the SLIM source, S. For each collection channel the local topology state consists of the number of active downstream branches and the system unique identifier of each branch. The local collection state and the state from each downstream node is used to compute the number of leaves, weight and height of each channel using the gather mechanism. Each gather message consists of the base values for l, w and h and in addition the number of packets and bytes received at the node for the flow identified by $<S, C>$. The base values at the root of the collection channel can be used to estimate the number of multicast receivers (leaves), longest path to a receiver (height) and the number of internal nodes in the multicast channel as $w - l$. Using the byte/packet values in a received gather message a node can estimate the link lossrate of each downstream link by comparing the downstream value with the number of bytes/packets received.

An initial distribution message is simply sent on the multicast channel being monitored. The distribute and gather messages are sent with the router alert IP-option and a special protocol ID which results in the active nodes intercepting the messages and dispatching them to the module implementing the mechanisms. The distribution mechanism can be used to distribute and update running code in the active nodes. Our implementation is in C++. The C++ code for the local collection, gather and distribute objects of the monitoring daemon can be introduced and updated through the use of dynamic C++ classes [15].

4.3 Bottleneck Discovery – Placement of Active Retransmission

Using our mechanisms discovering bottleneck links and deploying active retransmission is relatively easy. Each node transmits upstream the number of packets it receives on a given channel. By comparing this value to the local observation of packets received, the gather computation reveals if excessive losses are occurring on any of the downstream links. If so it deploys active retransmission on that particular link (using the Pronto packet processors this is very easy to do on a per branch basis).

5 Monitoring More General Virtual Topologies

In this section we give examples of how the mechanisms can be used for general service level topologies. A meshed topology structure does not have a distinguished root and has multiple paths between nodes in the topology. However, from any node a virtual topology a well defined (minimum cost) spanning tree will typically exist. A collection point initiates query processing by sending a distribute message over such a spanning tree.

Although a wide range of functions can be computed over general topologies using the mechanisms, computing link attributes is more difficult than computing node properties, as a spanning tree will visit all nodes but will not traverse all links. Of course this can be overcome, but the mechanisms do not provide explicit support to address this issue.

5.1 Monitoring SLIM Router Deployment Using a Control Plane Overlay

As part of our research on multicast we have been offering televisions distribution
services and teleconferencing experimentation over SLIM multicast for over a year
now. Although the number of SLIM-enabled routers is still small their number is
growing. To better exploit available SLIM routers, to keep track of their distribution,
to update the SLIM code, and as part of our ongoing research on advanced group
management the SLIM protocol now supports a control plane overlay.

By building a spanning tree from our local SLIM router, we can use our mechanisms over this overlay, to keep track of the number of routers, the diameter and density of the deployment, as well as to facilitate distribution of code updates. This is in
addition and separate from the flow level monitoring described in Section 4.

5.2 Applications to Service Level Routing

In [2] Anerousis et al employ a virtual topology of dynamically constructed tunnels to
route requests to a named service realized by a virtual host that, in theory, provides
the service. A virtual host has an IP address and appears to the rest of the Internet as a
regular host. A request from a client is routed to a particular (physical) server by a set
of service level (application level) nodes. The routing is determined in real time
through the service level routing map and may take into consideration user attributes
such as originating address, and network and server attributes such as load. Rather
than relying on modified DNS based redirection schemes at the edges of the network,
in the service level routing of [2] the service level nodes use service semantics, and
load and availability attributes to transparently routes service requests to the appropriate servers based on a variety of criteria.

Requests are routed over a layered virtual topology. Client requests are routed by
the IP infrastructure to the service level router (SLR) closest to the client (using standard destination based routing). The packets are then directed to an SLR one layer up
using IP-in-IP tunnels constructed dynamically if needed. This continues until the
SLR of a particular hosting site is reached. The SLR at the hosting site further tunnels
the packets to the host that is best suited for serving the request. Each server host
terminates the tunnel and recovers the original datagram exactly as it was sent from
the client. From the addresses in the original datagram the receiving server process
learns the client address as well as a the virtual host address. Acting as the virtual
host, it transmits its replies directly to the requesting user client, using the address of
the virtual host as its source address, and avoids the service level virtual structure.
The multiple levels improve scalability and load balancing effectiveness.

In the service level routing topology the availability and load of the service level
routers, and the server hosts play a dominant role in providing consistent dependable
service quality. Given appropriate policies to determine the local load metrics at the
SLR's or the servers, we employ our active mechanisms to propagate and update the
availability and load information in the SLR topology as follows. Each lowest layer
SLR is a collector that initiates a collection channel. The SLR at each hosting site
joins the collection channel of each leaf. At each hosting site the SLR computes a

load metric for each virtual host hosted at the site, and propagates using the gather mechanism. Intermediate SLR's collate the load metrics from below, combine them with a network load metric, and compute a load metric for the downstream tree that are propagated upstream. Each lowest layer SLR thereby receives a metric of load from each branch that it uses to perform load aware route selection (combined with other criteria).

6 Discussion

Insensitivity to non-cooperating nodes. In the heterogeneous Internet assuming uniform deployment is unrealistic. Even under active networking assumptions, homogeneity cannot be assumed, as nodes may vary in their capabilities, authentication policies, and access given to installed services. While the correct operation of our mechanisms does not require uniform cooperation across the virtual topology, the effectiveness of the mechanisms is reduced. As the ratio of non-cooperating nodes in the topology increases, it may become attractive to employ some of the techniques of [3,4] to infer the properties of the non-participating segments of the virtual topology. The same applies if physical topology attributes are of interest as metrics for a virtual topology that still consists only of relatively few nodes of the physical topology.

It is relatively easy to determine the density of the virtual topology over the physical one, by tracking the TTL count between virtual hops, and summing up all physical hops over a given channel. At a given collector, the density can then be defined as the physical hop count over the weight of the tree.

IP as a service level topology over the transport network. In traditional network operation models the physical network (e.g. the optical transport network) is viewed as providing physical transport to a number of service networks running over virtual topologies on top. In this model, IP is just another service constructing a service specific virtual topology. Alternate models assume that the routers manage the underlying physical resources [16]. Our mechanisms are agnostic to this and are suitable for such an environment by deploying our mechanism in IP routers, and could then provide the collection mechanisms described above for the IP network.

7 Conclusion

In this paper we have described extensible general purpose mechanisms to monitor and measure characteristics of a service level topology at the nodes of the topology. The mechanisms provide means to dynamically deploy a distributed observation function to the nodes of the topology and to collate the observations into a result given to the requestor on a subscription channel. The value of the mechanisms is validated by their extensive use in our experimentation with multicast. In addition we have given examples from our experimentation with the same mechanisms over general service topologies, including overlays for router discovery, and service level routing.

References

[1] N.G. Duffield, P. Goyal, A. Greenberg, P. Mishra, K.K. Ramakrishnan, and J. E. Van der Merwe, "A Flexible Model for Resource Management in Virtual Private Networks", IEEE/ACM Transactions on Networking, No.5, Oct. 2002.

[2] N. Anerousis and G. Hjálmtýsson, "Service Level Routing on the Internet," in proceedings of Globecom'99, Rio de Janeiro, Brazil, December 1999.

[3] A. Adams, T. Bu, R. Caceres, N.G. Duffield, T. Friedman, J. Horowitz, F. Lo Presti, S.B. Moon, V. Paxson, and D. Towsley. "The Use of End-to-End Multicast Measurements for Characterizing Internal Network Behavior", IEEE Communications Magazine, May 2000.

[4] T. Bu, N. Duffield, F. Presti, and D. Towsley, "Network tomography on general topologies," in proceedings of ACM SIGMETRICS, 2002

[5] Y. Chen, D. Bindel and R. H. Katz, "Tomography-based Overlay Network Monitoring", in proceedings of the 2003 ACM SIGCOMM conference on Internet measurement, Miami Beach, USA, 2003

[6] S. Ratnasamy and S. McCanne, "Inference of Multicast Routing Trees and Bottleneck Bandwidths using End-to-end Measurements," in proceedings of IEEE Infocom'99, Mar. 1999.

[7] W. Cui, I. Stoica, and R. H. Katz., "Backup path allocation based on a correlated link failure probability model in overlay networks". In the proceedings of ICNP 2002, November 2002.

[8] David G. Andersen, Hari Balakrishnan, M. Frans Kaashoek, Robert Morris, "Resilient Overlay Networks", in Proc. 18th ACM SOSP, Banff, Canada, October 2001.

[9] K. Sarac and K. Almeroth, "Supporting Multicast Deployment Efforts: A Survey of Tools for Multicast Monitoring", Journal of High Speed Networking - Special Issue on Management of Multimedia Networking, vol. 9, num. 3/4, pp. 191-211, March 2001.

[10] K. L. Calvert, J. Griffioen, B. Mullins, A. Sehgal and S. Wen, "Concast: Design and Implementation of an Active Network Service", IEEE Journal on Selected Area in Communications (JSAC). Volume 19, No. 3. March, 2001.

[11] S. Wen, J. Griffioen and K. L. Calvert, "Building Multicast Services from Unicast Forwarding and Ephemeral State", Computer Networks: the International Journal of Computer and Telecommunications Networking. Elsevier Science. Vol.38, Issue 3. February, 2002. pp.327-45.

[12] G. Hjálmtýsson, B. Brynjúlfsson and Ó. R. Helgason, "Self-configuring Lightweight Internet Multicast", accepted for publication at IEEE SMC 2004, Netherlands, october 2004.

[13] G. Hjálmtýsson, "The Pronto Platform - A Flexible Toolkit for Programming Networks using a Commodity Operating System," in the proceedings of OpenArch 2000, Tel Aviv, Israel, March 2000.

[14] G. Hjálmtýsson, H. Sverrisson, B. Brynjúlfsson and Ó. R. Helgason, "Dynamic packet processors - A new abstraction for router extensibility", in proceedings of OPENARCH-2003, San Francisco, April 2003.

[15] R. Gray and G. Hjálmtýsson, "Dynamic C++ classes - A Lightweight mechanism to update code in a running program," in proceedings of the USENIX Annual Technical Conference, pp. 65-76, June, 1998

[16] A. Greenberg, G. Hjálmtýsson and J. Yates, "Smart Routers - Simple Optics. A Network Architecture for IP over WDM," in the proceedings of the OFC 2000, Baltimore, March 2000.

Author Index

Lecture Notes in Computer Science

For information about Vols. 1–4329

please contact your bookseller or Springer

Vol. 4378: I. Virbitskaite, A. Voronkov (Eds.), Perspectives of Systems Informatics. XIV, 496 pages. 2007.

Vol. 4377: M. Abe (Ed.), Topics in Cryptology – CT-RSA 2007. XI, 403 pages. 2006.

Vol. 4376: E. Frachtenberg, U. Schwiegelshohn (Eds.), Job Scheduling Strategies for Parallel Processing. VII, 257 pages. 2007.

Vol. 4374: J.F. Peters, A. Skowron, I. Düntsch, J. Grzymała-Busse, E. Orłowska, L. Polkowski (Eds.), Transactions on Rough Sets VI, Part I. XII, 499 pages. 2007.

Vol. 4373: K. Langendoen, T. Voigt (Eds.), Wireless Sensor Networks. XIII, 358 pages. 2007.

Vol. 4372: M. Kaufmann, D. Wagner (Eds.), Graph Drawing. XIV, 454 pages. 2007.

Vol. 4371: K. Inoue, K. Satoh, F. Toni (Eds.), Computational Logic in Multi-Agent Systems. X, 315 pages. 2007. (Sublibrary LNAI).

Vol. 4370: P.P Lévy, B. Le Grand, F. Poulet, M. Soto, L. Darago, L. Toubiana, J.-F. Vibert (Eds.), Pixelization Paradigm. XV, 279 pages. 2007.

Vol. 4369: M. Umeda, A. Wolf, O. Bartenstein, U. Geske, D. Seipel, O. Takata (Eds.), Declarative Programming for Knowledge Management. X, 229 pages. 2006. (Sublibrary LNAI).

Vol. 4368: T. Erlebach, C. Kaklamanis (Eds.), Approximation and Online Algorithms. X, 345 pages. 2007.

Vol. 4367: K. De Bosschere, D. Kaeli, P. Stenström, D. Whalley, T. Ungerer (Eds.), High Performance Embedded Architectures and Compilers. XI, 307 pages. 2007.

Vol. 4366: K. Tuyls, R. Westra, Y. Saeys, A. Nowé (Eds.), Knowledge Discovery and Emergent Complexity in Bioinformatics. IX, 183 pages. 2007. (Sublibrary LNBI).

Vol. 4364: T. Kühne (Ed.), Models in Software Engineering. XI, 332 pages. 2007.

Vol. 4362: J. van Leeuwen, G.F. Italiano, W. van der Hoek, C. Meinel, H. Sack, F. Plášil (Eds.), SOFSEM 2007: Theory and Practice of Computer Science. XXI, 937 pages. 2007.

Vol. 4361: H.J. Hoogeboom, G. Păun, G. Rozenberg, A. Salomaa (Eds.), Membrane Computing. IX, 555 pages. 2006.

Vol. 4360: W. Dubitzky, A. Schuster, P.M.A. Sloot, M. Schroeder, M. Romberg (Eds.), Distributed, High-Performance and Grid Computing in Computational Biology. X, 192 pages. 2007. (Sublibrary LNBI).

Vol. 4358: R. Vidal, A. Heyden, Y. Ma (Eds.), Dynamical Vision. IX, 329 pages. 2007.

Vol. 4357: L. Buttyán, V. Gligor, D. Westhoff (Eds.), Security and Privacy in Ad-Hoc and Sensor Networks. X, 193 pages. 2006.

Vol. 4355: J. Julliand, O. Kouchnarenko (Eds.), B 2007: Formal Specification and Development in B. XIII, 293 pages. 2006.

Vol. 4354: M. Hanus (Ed.), Practical Aspects of Declarative Languages. X, 335 pages. 2006.

Vol. 4353: T. Schwentick, D. Suciu (Eds.), Database Theory – ICDT 2007. XI, 419 pages. 2006.

Vol. 4352: T.-J. Cham, J. Cai, C. Dorai, D. Rajan, T.-S. Chua, L.-T. Chia (Eds.), Advances in Multimedia Modeling, Part II. XVIII, 743 pages. 2006.

Vol. 4351: T.-J. Cham, J. Cai, C. Dorai, D. Rajan, T.-S. Chua, L.-T. Chia (Eds.), Advances in Multimedia Modeling, Part I. XIX, 797 pages. 2006.

Vol. 4349: B. Cook, A. Podelski (Eds.), Verification, Model Checking, and Abstract Interpretation. XI, 395 pages. 2007.

Vol. 4348: S.T. Taft, R.A. Duff, R.L. Brukardt, E. Ploedereder, P. Leroy (Eds.), Ada 2005 Reference Manual. XXII, 765 pages. 2006.

Vol. 4347: J. Lopez (Ed.), Critical Information Infrastructures Security. X, 286 pages. 2006.

Vol. 4346: L. Brim, B. Haverkort, M. Leucker, J. van de Pol (Eds.), Formal Methods: Applications and Technology. X, 363 pages. 2007.

Vol. 4345: N. Maglaveras, I. Chouvarda, V. Koutkias, R. Brause (Eds.), Biological and Medical Data Analysis. XIII, 496 pages. 2006. (Sublibrary LNBI).

Vol. 4344: V. Gruhn, F. Oquendo (Eds.), Software Architecture. X, 245 pages. 2006.

Vol. 4342: H. de Swart, E. Orłowska, G. Schmidt, M. Roubens (Eds.), Theory and Applications of Relational Structures as Knowledge Instruments II. X, 373 pages. 2006. (Sublibrary LNAI).

Vol. 4341: P.Q. Nguyen (Ed.), Progress in Cryptology - VIETCRYPT 2006. XI, 385 pages. 2006.

Vol. 4340: R. Prodan, T. Fahringer, Grid Computing. XXIII, 317 pages. 2007.

Vol. 4339: E. Ayguadé, G. Baumgartner, J. Ramanujam, P. Sadayappan (Eds.), Languages and Compilers for Parallel Computing. XI, 476 pages. 2006.

Vol. 4338: P. Kalra, S. Peleg (Eds.), Computer Vision, Graphics and Image Processing. XV, 965 pages. 2006.

Vol. 4337: S. Arun-Kumar, N. Garg (Eds.), FSTTCS 2006: Foundations of Software Technology and Theoretical Computer Science. XIII, 430 pages. 2006.

Vol. 4336: V.R. Basili, D. Rombach, K. Schneider, B. Kitchenham, D. Pfahl, R.W. Selby, Empirical Software Engineering Issues. XVII, 193 pages. 2007.

Vol. 4335: S.A. Brueckner, S. Hassas, M. Jelasity, D. Yamins (Eds.), Engineering Self-Organising Systems. XII, 212 pages. 2007. (Sublibrary LNAI).

Vol. 4334: B. Beckert, R. Hähnle, P.H. Schmitt (Eds.), Verification of Object-Oriented Software. XXIX, 658 pages. 2007. (Sublibrary LNAI).

Vol. 4333: U. Reimer, D. Karagiannis (Eds.), Practical Aspects of Knowledge Management. XII, 338 pages. 2006. (Sublibrary LNAI).

Vol. 4332: A. Bagchi, V. Atluri (Eds.), Information Systems Security. XV, 382 pages. 2006.

Vol. 4331: G. Min, B. Di Martino, L.T. Yang, M. Guo, G. Ruenger (Eds.), Frontiers of High Performance Computing and Networking – ISPA 2006 Workshops. XXXVII, 1141 pages. 2006.

Vol. 4330: M. Guo, L.T. Yang, B. Di Martino, H.P. Zima, J. Dongarra, F. Tang (Eds.), Parallel and Distributed Processing and Applications. XVIII, 953 pages. 2006.